Frommer's

Vienna day by day®

3rd Edition

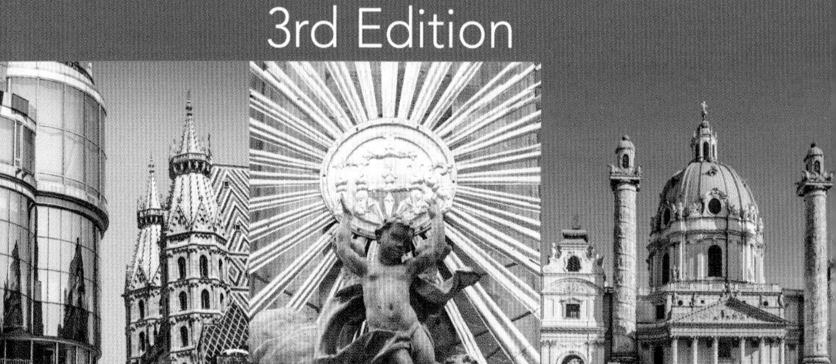

by Margaret Childs

FrommerMedia LLC

Contents

Published by:
Frommer Media LLC

ISBN: 978-1-628-87304-7 (paper); 978-1-628-87305-4 (ebk)

Editorial Director: Pauline Frommer
Editor: Lorraine Festa
Production Editor: Donna Wright
Photo Editor: Helen Stallion
Cartographer: Elizabeth Puhl
Indexer: Maro Riofrancos

Front cover photos, left to right: canadastock/Shutterstock.com, Zvonimir Atletic/Shutterstock.com, pavel dudek/Shutterstock.com

Back cover photo: © Eis Greissler

For information on our other products and services, please go to Frommers.com.

Frommer's also publishes its books in a variety of electronic formats. Some content that appears in print may not be available in electronic formats.

Manufactured in China

5 4 3 2 1

About This Guide

Organizing your time. That's what this guide is all about.

Other guides give you long lists of things to see and do and then expect you to fit the pieces together. The Day by Day guides are different. These guides tell you the best of everything, and then they show you how to see it in the smartest, most time-efficient way. Our authors have designed detailed itineraries organized by time, neighborhood, or special interest. And each tour comes with a bulleted map that takes you from stop to stop.

Would you like to wind back the clock to Imperial times at the Hofburg, visit Mozart's house, cruise the Blue Danube, or admire Lipizzaner horses strutting to Waltz music? Or catch a tram along epic Viennese legendary coffeehouses or snack on a large Wiener schnitzel? Whatever your interest or schedule, the Day by Days give you the smartest routes to follow. Not only do we take you to the top attractions, hotels, and restaurants, but we also help you access those special moments that locals get to experience—those "finds" that turn tourists into travelers.

The Day by Days are also your top choice if you're looking for one complete guide for all your travel needs. The best hotels and restaurants for every budget, the greatest shopping values, the wildest nightlife—it's all here.

Why should you trust our judgment? Because our authors personally visit each place they write about. They're an independent lot who say what they think and would never include places they wouldn't recommend to their best friends. They're also open to suggestions from readers. If you'd like to contact them, please send your comments our way at Support@FrommerMedia.com, and we'll pass them on.

Enjoy your Day by Day guide—the most helpful travel companion you can buy. And have the trip of a lifetime.

About the Author

Margaret Childs is the founder and Editor in Chief of *Metropole—Vienna in English.* Originally from New York, she has called Vienna home for 18 years. She is the co-author of *Frommer's Vienna & the Danube Valley* and *Frommer's Complete Guide to Austria.*

An Additional Note

Please be advised that travel information is subject to change at any time—and this is especially true of prices. We therefore suggest that you write or call ahead for confirmation when making your travel plans. The authors, editors, and publisher cannot be held responsible for the experiences of readers while traveling. Your safety is important to us, however, so we encourage you to stay alert and be aware of your surroundings.

Star Ratings, Icons & Abbreviations

Every hotel, restaurant, and attraction listing in this guide has been ranked for quality, value, service, amenities, and special features using a **star-rating system.** Hotels, restaurants, attractions, shopping, and nightlife are rated on a scale of zero stars (recommended) to three stars (exceptional). In addition to the star-rating system, we also use a **kids icon** to point out the best bets for families. Within each tour, we recommend cafes, bars, or restaurants where you can take a break. Each of these stops appears in a shaded box marked with a coffee-cup-shaped bullet.

The following **abbreviations** are used for credit cards:

AE	American Express	MC	MasterCard
DC	Diners Club	V	Visa

A Note on Prices

In the "Take a Break" listings denoted by a coffee cup, we have used a system of euro symbols to show a range of costs for an entree at a restaurant. Use the following table to decipher the euro symbols:

Cost	Restaurants
€	under €10
€€	€10–€15
€€€	€15–€24
€€€€	over €24

Travel Resources at Frommers.com

Frommer's travel resources don't end with this guide. Frommer's website, **www.frommers.com,** has travel information on more than 4,000 destinations. We update features regularly, giving you instant access to the most current trip-planning information available, and the best airfares, lodging rates, and car rental bargains. You can listen to podcasts, connect with other Frommers.com members through our active-reader forums, share your travel photos, read blogs from guidebook editors and fellow travelers, and much more.

How to Contact Us

In researching this book, we discovered many wonderful places—hotels, restaurants, shops, and more. We're sure you'll find others. Please tell us about them, so we can share the information with your fellow travelers in upcoming editions. If you were disappointed with a recommendation, we'd love to know that, too. Please write to: Support@FrommerMedia.com

14 Favorite Moments

14 Favorite Moments

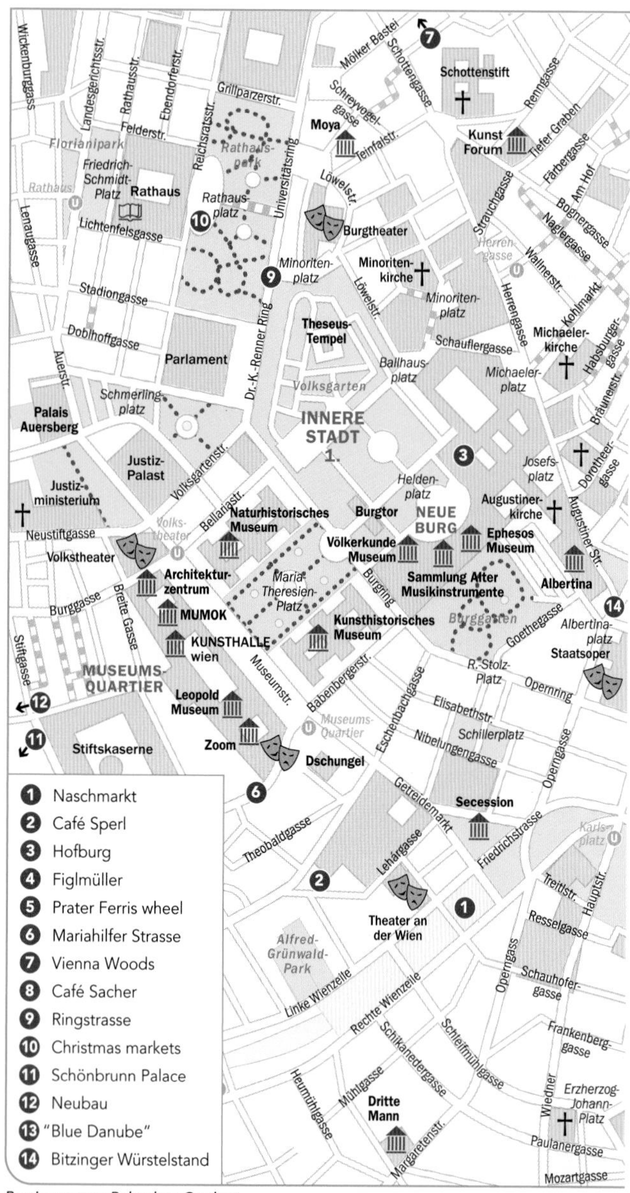

Previous page: Belvedere Gardens.

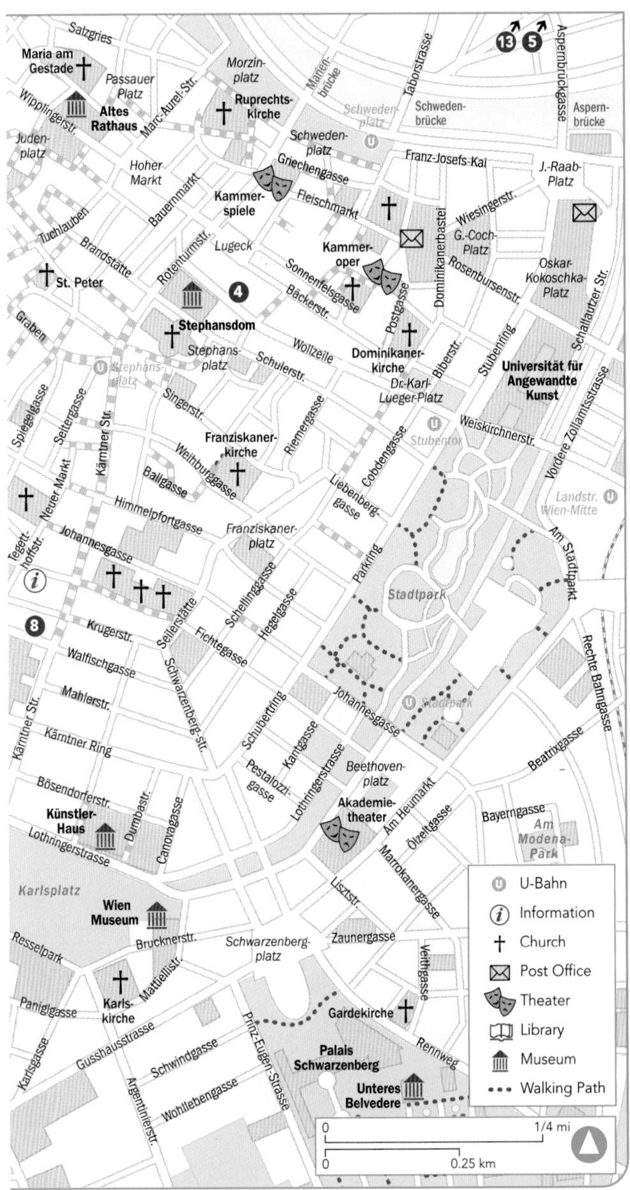
Salzgries
Maria am Gestade
Passauer Platz
Wipplingerstr.
Altes Rathaus
Marc-Aurel-Str.
Morzinplatz
Ruprechtskirche
Marienbrücke
Taborstrasse
Schwedenplatz
Schwedenbrücke
Aspernbrückgasse
Aspernbrücke
Judenplatz
Hoher Markt
Griechengasse
Franz-Josefs-Kai
J.-Raab-Platz
Kammerspiele
Fleischmarkt
Bauernmarkt
Tuchlauben
Brandstätte
Rotenturmstr.
Lugeck
Kammeroper
Wiesingerstr.
G.-Coch-Platz
Dominikanerbastei
Oskar-Kokoschka-Platz
Rosenbursenstr.
Sonnenfelsgasse
Bäckerstr.
Postgasse
St. Peter
Stephansdom
Schallautzer Str.
Graben
Stephansplatz
Wollzeile
Schulerstr.
Dominikanerkirche
Dr.-Karl-Lueger-Platz
Biberstr.
Stubenring
Universität für Angewandte Kunst
Singerstr.
Spiegelgasse
Seilergasse
Kärntner Str.
Franziskanerkirche
Riemergasse
Cobdengasse
Stubentor
Weiskirchnerstr.
Vordere Zollamtsstrasse
Weihburggasse
Ballgasse
Neuer Markt
Liebenberggasse
Landstr. Wien-Mitte
Himmelpfortgasse
Franziskanerplatz
Johannesgasse
Tegetthoffstr.
Parkring
Am Stadtpark
Stadtpark
Schellinggasse
Hegelgasse
Seilerstätte
Krugerstr.
Fichtegasse
Walfischgasse
Schwarzenberg-str.
Mahlerstr.
Rechte Bahngasse
Kärntner Str.
Kärntner Ring
Schubertring
Kantgasse
Beatrixgasse
Pestalozzigasse
Lothringerstrasse
Beethovenplatz
Bösendorferstr.
Akademietheater
Am Heumarkt
Künstler-Haus
Dumbastr.
Canovagasse
Ölzeltgasse
Bayerngasse
Am Modena-Park
Lothringerstrasse
Marrokanergasse
Karlsplatz
Lisztstr.
Wien Museum
Resselpark
Brucknerstr.
Schwarzenbergplatz
Zaunergasse
Veithgasse
Mattiellistr.
Paniglgasse
Karlskirche
Prinz-Eugen-Strasse
Gardekirche
Gusshausstrasse
Rennweg
Karlsgasse
Schwindgasse
Palais Schwarzenberg
Argentinierstr.
Wohllebengasse
Unteres Belvedere
U-Bahn
Information
Church
Post Office
Theater
Library
Museum
Walking Path
0
1/4 mi
0
0.25 km

Like a catchy waltz tune, Vienna makes my heart beat faster. Much more than music and museums, this stately city is constantly reinventing itself. Modern art and vibrant nightlife are as much part of the Vienna of today as the grand concert halls and baroque architecture of its imperial heyday. Amid the pomp and splendor of its stately parks and palaces drifts an air of romance and easy living—a seductive charm at once relaxing yet compelling.

❶ Nibble your way through the culinary world of the Naschmarkt. On any weekday the stalls of the giant Naschmarkt are brimming with fresh fruit and vegetables, spices, meats, cheeses, olives, nuts, and baked goods. There are plenty of cafes and restaurants to grab a full meal, but it can be even more fun to sample as you go. On Saturdays a sprawling flea market promises all kinds of treasures—just get there early, as the best stuff goes fast. *See p 17,* ❸.

❷ Crack the code of the coffee menu at a legendary Viennese Kaffeehäuser. Viennese coffee houses range from basic, boho, and nicotine-stained to the sophisticated *fin-de-siècle* grandeur of my favorite, **Café Sperl.** Many have long literary associations. Coffee-drinking is virtually an art form in Vienna: choose a *Melange* (coffee with frothy milk); a *kleiner* or *grosser Brauner* (large or small coffee with cream); an *Einspänner* (mocha with whipped cream); a *Fiaker* (mocha with brandy) . . . the list goes on. *See "The Best Dining," p 109.*

❸ Wind back the clocks to imperial times at the Hofburg and see how the 19th-century Habsburg Empress Sisi, darling of Viennese society, lived in these grandiose palace apartments. Discover how all that glittered was not gold for Vienna's "Princess Diana" figure, whose tragic life came to an abrupt end in 1898. *See p 10,* ❶.

❹ Tuck into what must be the largest Wiener schnitzel in the world at Figlmüller. This tiny, *pseudo-rustique* restaurant is always crowded and a bit touristy. But who cares when the

Kids large and small love to ride the Riesenrad.

legendary schnitzels are so big that they overlap the plates? They taste pretty good too, washed down with a *G'spritzter* (white wine spritzer). If they're full, try the nearby Lugeck. *See p 10,* 2.

5 Take photos from the top of the Prater Ferris wheel (Riesenrad). Aerial views of the city and the Vienna Woods beyond are especially enticing at sunset, when the city glows in mellow evening light and lamps begin to twinkle. You can also relive the key scene in Vienna's cult movie, *The Third Man,* when the two anti-heroes finally meet on the wheel. *See p 98,* 5.

6 Indulge in some serious retail therapy in the side streets of Mariahilferstrasse. Take the pulse of the city's young fashion designers in the trendy Neubau district; gather home-furnishing ideas at the MAK (the Museum of Applied Arts) boutique; then shop for a picnic at the bustling Naschmarkt, where the photogenic food stalls are a feast for the senses. *See "The Best Shopping," p 79.*

7 Stroll through the Vienna Woods and taste some local wines. Few of the world's capitals grow wine within the city limits. A visit to some of the cozy *Heurigen* (wine taverns) in the romantic wine-growing villages on Vienna's outskirts always makes an enjoyable excursion. Take your camera to capture stunning views over Vienna from the vine-striped hills. *See "The Great Outdoors," p 93.*

8 Forget the calories and enjoy "Kuchen mit Schlag." Vienna is cake-and-whipped-cream heaven. It's hard to stick to the straight and narrow when confronted by a formidable choice of gooey gâteaux. Some of the most popular cakes include Mozarttorte and Esterhazytorte Then there's a divine specialty

Vienna's vineyards are a short tram ride away.

known as *Mohr im Hemd* (warm chocolate cake with fudge sauce) and of course the ubiquitous *Apfelstrudel* (apple strudel). If you can manage only one cake during your stay, make it the city's most famous indulgence—the irresistible chocolate *Sachertorte* created at **Café Sacher.** *See "The Best Dining," p 109.*

9 Take a tram ride round the Ringstrasse. Ride the Ring Tram for a complete circuit of the epic boulevard surrounding the medieval city, trundling past a monumental assortment of palaces, parliament buildings, and grand hotels. Captivating by day or by night—when many of the edifices are spectacularly lit up. *See the Ringstrasse tour, p 58.*

10 Soak up the magical atmosphere of the Christmas markets. Search for Christmas goodies, decorations, and expertly carved cribs amid a winter wonderland of twinkling trees and snow-capped wooden huts. After buying your stocking-stuffers, gather round the market stalls for *Glühwein* (mulled wine) and warm gingerbread, or *Lebkuchen.* Christkindlmarkt, the most famous Christmas market,

Tour the Ringstrasse on tram 1 and 2.

takes place at Rathausplatz. *See p 60,* ❼.

⓫ **Get lost in the maze of the Schönbrunn Palace.** Join the Viennese in one of their favorite pastimes—strolling in Schönbrunn's magnificent formal gardens. This massive park is larger than the Principality of Monaco. Don't miss the world's oldest zoo tucked in one corner with its adorable polar bears and pandas, and Maria Theresa's grand apartments inside the palace. *See p 108,* ❺.

⓬ **Mingle with the creative crowd on the sidewalk tables of a cafe in Neubau.** Take an afternoon to don some round shades and a brimmed hat of some sort and sip wine, coffee, or tea at one of the many cafes in the side streets of Mariahilferstrasse, Vienna's new in 2015 pedestrian zone. Take in some art at the galleries and check out the local and international fashion in the neighborhood's many boutiques. *See "Bobo Vienna," p 54.*

⓭ **Swim in the Danube and chill out on the beach.** Yes . . . there really is a beach in Vienna, and in the summer it's packed with sunbathers, swimmers, and watersports fanatics. If you'd rather be on the water than in it, rent a motor- or sailboat or take a mini-cruise along the river. *See "The Great Outdoors," p 93.*

⓮ **Devour a Viennese sausage at a Würstelstand near you.** They're all over town, and you shouldn't leave Vienna without having sampled one of the local *Wurst* specialties. Go for a spicy Debreziner or a classic Frankfurter. *See p 65,* 12.

Johann Strauss—the most celebrated statue in town.

1 The Best Full-Day Tours

The Best **in One Day**

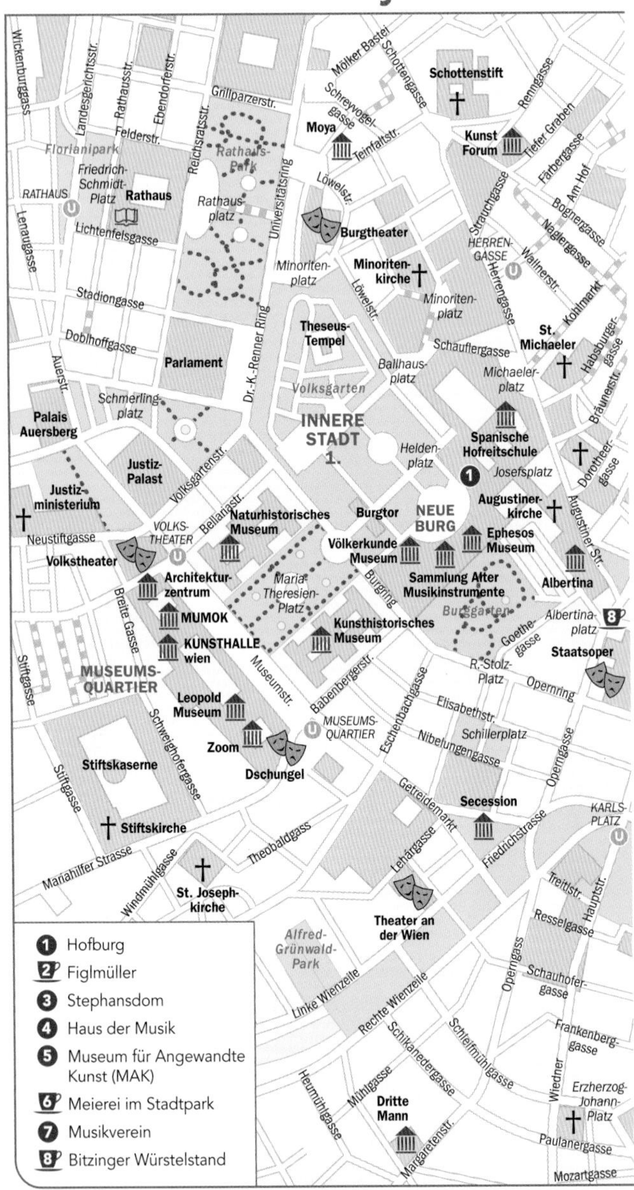

Previous page: Vienna's fiaker (horse and buggy) horses.

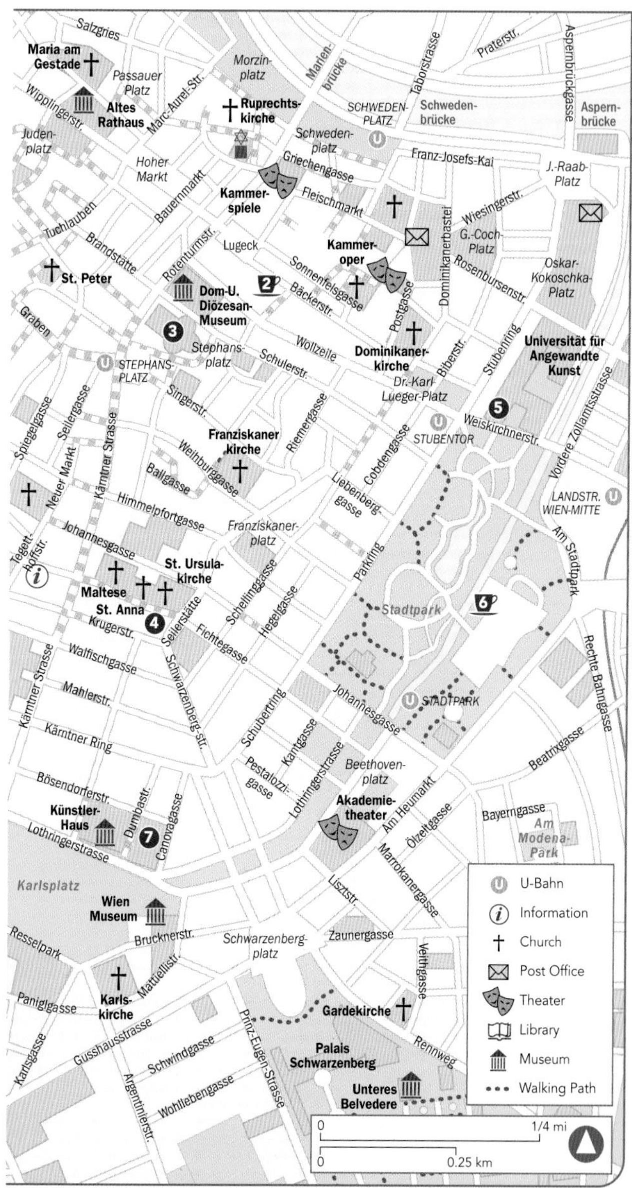

Salzgries
Maria am Gestade
Passauer Platz
Altes Rathaus
Wipplingerstr.
Marc-Aurel-Str.
Morzinplatz
Ruprechtskirche
Marienbrücke
Taborstrasse
Praterstr.
Aspernbrückgasse
Aspernbrücke
SCHWEDENPLATZ
Schwedenbrücke
Schwedenplatz
Judenplatz
Hoher Markt
Griechengasse
Franz-Josefs-Kai
J.-Raab-Platz
Kammerspiele
Fleischmarkt
Bauernmarkt
Tuchlauben
Wiesingerstr.
G.-Coch-Platz
Brandstätte
Rotenturmstr.
Lugeck
Kammeroper
Dominikanerbastei
Rosenbursenstr.
Oskar-Kokoschka-Platz
St. Peter
Dom-U. Diözesan-Museum
Sonnenfelsgasse
Bäckerstr.
Postgasse
Graben
Stephansplatz
STEPHANSPLATZ
Wollzeile
Schulerstr.
Dominikanerkirche
Biberstr.
Stubenring
Universität für Angewandte Kunst
Dr.-Karl-Lueger-Platz
Singerstr.
Spiegelgasse
Seilergasse
Kärntner Strasse
Riemergasse
Weiskirchnerstr.
STUBENTOR
Franziskaner kirche
Weihburggasse
Cobdengasse
Vordere Zollamtsstrasse
Neuer Markt
Ballgasse
Liebenberggasse
LANDSTR. WIEN-MITTE
Himmelpfortgasse
Johannesgasse
Franziskanerplatz
Am Stadtpark
Tegetthoffstr.
Parkring
St. Ursula-kirche
Maltese
St. Anna
Schellinggasse
Hegelgasse
Stadtpark
Krugerstr.
Seilerstätte
Fichtegasse
Walfischgasse
Kärntner Strasse
Rechte Bahngasse
Mahlerstr.
Schwarzenberg-Str.
Johannesgasse
STADTPARK
Kärntner Ring
Schubertring
Kantgasse
Beatrixgasse
Pestalozzigasse
Lothringerstrasse
Beethovenplatz
Bösendorferstr.
Akademietheater
Am Heumarkt
Künstler-Haus
Dumbastr.
Canovagasse
Ölzeltgasse
Bayerngasse
Am Modena-Park
Lothringerstrasse
Marrokanergasse
Karlsplatz
Lisztstr.
Wien Museum
Resselpark
Brucknerstr.
Schwarzenbergplatz
Zaunergasse
Veithgasse
Mattiellistr.
Paniglgasse
Karlskirche
Gardekirche
Gusshausstrasse
Prinz-Eugen-Strasse
Rennweg
Karlsgasse
Schwindgasse
Palais Schwarzenberg
Argentinierstr.
Wohllebengasse
Unteres Belvedere
U-Bahn
Information
Church
Post Office
Theater
Library
Museum
Walking Path
0
1/4 mi
0
0.25 km

Where better to start exploring Vienna than at its historic heart? On this tour you can soak up the architecture and lifestyle of imperial Vienna; admire the Stephansdom (St. Stephen's Cathedral and national emblem of Austria); discover the best schnitzels in town; dabble in Vienna's musical identity; and eat at one of the finest restaurants in the world . . . all in a single day. START: **Hofburg (U-Bahn 3 Herrengasse).**

---

❶ ★★★ **Hofburg.** Home to the powerful Habsburg dynasty, which ruled Austria for 6 centuries, the grandiose Hofburg buildings provide a remarkable record of Vienna's imperial lifestyle and architecture at the end of the 19th century. Don't be put off by the daunting tally of 18 wings, 19 courtyards, and 2,600 rooms. This rambling complex has been neatly packaged into clusters of manageable attractions. The Sisi Museum vividly portrays the moving life of Vienna's beloved empress, Elisabeth of Bavaria (1837–98). With a collection of her personal effects and accessories, such as gloves and a parasol, visitors get an intimate picture of the empress. There is also a room dedicated to the details of her assassination. The Imperial Apartments include the study, waiting room, and audience room of Sisi's husband, the Emperor Franz Joseph I (1848–1916). Make sure you don't miss the Schatzkammer (located in the Treasury, p 30), a glittering hoard of Habsburg jewels amassed over more than a millennium, and the celebrated **Spanische Reitschule** (Spanish Riding School), where magnificent Lipizzaner stallions perform dance-like exercises and formations. *Audio guides for adults and kids are included in the price.* ⏱ *1–4 hr. Hofburg. www.hofburg-wien.at. U-Bahn 3 (Herrengasse).* *See p 28–31, 44 ❻.*

2 ★★ kids **Figlmüller.** Tucked inside a narrow arcade, this legendary schnitzel joint is no secret. Yet while crowded, it reputedly serves the best schnitzels in Vienna, that will exceed the edges of your dinner plate. The culinary treasure is accompanied by a mixed salad and

The Hofburg's central courtyard.

Sisi—A Tragic Empress

The eccentric, reclusive, and beautiful Empress "Sisi" was born Elisabeth, Duchess of Bavaria, in 1837. At the tender age of 15, she agreed to marry her cousin, Franz Joseph of Austria, and took up residence at the Hofburg. Thrust unwillingly into the public eye, she hated imperial life and declined to fulfill the traditional roles of empress, wife, and mother. Her eldest child died aged two, and her fourth child committed suicide in 1889 at age 31. She eventually became estranged from her husband, wrote increasingly melancholic poetry, and traveled incessantly. In 1885 she wrote: "I am a seagull, of no land, I call no shore my home, I am bound to no place, I fly from wave to wave." She was assassinated in Geneva in 1898 by an Italian anarchist, who later remarked: "I wanted to kill a royal. It did not matter which one."

either beer or wine from the owner's own vineyard in Grinzing (p 103). If you can't get a seat, try Lugeck around the corner, which also serves traditional Austrian in a more modern setting and belongs to the Figlmüller family. *Wollzeile 5.* ☎ *01 512 6177. €€.*

❸ ★★ **Stephansdom.** The Viennese affectionately call their majestic cathedral the "Steffl." Dominating the city center, its skeletal spire towers 137m (450 ft) above the rooftops. Literally and figuratively, it represents a high point in Viennese Gothic architecture. The cathedral is now a national emblem. Its graceful pillars and lofty ribbed vaulting were described by architect Adolf Loos as "the most spiritual church interior in the world." Take the elevator up the north tower for exceptional views of the city center and the cathedral's eye-catching yellow, blue, and green rooftop, which consists of a quarter of a million brilliantly glazed tiles. The Stephansdom's "Pummerin" (Boomer)

St. John Capistrano rallied the people to crusade in 1454 to hold back the Muslim invasions of Christian Europe.

bell is Austria's largest and heaviest. It is used just once annually—to ring in the New Year. Beethoven discovered the totality of his deafness when he realized he could no longer hear the bells. The square in front of the cathedral was once a marketplace. Medieval measuring marks are still visible in the masonry

The stunning Stephansdom cathedral.

by the main west entrance. Two are ancient measures of length (the shorter "Bohemian" and the longer "Viennese" ell), while another indicates the correct size for a loaf of bread. *1 hr; go early on weekdays or during the evening to avoid the tour groups. Stephansplatz 3. ☎ 01 515 52 3526. www.stephanskirche.at. Free admission. Mon–Sat 6am–10pm; Sun 7am–10pm. Elevator: daily 9am–5:30pm. €5.50 adults, €2 kids. U-Bahn 1/3 (Stephansplatz).*

4 ★★ kids Haus der Musik. There's no escaping Vienna's influence on the world of classical music. From Strauß walzes to Mozart's distinct footprint, music is part of Vienna's DNA. The "sound Museum" takes on not only the history of music, but is a hands-on way to experience how sounds and instruments work. Visitors can even record their own tracks using easy-interface composing software. The museum has lots of history as well, including plenty on Vienna Wunderkind, Wolfgang Amadeus Mozart. *1–3 hr. Seilerstätte 30. ☎ 01 513 48 50. www.hausdermusik.com. €13 adults, €9 concessions, €9 students, €6 kids under 12, €29 family (2 adults, 3 kids under 12), €18/8 adults/kids for a combined ticket with Mozarthaus, see p 39; audio guides for adults and kids are included in the price. Daily 10am–10pm. U-Bahn 1/2/4 (Karlsplatz).*

5 ★★ Museum für Angewandte Kunst (MAK). The Applied Arts Museum is one of Vienna's most eclectic museums, showcasing 8 centuries of Austrian decorative arts and design. Treasures range from Renaissance jewelry and Biedermeier furniture to the world's first fitted kitchen—the *Frankfurter Küche* (Frankfurt Kitchen). The rooms are arranged in chronological order from the Gothic era to the present day. Besides the innovative contemporary exhibits, highlights include the Jugendstil rooms, and the exquisite Arts and Crafts exhibits from the Wiener Werkstätte (p 35). Allow time to visit the museum shop, full of design objects, arty gifts, and weird and wonderful gadgets and gizmos. *1 hr. Stubenring 5. ☎ 01 711 36-0. www.mak.at. €9 adults, €7.50 concessions, free under 19, €13 family ticket. Tues 10am–10pm; Wed–Sun 10am–6pm. Admission free Tue 6–10pm. U-Bahn 3 (Stubentor).*

6 ★★★ Meierei im Stadtpark. Stroll through the picturesque Stadtpark to Steirereck, arguably one of the top 10 restaurants in town. But downstairs from the main event is Meierei, its more affordable little brother, which serves high-end versions of Viennese classics, plus seasonal menus. The view of dusk over the park is a perfect way to welcome the evening. In warm weather, ask for a seat on the terrace. *Am*

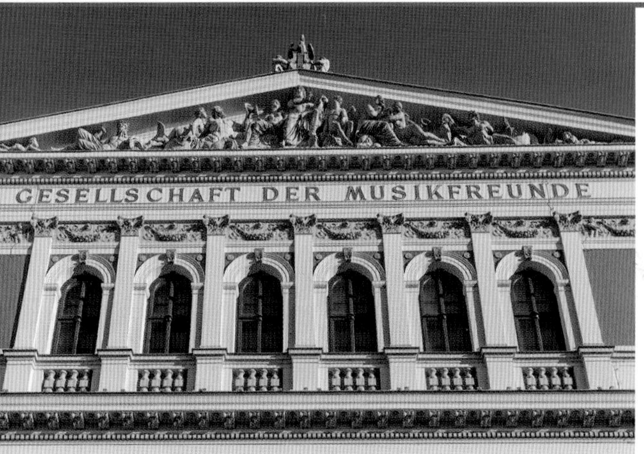

Building detail from the Musikverein.

Heumarkt 2A/im Stadtpark. ☎ *01 713 3168 - 10. €€€.*

❼ ★★ **Musikverein.** If you only go to one concert in Vienna, make sure it's at the Musikverein—the city's most prestigious classical music venue. Each year, the sumptuously decorated Golden Hall hosts Vienna's celebrated New Year's Day concert, performed by its world-famous resident orchestra, the Vienna Philharmonic. An awe-inspiring roll call of former concert directors includes Johannes Brahms, Herbert von Karajan and, more recently, Leonard Bernstein, Claudio Abbado, and Riccardo Muti. The building itself, designed by Theophil Hansen in Greek Renaissance style, with lavish use of terracotta capitals, balustrades, and gilded statuary, was opened in 1870 for the Viennese Society of Friends of Music. *Bösendorferstrasse 12.* ☎ *01 505 8190. www.musikverein.at. Tickets €6 (standing room) to €85. U-Bahn 1/2/4 (Karlsplatz).*

8 ★★ **Bitzinger.** The Viennese *würstelstand* (sausage stand) is as much part of local culture as schnitzel or the ball season. Join the post-opera crowd at the classiest stand of them all right next to the Albertina (p 30). Grab a Debreziner (slightly spicy) or a Käsekainer (with melted cheese) and a glass of wine, or even Perrier champagne to end the day in urban style, just like a local. *Albertinaplatz.* ☎ *0660 815 24 13. €.*

The Best in Two Days

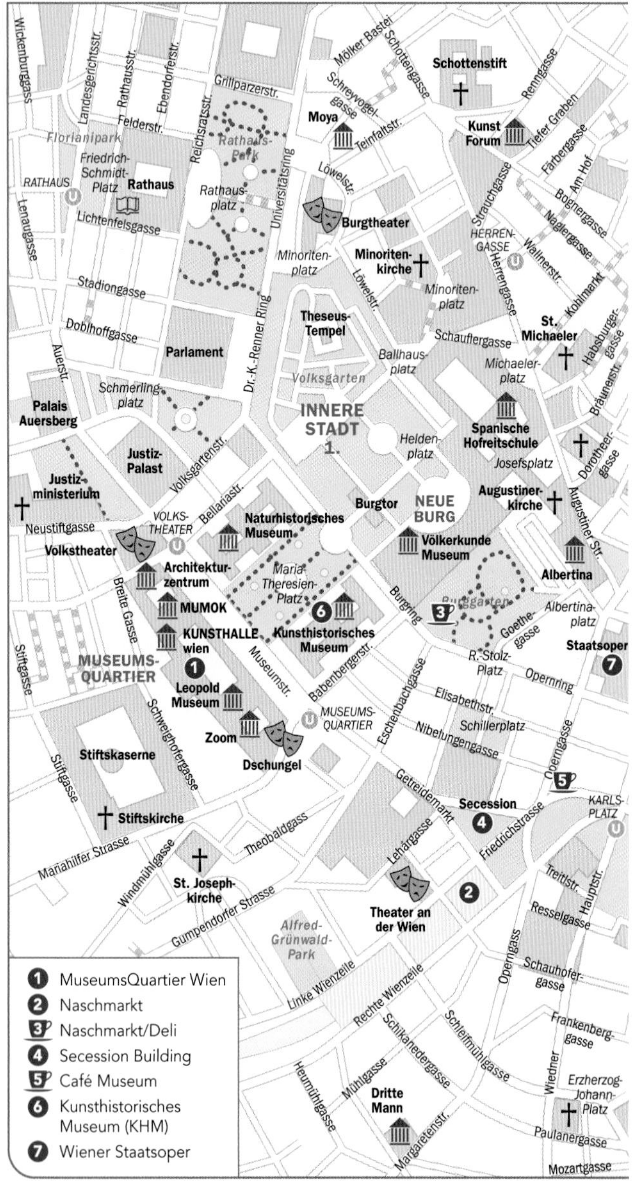

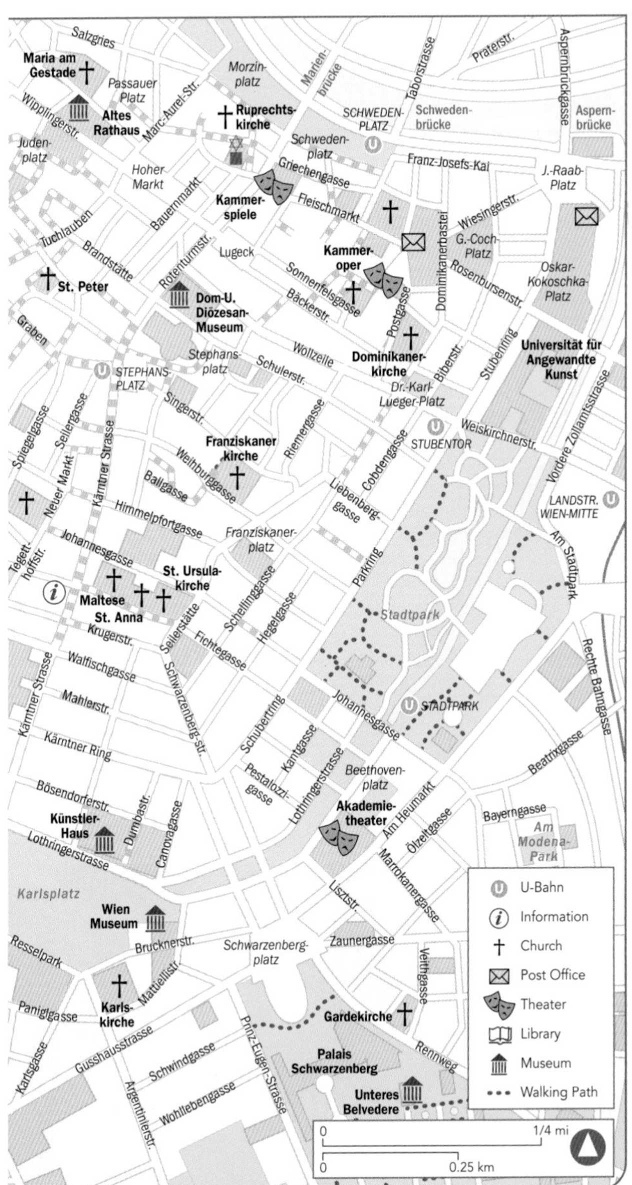
Salzgries
Maria am Gestade
Passauer Platz
Altes Rathaus
Wipplingerstr.
Juden-platz
Marc-Aurel-Str.
Morzin-platz
Ruprechts-kirche
Marien-brücke
Taborstrasse
Praterstr.
Asperbrückgasse
Aspern-brücke
SCHWEDEN-PLATZ
Schweden-brücke
Schweden-platz
Franz-Josefs-Kai
Hoher Markt
Griechengasse
Kammer-spiele
Fleischmarkt
J.-Raab-Platz
Bauernmarkt
Tuchlauben
Brandstätte
Rotenturmstr.
Lugeck
Kammer-oper
Wiesingerstr.
G.-Coch-Platz
Dominikanerbastei
Rosenbursenstr.
Oskar-Kokoschka-Platz
St. Peter
Dom-U. Diözesan-Museum
Sonnenfelsgasse
Bäckerstr.
Postgasse
Graben
Stephans-platz
Wollzeile
Schulerstr.
Dominikaner-kirche
Biberstr.
Stubenring
Universität für Angewandte Kunst
STEPHANS-PLATZ
Singerstr.
Dr.-Karl-Lueger-Platz
Vordere Zollamtsstrasse
Spiegelgasse
Seilergasse
Kärntner Strasse
Franziskaner kirche
Riemergasse
STUBENTOR
Weiskirchnerstr.
Neuer Markt
Weihburggasse
Ballgasse
Cobdengasse
Liebenberg-gasse
LANDSTR. WIEN-MITTE
Himmelpfortgasse
Johannesgasse
Franziskaner-platz
Am Stadtpark
Tegett-hoffstr.
St. Ursula-kirche
Maltese
St. Anna
Parkring
Schellinggasse
Hegelgasse
Seilerstätte
Stadtpark
Krugerstr.
Fichtegasse
Walfischgasse
Kärntner Strasse
Mahlerstr.
Schwarzenberg-str.
Schubertring
Johannesgasse
STADTPARK
Rechte Bahngasse
Kärntner Ring
Kantgasse
Lothringerstrasse
Beethoven-platz
Beatrixgasse
Pestalozzi-gasse
Bösendorferstr.
Akademie-theater
Am Heumarkt
Bayerngasse
Künstler-Haus
Dumbastr.
Canovagasse
Ölzeltgasse
Am Modena-Park
Lothringerstrasse
Marokanergasse
Karlsplatz
Lisztstr.
Wien Museum
Bruckner.str.
Schwarzenberg-platz
Zaunergasse
Resselpark
Mattiellistr.
Veithgasse
Karls-kirche
Paniglgasse
Gardekirche
Gusshausstrasse
Prinz-Eugen-Strasse
Rennweg
Karlsgasse
Schwindgasse
Palais Schwarzenberg
Argentinierstr.
Wohllebengasse
Unteres Belvedere
U-Bahn
Information
Church
Post Office
Theater
Library
Museum
Walking Path
0
1/4 mi
0
0.25 km

On your second day, you will start to get under the skin of the city. This tour unveils more of Vienna's remarkable history and dazzling art treasures, with a relaxing interlude to soak up the atmosphere and flavors of the Naschmarkt, Vienna's most colorful market. Some of the world's finest museums and art galleries await you after a snack or picnic lunch in the park. In the evening, a visit to the opera rounds off a perfect day. START: **Wien Museum (U-Bahn 1/2/4 Karlsplatz).**

❶ ★★★ kids **MuseumsQuartier Wien.** This vast art and recreational complex comprises several art galleries surrounding a vast central courtyard. Younger tourists and stylish Viennese use the courtyard as their personal urban backyard. The Leopold Museum contains Austrian art from the 19th and 20th centuries; MUMOK is the nation's largest modern-art museum; and the Kunsthalle stages temporary art exhibitions. Add to this an architecture center, a kids' museum, and a cluster of shops, open-air restaurants, cafes, and bars, and you have one of the most popular cultural venues in town for locals and visitors alike (p 136). In warm weather it's a great place to reconvene or sip spritzers while lounging on the deck chairs ("enzis") at dusk. *1–6 hr. Museumsplatz 1. ☎ 01 523 5881. www.mqw.at. U-Bahn 2 (MuseumsQuartier).*

❷ ★★★ kids **Naschmarkt.** The colorful Naschmarkt is Vienna's largest and liveliest market, and a perfect place to buy picnic provisions. Mouthwatering displays of fresh and seasonal produce—flowers, fish, cheese, and wine—give visitors an extraordinary culinary tour around the world; the more far-reaching the further you delve. It stands in the valley of the River Wien, a site once occupied by medieval vineyards and an 18th-century milk market. Traditional wooden stalls lend it an old-fashioned air. It has a dazzling choice of eateries to suit all tastes and budgets, ranging from the snack bars that kick-start market traders with early-morning caffeine shots to seafood brasseries that seduce city sophisticates with platters of oysters. The Karlsplatz end tends to have the smartest (and most expensive) Viennese-run

Strolling the famed Naschmarkt.

The Secession Building continues to exhibit contemporary art.

stalls, along with luxury delicatessens and elegant pavement cafes. The less formal multi-ethnic section sells exotic produce and spices from all over the world. Farther west (near Kettenbrückengasse), a popular farmers market takes place on Fridays and Saturdays (Mar–Oct), and a Saturday morning flea market hawks a motley array of antiques, clothing, and bric-a-brac to bargain hunters. ⏲ *1 hr. Naschmarkt. Stalls: Mon–Fri 8am–6pm; Sat 6am–1pm. Snack bars: times vary, some open until 10 or 11pm, closed Sun. U-Bahn 1/2/4 (Karlsplatz) or U-Bahn 4 (Kettenbrückengasse).*

3 ★ **Naschmarkt/Deli.** This part of the Naschmarkt is the ultimate location for people-watching. The collection of cafes surrounding and including Deli have become the meeting point for students and people from the creative industries. The breakfast at Deli is popular and throughout the day you can get Middle Eastern fare, from hummus to pastrami sandwiches. *Naschmarkt Stand 421–436.* ☎ *01 585 0823. €–€€.*

4 ★★ **Secession Building.** This unusual white block was created in 1898 by Otto Wagner's student Joseph Maria Olbrich as a "Temple of Art"—a celebration of the Secessionist artistic movement—reflecting the fluid, functional yet decorative style of a new generation of artists (led by Gustav Klimt) who rebelled against the meaningless excesses of Viennese ornamentation. An inscription above the door proclaims *"Der Zeit ihre Kunst, der Kunst ihre Freiheit"* ("To the age, its own art; to art, its own freedom"). Garlands and floral patterns adorn the facade, while the entrance is decorated with a golden tree and the heads of the three Gorgons (representing architecture, sculpture, and painting). The crowning glory, however, is a dome of gilded laurel leaves—supposedly symbolizing the interdependence of art and nature—which has earned the Secession Building the affectionate nickname the "Golden Cabbage." The airy interior remains true to its original purpose, hosting exhibitions of contemporary art. In the basement, Klimt's Beethoven frieze is essential viewing (p 33, 3). ⏲ *30 min. Friedrichstrasse 12.* ☎ *01 587 5307. www.secession.at. €9.50 adults, €6 concessions, free under 10. Tues–Sun 10am–6pm; guided tours (in English) Sat 11am. U-Bahn 1/2/4 (Karlsplatz).*

5 **Café Museum.** Enjoy coffee and cake whilst watching the world go by from the sunny sidewalk terrace of this classic Viennese cafe, once frequented by artists Klimt, Kokoschka, and Schiele. Seating is also available in the cafe's cozy classic interior. *Friedrichstrasse 6/Operngasse. ☎ 01 2410 0620. €–€€.*

6 ★★★ Kunsthistorisches Museum (KHM). Vienna's superlative Museum of Fine Arts occupies a monumental Renaissance-style building on the Ringstrasse. It contains the Imperial collection assembled over centuries by the Habsburgs, who were keen patrons and avid collectors of art. It's a staggering haul of treasures from all around the globe, displayed in room after room on three floors. There's far too much to see properly in a single visit, but try at least to view the Old Masters in the Gemäldegalerie (Picture Gallery). *2 hr. Maria-Theresien-Platz. ☎ 01 525 240. www.khm.at. €15 adults, €11 concessions, free under 19 (tickets also valid for the Neue Burg, p 60). Sept–May Tues–Sun 10am–6pm (Thurs until 9pm); June–Aug daily 10am–6pm (Thurs until 9pm). U-Bahn 2/3 (Volkstheater).*

7 ★★★ Wiener Staatsoper. The Vienna State Opera holds a special place in the hearts of the Viennese, and it is recognized by music-lovers everywhere as one of the world's most illustrious opera houses. You can visit the interior, with its grand staircase and plush red-and-gold auditorium, on a guided tour. Even if you wouldn't normally consider seeing an opera, you may well be lured by the glitz and glamour of the Staatsoper. Also, standing room costs around €10; you just need to line up 30 minutes before the performance. This is an ideal way to get a taste of the experience without the black tie or needing to stay for the whole performance. *40 min. tour (start times vary and are advertised on a board at the box office). Opernring 2. ☎ 01 514-44 7810 (box office). www.staatsoper.at. U-Bahn 1/2/4 (Karlsplatz), Tram 1/2/D (Oper).*

Egyptian friezes adorn the walls of the Kunsthistorisches Museum.

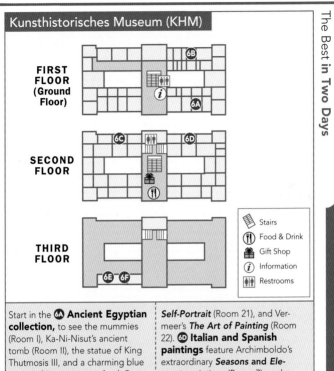

Kunsthistorisches Museum (KHM)

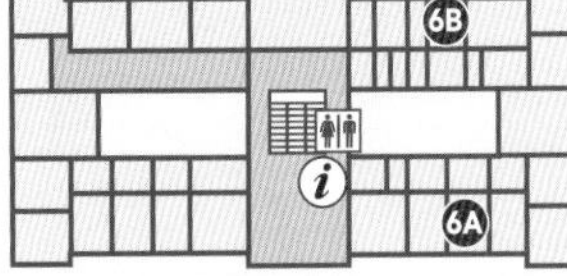

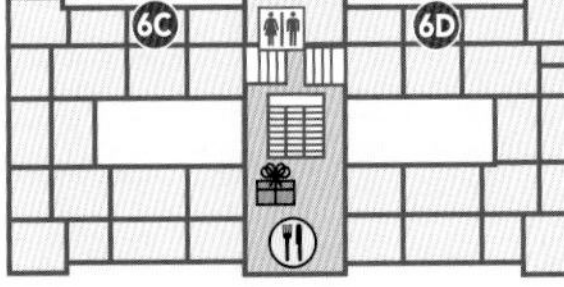

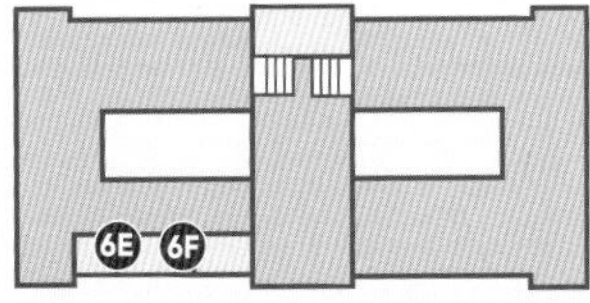

Start in the 6A **Ancient Egyptian collection,** to see the mummies (Room I), Ka-Ni-Nisut's ancient tomb (Room II), the statue of King Thutmosis III, and a charming blue ceramic hippopotamus (both Room IX). In 6B **Greek and Roman Antiquities,** look out for the impressive 2nd-century mosaic of *Theseus and the Minotaur* (Room XII), exquisite Roman cameos (Room XVI), and rare textiles (Room XVIII). The picture gallery upstairs represents all the major schools of European art and many of the world's greatest artists too. 6C **German, Flemish, and Dutch paintings** include Brueghel the Elder's ***The Seasons*** cycle (Room X), Dürer's ***Madonna with the Pear*** (Room 16), Rembrandt's ***Large Self-Portrait*** (Room 21), and Vermeer's ***The Art of Painting*** (Room 22). 6D **Italian and Spanish paintings** feature Archimboldo's extraordinary ***Seasons and Elements*** paintings (Room 7), and Velázquez's portrait of the 8-year-old ***Infanta Margarita Teresa in Blue Dress*** (Room 10), who married Leopold I just 7 years later. The paintings of early 18th-century imperial palaces and Viennese views by Canaletto's nephew Bellotto commissioned for the Empress Maria Theresa (Room VII) are especially fascinating. The top floor contains one of the world's most extensive 6E **coin collections** and over 1,000 6F **miniature portraits** collected by Emperor Ferdinand II.

The Best in Three Days

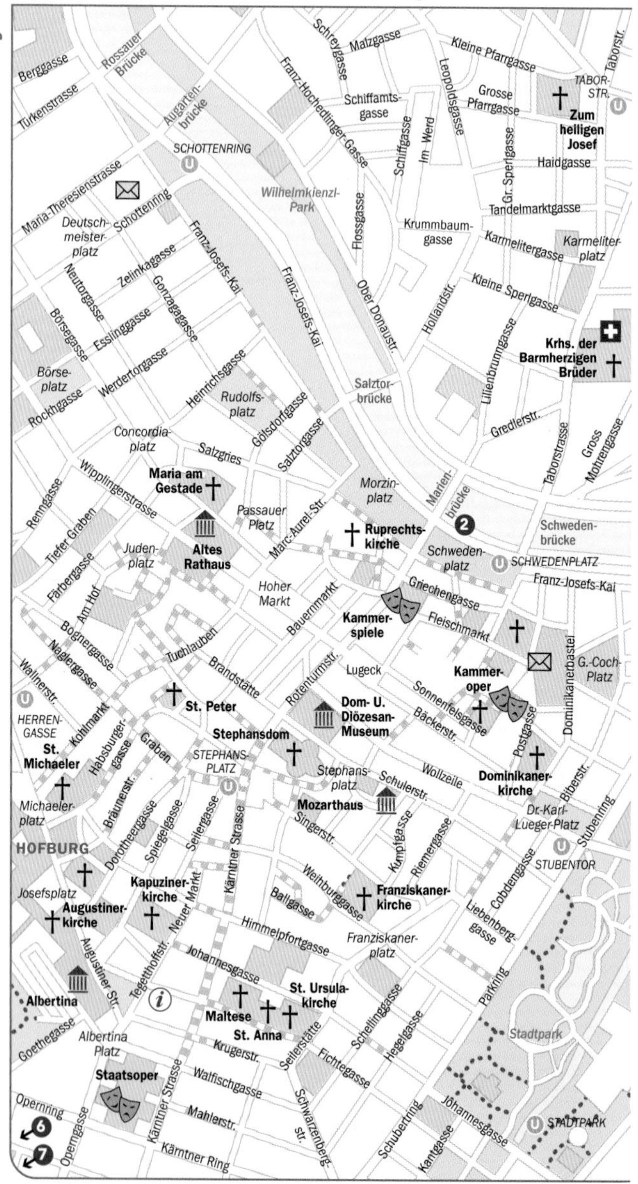

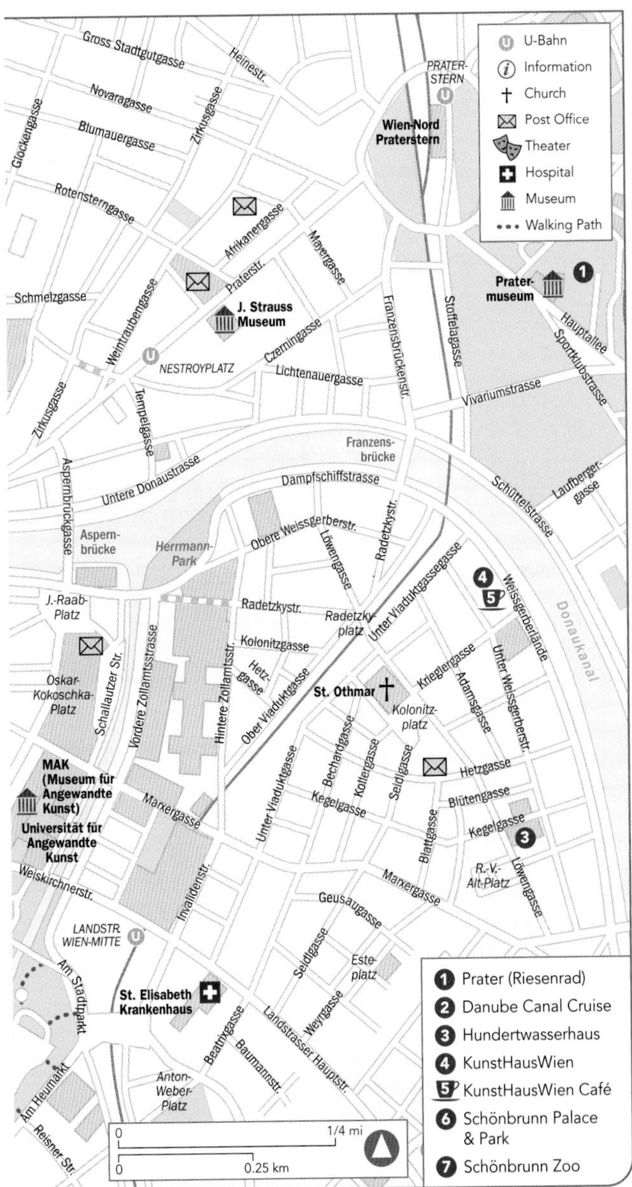
U-Bahn
Information
Church
Post Office
Theater
Hospital
Museum
Walking Path
Gross Stadtgutgasse
Novaragasse
Blumauergasse
Glockengasse
Heinestr.
Zirkusgasse
PRATER-STERN
Wien-Nord Praterstern
Rotensterngasse
Afrikanergasse
Mayergasse
Praterstr.
Schmelzgasse
Weintraubengasse
J. Strauss Museum
Prater-museum
Franzensbrückenstr.
Stoffelagasse
Hauptallee
Sportklubstrasse
NESTROYPLATZ
Czerningasse
Lichtenauergasse
Vivariumstrasse
Zirkusgasse
Tempelgasse
Franzens-brücke
Untere Donaustrasse
Dampfschiffstrasse
Schüttelstrasse
Laufberger-gasse
Asperbrückgasse
Aspern-brücke
Herrmann-Park
Obere Weissgerberstr.
Löwengasse
Radetzkystr.
Unter Viaduktgassegasse
Weissgerberlände
Donaukanal
J.-Raab-Platz
Radetzkystr.
Radetzky-platz
Kolonitzgasse
Hetz-gasse
Krieglergasse
Adamsgasse
Unter Weissgerberstr.
Oskar-Kokoschka-Platz
Schallautzer Str.
Vordere Zollamtsstrasse
Hintere Zollamtsstr.
Ober Viaduktgasse
St. Othmar
Kolonitz-platz
MAK (Museum für Angewandte Kunst)
Universität für Angewandte Kunst
Unter Viaduktgasse
Bechardgasse
Koltergasse
Seidlgasse
Hetzgasse
Blütengasse
Kegelgasse
Kegelgasse
Marxergasse
Blattgasse
R.-V.-Alt-Platz
Löwengasse
Weiskirchnerstr.
Invalidenstr.
Marxergasse
Geusaugasse
LANDSTR. WIEN-MITTE
Seidlgasse
Este-platz
Am Stadtpark
St. Elisabeth Krankenhaus
Beatrixgasse
Weyrgasse
Landstrasser Hauptstr.
Baumannstr.
Am Heumarkt
Anton-Weber-Platz
Reisner Str.
0
1/4 mi
0
0.25 km
1 Prater (Riesenrad)
2 Danube Canal Cruise
3 Hundertwasserhaus
4 KunstHausWien
5 KunstHausWien Café
6 Schönbrunn Palace & Park
7 Schönbrunn Zoo

After 2 days of art, architecture, history, and culture, today's trip takes in some of the city's best-loved attractions, including the famous Prater Riesenrad (Ferris wheel), the Danube Canal, the city zoo, and Schönbrunn, the most-visited palace in Austria. It requires an early start and a bit of stamina, but you will be well-rewarded for your efforts. START: **Prater (U-Bahn 1/2 Praterstern).**

❶ ★★★ kids Prater (Riesenrad). Vienna's world-famous Ferris wheel. *See p 98,* ❺.

❷ ★★ kids Danube Canal Cruise. The Danube, Vienna's lifeblood since Roman times, was partly canalized at the end of the 19th century to reduce flooding in the built-up areas of the city. A mini-cruise provides an entirely new perspective of the city. The DDSG (Blue Danube Shipping Company) offers a 1½-hour trip on the canal, which starts from the Schiffstation Wien/City at Schwedenplatz, and passes some of Vienna's lesser known but nonetheless intriguing sights.

The Prater amusement park is fun for the whole family.

See the sights by boat.

❸ ★★ kids Hundertwasserhaus. You can't fail to spot the Hundertwasserhaus! With its vividly colored patchwork facade, gleaming gold onion-domes, distinct lack of straight lines (even inside), and tree-clad roof, the Hundertwasserhaus stands out among the dull Austro-Hungarian empire architecture that surrounds it. Designed by Austrian artist Friedensreich Hundertwasser in 1986 as a public housing complex, it provoked fierce debate among the Viennese who described it as "an unbearable display of new-money pomposity." Now it is a much-loved part of the Viennese cityscape. *Löwengasse/corner of Kegelgasse. www.hundertwasserhaus.at. Tram 1 (Hetzgasse).*

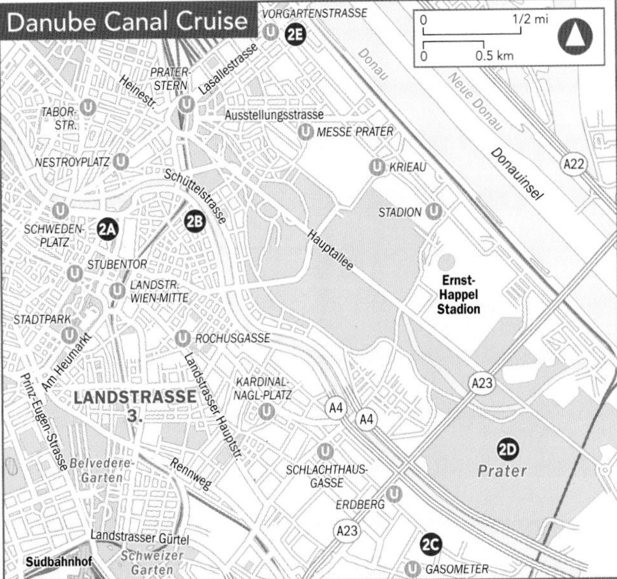

The first eye-catching sight on this tour is the cupola of the 2A ★ **Sternwarte Urania.** Built in 1910, this is Austria's oldest astronomical observatory and also contains a cinema, a puppet theater, and a cafe with superb canal vistas. Farther east, look out for glimpses of the 2B ★★★ **KunstHausWien** (below), designed by Vienna's radical architect, Hundertwasser. Beyond lies a curious structure known as the 2C ★ **Gasometer.** These four rotund brick towers were used to store the city's gas supply from 1899 to 1969. In the 1990s, they were converted into 615 apartments, a vast shopping center, and leisure complex. As you pass through the massive Freudenau lock and on to the New Danube, you'll see the gravel beaches of the Donauinsel (Danube Island) to your right and the 2D **Prater** park (p 97) on your left. Keep an eye open for three Prater landmarks: the Buddhist pagoda, the Ernst Happel Stadium (venue of the Euro 2008 football tournament), and the Riesenrad (p 98, 5). The tour ends at the Reichsbrücke, a bridge near Mexikoplatz. The most prominent building on this square is the multi-turreted 2E **Franz-von-Assisi-Kirche,** built in 1898 by Emperor Franz Joseph I to commemorate his golden anniversary. *DDSG Information Desk, Handelskai 265. ☎ 01 58880. www.ddsg-blue-danube.at. U-Bahn 1 (Vorgartenstrasse).*

4 ★★★ kids **KunstHausWien.** Just round the corner from the Hundertwasserhaus is one of my favorite museums—the KunstHausWien. This is not your usual museum experience but rather an adventure in architecture, and the chance to experience the

KunstHausWien, designed by the undeniably eccentric Friedensreich Hundertwasser.

extraordinary range of Hundertwasser's creative genius, which encompassed art, graphics, models, tapestry, kites, sculpture, even postage stamps. His brightly colored paintings are as distinctive as his architectural constructions. The building (a converted furniture factory) features all the artist's characteristic trademarks—vivid colors contrasting with black and gold; shiny, irregularly shaped pillars; a roof garden; and no straight lines (even the floor is uneven). When it was created in 1989, critics described it as "tasteless," resembling "a half-melted slab of liquorice." Come and see what you think. *1 hr. Untere Weissgerberstrasse 13. ☎ 01 712 0495. www.kunsthauswien.com. €10 adults, €5 kids (11–18), free under 11. Daily 10am–6pm. Tram 1/O (Radetzkyplatz).*

5 ★★★ kids KunstHausWien Café. As you might expect from Hundertwasser, this cafe is innovative and informal, with a delightful shaded patio area. Its simple menu includes a good choice of vegetarian dishes. *Untere Weissgerberstrasse 13. ☎ 01 713 8620. €–€€.*

6 ★★★ kids Schönbrunn Palace & Park. *See p 45.*

7 ★★ kids Schönbrunn Zoo. *See p 108, 7.* ●

Vienna's Playground

First mentioned in 1162 and gifted to the public by Emperor Josef II on April 7, 1776, the beloved retreat-within-the-city serenaded through the centuries by Mozart, Strauss, and Robert Stolz, celebrated its 250th anniversary in 2016. In addition to the famous amusement park (including the legendary Riesenrad, or Giant Ferris Wheel), the former imperial hunting grounds are a vast recreation area, popular for sports. On foot, wheels, and horseback, Viennese frequent the 4.4km-long (2¾ miles) Hauptallee (promenade). Centrally located are the nation's largest stadium, a velodrome, and swimming pool (all built for the 1931 International Worker's Olympiad, a proletarian Olympic games). There are two horseracing tracks, a golf course, a BMX track, and numerous playgrounds. The main entrance is at Praterstern (*U-Bahn 1/2 Pratestern*).

2 The Best Special-Interest Tours

Imperial Vienna

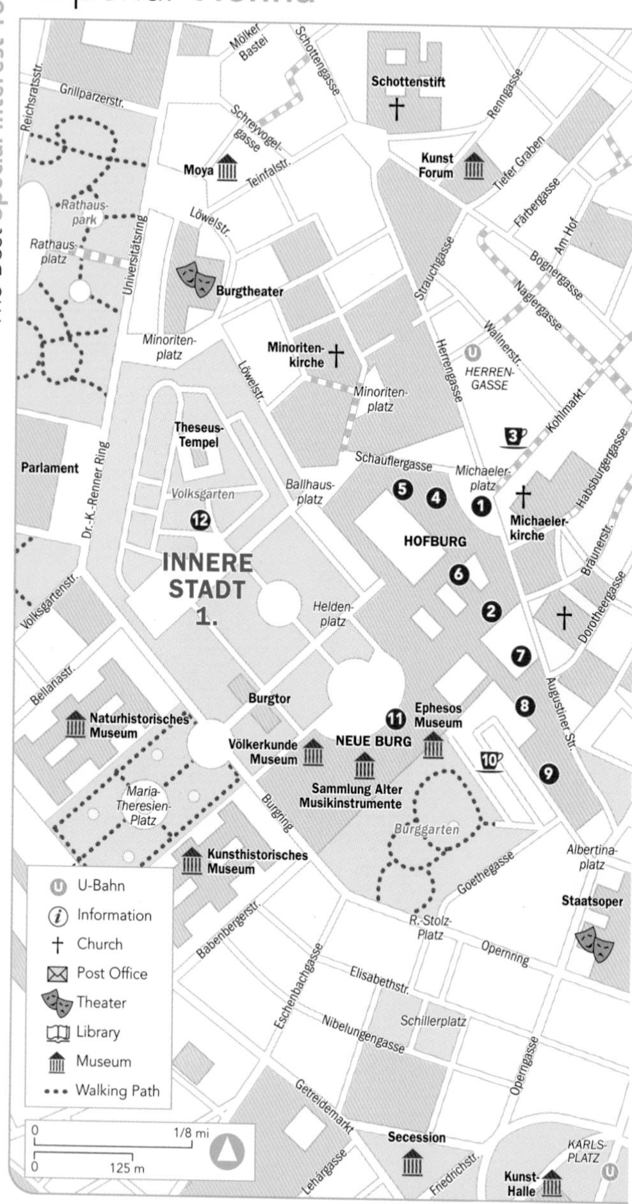

Previous page: Borromeo—the patron saint of Karlskirche.

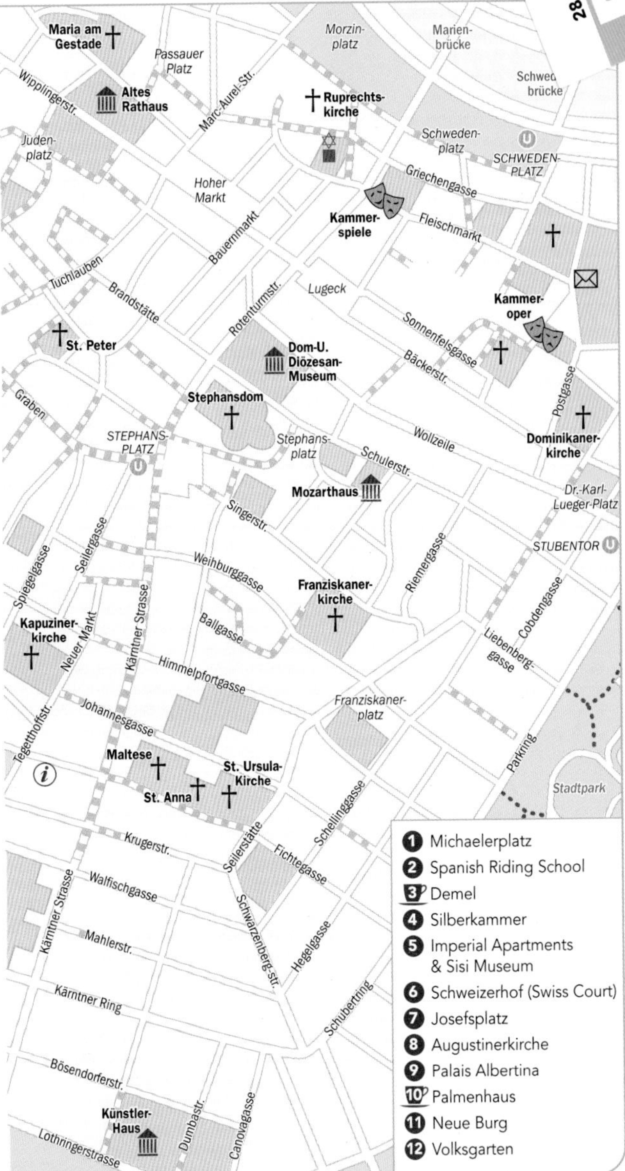
Maria am Gestade
Altes Rathaus
Passauer Platz
Wipplingerstr.
Marc-Aurel-Str.
Morzinplatz
Ruprechtskirche
Marienbrücke
Schwedenbrücke
Schwedenplatz
SCHWEDENPLATZ
Judenplatz
Hoher Markt
Griechengasse
Kammerspiele
Fleischmarkt
Bauernmarkt
Tuchlauben
Brandstätte
Rotenturmstr.
Lugeck
Kammeroper
Sonnenfelsgasse
St. Peter
Dom-U. Diözesan-Museum
Bäckerstr.
Graben
Stephansdom
Postgasse
Dominikanerkirche
STEPHANSPLATZ
Stephansplatz
Wollzeile
Schulerstr.
Mozarthaus
Dr.-Karl-Lueger-Platz
Singerstr.
STUBENTOR
Seilergasse
Spiegelgasse
Weihburggasse
Riemergasse
Franziskanerkirche
Cobdengasse
Kärntner Strasse
Kapuzinerkirche
Neuer Markt
Ballgasse
Liebenberggasse
Himmelpfortgasse
Franziskanerplatz
Johannesgasse
Tegetthoffstr.
Maltese
St. Ursula-Kirche
St. Anna
Parkring
Stadtpark
Krugerstr.
Seilerstätte
Schellinggasse
Fichtegasse
Walfischgasse
Kärntner Strasse
Schwarzenberg-Str.
Mahlerstr.
Hegelgasse
Kärntner Ring
Schubertring
Bösendorferstr.
Künstler-Haus
Dumbastr.
Canovagasse
Lothringerstrasse
1 Michaelerplatz
2 Spanish Riding School
3 Demel
4 Silberkammer
5 Imperial Apartments & Sisi Museum
6 Schweizerhof (Swiss Court)
7 Josefsplatz
8 Augustinerkirche
9 Palais Albertina
10 Palmenhaus
11 Neue Burg
12 Volksgarten

The Hofburg, residence of the mighty Habsburg dynasty for over 600 years, should be on every visitor's itinerary. Originally a medieval castle, it was extended by each successive emperor to demonstrate the power and riches of the Habsburgs, until it effectively became a "city within a city." The resulting labyrinthine complex, and the astounding treasures within it, established Vienna's reputation worldwide as a place of unrivalled elegance, wealth, and splendor. START: **Michaelerplatz (U-Bahn 3 Herrengasse).**

1 ★ Michaelerplatz. Layer upon layer of history has been unearthed in Michaelerplatz—the monumental square adjacent to the Hofburg—and Roman remains and medieval foundations have been excavated at its center. Then there's the grandly colonnaded Michaelertrakt (St. Michael's Wing) and Michaelertor (St. Michael's Gate) entrances to the Hofburg, both added by Emperor Franz Joseph in 1893. The fountains on the outer limits of the main gateway (see below) symbolize Habsburg power both on land and at sea. The gigantic copper-clad cupola above the Michaelertor looks especially striking (and photogenic) from Kohlmarkt. The Michaelerkirche opposite, was once the parish church of the Imperial Court. Also in the square, Loos Haus (designed by Adolf Loos) broke architectural boundaries in 1912 with its functional design and unadorned green marble facade (p 34, 7).

2 ★★★ kids Spanish Riding School. *See p 44, 6.*

3 Demel. This opulent cafe and cake shop was founded in 1786. For centuries it has drawn wealthy Viennese shoppers to its mirrored and gilded interior for exquisite coffee, cakes, and confectionery, including Empress Sisi's favorite, candied violets. The beautiful candy and chocolate boxes make great gifts and souvenirs. *Kohlmarkt 14.* ☎ *01 535 1717-0. Daily 9am–7pm. Entrees €–€€.*

Mastery of the Seas sculpture in Michaelerplatz.

4 ★ Silberkammer. The Imperial Silver Collection is a dazzling array of priceless tableware in glass, silver, and porcelain. Some of these precious pieces are still used today for state banquets. The Grand Vermeil dinner service (Room 7), containing 4,500 pieces, is one of the world's largest silver-gilt services. Porcelain highlights include the flower plates of keen botanist, Emperor Franz II (Room D); the Hunting Lodge porcelain given to Franz Joseph by Sisi in 1870 (Room 6); floral baroque Meissen, Minton, and Sèvres porcelain services (Rooms H and J); and 60 pictorial plates from the Viennese Manufactory (Room 23), decorated with local scenes, including Schönbrunn, Belvedere, and Prater. *45 min; arrive before opening time to beat the crowds in high season. Hofburg. 01 533 7570. www.hofburg-wien.at. €13 adults, €12 concessions, €7.70 kids (6–18), audio guides available free of charge. Ticket price includes the Imperial Apartments and Sisi Museum. Daily 9am–5:30pm (July–Aug until 6pm). U-Bahn 3 (Herrengasse).*

5 ★★★ kids Imperial Apartments & Sisi Museum. The Imperial Palace accommodated the Habsburg royals for over 6 centuries (1282–1918), during which time the Hofburg complex developed into one of the great powerhouses of Europe. The first six rooms form the Sisi Museum, where a host of artifacts (poems, recipes, dresses, toiletries, portraits, jewelry, and so forth) offer a fascinating insight into the tragic empress's private life. Some items reveal her passions for travel, poetry, and sport, as well as her obsession with beauty and diet. Among her favorite beauty treatments were a leather face mask lined with raw veal and worn overnight, and a recipe for egg yolk and cognac shampoo with which to wash her floor-length hair, a process that took all day. From her early thirties onwards she refused to allow her portrait to be painted, so that she would always be remembered as a great beauty. *1 hr; visit early to avoid the crowds. Hofburg. 01 533 7570. www.hofburg-wien.at. €13 adults, €12 concessions, €7.70 kids (6–18), audio guides free of charge. Ticket price includes admission to the Silberkammer. Daily 9am–5:30pm (July–Aug until 6pm); kids' tours: 10:30am, 2:30pm Sat–Sun and public holidays. U-Bahn 3 (Herrengasse).*

6 ★★★ kids Schweizerhof (Swiss Court). The oldest part of the Hofburg, the Swiss Court was originally a 13th-century fortress complete with a moat and drawbridge, built by King Ottokar of Bohemia to defend himself against Rudolf von Habsburg. The king failed, and the Habsburgs moved in. The name recalls the Swiss

Traditional costumes on display in Franz Josef's waiting room.

The grandiose Prunksaal once house the Imperial Library.

Guards who were once posted here. Enter through the striking red, black, and gold **Schweizertor** (Swiss Gate), one of Vienna's finest Renaissance constructions, into the ancient courtyard. The Gothic **Burgkapelle** (Castle Chapel), up the steps to your right, was restored in baroque style in the 17th and 18th centuries. Mass is famously performed here every Sunday (Oct–June) by the **Wiener Sängerknaben** (Vienna Boys' Choir, p 137). The sparkling **Schatzkammer** (Treasury), whose entrance is beneath the chapel, is one of the world's most impressive national collections, containing a breathtaking hoard of jewels, crowns, and sacred relics spanning 1,000 years of both the Habsburg and the Holy Roman empires. 🕓 *Schatzkammer: 45 min. Schweizerhof, Hofburg. ☎ 01 525 24-0. www.khm.at, www.hofburgkapelle.at. €12 adults, €9 concessions, free under 19, €11 Vienna Card, €4 audio guide. Wed–Mon 10am–6pm (May–Oct from 9:30am). Chapel: €1.50. Open Mon–Thurs 11am–3pm; Fri 11am–1pm. U-Bahn 2/3 (Volkstheater) Tram 1/2/D (Burgring).*

7 ★ Josefsplatz. An equestrian statue of Emperor Joseph II marks the center of this sun-baked square, once used as a training ground for the Spanish Riding School. It is flanked by two fine palaces, the Renaissance **Stallburg** (stables) and the **Prunksaal** (State Hall). This magnificent building is a gem of baroque architecture, decked with marble statuary, walnut bookcases, and lavish frescoes. Once the Imperial Library, it remains the largest room of its kind in Europe, and contains a major part of the National Library's extensive collection of manuscripts, maps, books, and music scores. 🕓 *20 min. Prunksaal, Josefsplatz 1. www.onb.ac.at. €7 adults, €4.50 concessions. Guided tour by appointment, ☎ 01 534 10-464. Tues–Sun 10am–6pm (Thurs until 9pm). U-Bahn 2/3 (Volkstheater) Tram 1/2/71/D (Burgring).*

8 ★ Augustinerkirche. The former Court Church has witnessed numerous imperial weddings over the centuries, including Marie Louise's marriage to Napoleon in 1810 and that of Franz Joseph I to Sisi in 1854. Besides a stunning Gothic interior, it is renowned for the pyramidal tomb of Maria Christina by the Italian neoclassical sculptor Antonio Canova. Its crypt houses 54 silver casks containing the hearts of the Habsburgs (see above). 🕓 *20 min. Augustinerstrasse 3 (entrance on Josefsplatz). ☎ 01 533 7099. www.augustinerkirche.at. Free admission. Daily 8am–6pm. U-Bahn 3 (Herrengasse).*

9 ★★ Albertina. One of the world's finest collections of graphic art is housed in the Albertina Palace at the southern end of the Hofburg. Famous as the home of the Albrecht Dürer's "Young Hare" painting (which the museum uses as its mascot), it contains around a million etchings, engravings, and

The lovely Palmenhaus brasserie in the emperor's greenhouse.

lithographs; over 65,000 watercolors and drawings; and some 70,000 photographs. Due to the collection's sheer volume—it features virtually every major artist from the 15th century to the present day—it is displayed in temporary exhibitions in the magnificent neoclassical Habsburg State Rooms. The sections spanning Impressionism to Classical Modernism, and Contemporary Art are especially impressive. ⏱ *1 hr; quietest at lunchtime.* *Albertinaplatz 1.* ☎ *01 534 83-0. www.albertina.at. €13 adults, €9.90 concessions, €8.50 students, free under 19. Daily 10am–6pm (Wed until 9pm). U-Bahn 1/2/4 (Karlsplatz).*

10 ★★ **Palmenhaus.** This charming brasserie is housed in a giant Jugendstil greenhouse with gargantuan palm trees and Jugendstil flair, in the former Imperial Garden. Serving delicious Viennese and Mediterranean dishes and fine wines, it is a stylish setting for lunch. Palmenhaus's generous outdoor seating is a local favorite, especially in summertime. *Burggarten.* ☎ *01 533 1033. Tram 1/2/71/D (Burgring). €–€€.*

⓫ ★ **Neue Burg.** *See p 60, ❺.*

⓬ ★★ **Volksgarten.** This breathtaking garden between Heldenplatz (p 48, ❺) and the Burgtheater (p 60, ❽) is surely Vienna's most romantic, famed for its beautiful roses (each carefully labeled) and its Theseus temple, built for Sisi in 1822 as a gift from her husband, Franz Joseph. ⏱ *30 min. Tram 1/2/71/D (Stadiongasse/Parlament).*

The mighty equestrian statue of Franz Josef dominates the entrance to the Palais Albertina.

Jugendstil Vienna

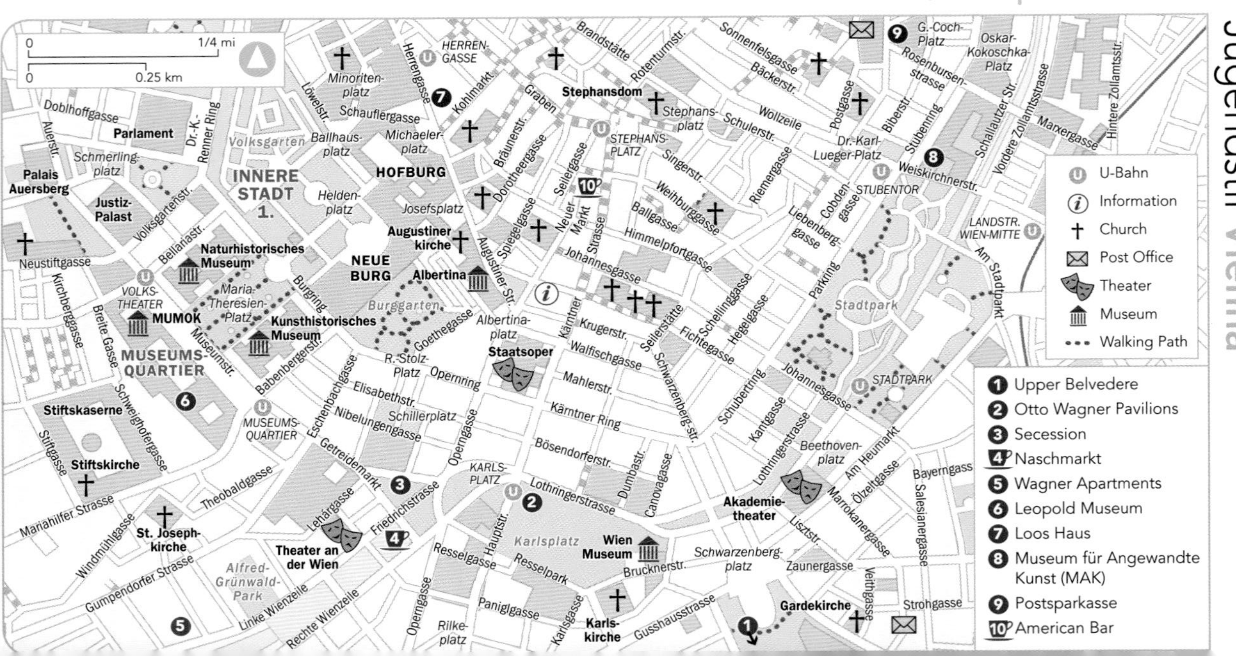

Vienna is the birthplace of Jugendstil—Austria's answer to Art Nouveau—and its spin-off movement, the **Secession.** This tour takes you on a "greatest hits" trip of groundbreaking Modernist art and architecture from *fin-de-siècle* Vienna, including the Secession Building—a daring structure with a cupola of golden laurel leaves, known locally as the "Golden Cabbage." START: **Upper Belvedere (Tram D Schloss Belvedere).**

❶ ★★★ Upper Belvedere. The best collection of Austrian Modernism can be found in the Belvedere (www.belvedere.at), a glorious baroque palace, where pride of place goes to the celebrated work known as ***The Kiss*** by Gustav Klimt (founder of the Secession movement), alongside paintings by French Impressionists and Austrian contemporaries Egon Schiele and Oskar Kokoschka. *See p 68,* ❽.

❷ ★★ Otto Wagner Pavilions. These two symmetrical Jugendstil railway stations were built as part of Otto Wagner's scheme for Vienna's horse-drawn rail network. Made of green-painted steel with white marble slabs, they have striking decorative golden flower motifs. Both stations fell into disuse when the modern U-Bahn was built. They were dismantled in the 1960s but re-erected in 1977, following extensive protests. One is now a simple cafe; the other contains a small museum devoted to Wagner. 🕓 *20 min. Karlsplatz.* ☎ *01 505 87 47-85 177. www.wienmuseum.at. €5 adults, €4 concessions, free under 19, also free on the first Sun of the month. Apr–Oct Tues–Sun 10am–6pm. U-Bahn 1/2/4 (Karlsplatz).*

❸ ★★★ Secession. This gallery is the finest example of Jugendstil architecture in Vienna, reflecting the Secessionist ideals of purity and functionalism. Be sure to visit the fascinating interior, if only to see Gustav Klimt's remarkable 34m-long (111 ft.) Beethoven frieze in the basement. Based on the composer's 9th Symphony (and, in particular, his musical setting of German poet Schiller's *Ode to Joy*), it is one of the masterpieces of Viennese Art Nouveau. *See p 17,* ❹.

The sunflower motif on Wagner's pavilion is a recurring Jugendstil theme.

❹ ★★★ kids Naschmarkt. Look up as you stroll through Vienna's top market. You'll some of the most beautiful Jugendstil facades as you pass stands serving everything from hummus and Turkish olives to sushi and vindaloo. Local favorites include the Naschmarkt Deli for brunch (Stand 421–436, ☎ 01 585 0823, €); Umar Fisch (Stand 76–79, ☎ 01 587 0456, €€) for shellfish; and the Indian Pavillion (Stand 74–75, ☎ 01 587 8561, €–€€) for a taste of the exotic. *See "The Best Dining," p 109.*

The striking Secession building.

5 ★ Wagner Apartments. Few facades in Vienna are as captivating as the Jugendstil Majolikahaus. Designed by pioneering architect Otto Wagner in 1899, it is named after the majolica tiles he used to create the colorful, flowing, floral patterns covering the exterior. Together with its neighbor (on the corner of Köstlergasse), whose curvaceous facade is further embellished with gold embossing by Secessionist artist Koloman Moser, they represent Wagner's ultimate fusion of Art Nouveau decoration with modern materials. *5 min. Linke Wienzeile 40 and 38. No phone. Closed to the public. U-Bahn 4 (Kettenbrückengasse).*

Wagner's ornate Majolikahaus.

6 ★★★ Leopold Museum. The main draw of this gallery of 19th- and 20th-century Austrian art is the world's largest collection of works by the provocative artist Egon Schiele. It also contains some significant Klimt canvases. While you're here, check out the exquisite Arts and Crafts furniture designs of the Wiener Werkstätte. *See p 76,* 2.

7 ★ Loos Haus. Loos Haus, designed by Adolf Loos in 1921, caused an outcry when it was first built. Its austere design, geometric lines, and lack of ornamentation offended public taste during a period when florid facades were still *de rigueur*. The ornament-loving Emperor Franz Joseph found the house so hideous that he kept the curtains of rooms overlooking Michaelerplatz drawn shut and refused to use the Hofburg's Michaelertor exit ever again. Nicknamed "the house without eyebrows," it is now considered a masterpiece of modern design. The interior (currently a bank) reflects the exterior's simple, stylish elegance. *10 min. Herrengasse 2–4. No phone. www.adolfloos.at. Bank opening hours (to glimpse inside): Mon–Wed, Fri 9am–3pm; Thurs 9am–5:30pm. U-Bahn 3 (Herrengasse).*

8 ★★ Museum für Angewandte Kunst (MAK). Design

buffs will devour the Jugendstil and Wiener Werkstätte rooms here. *See p 12,* ❺.

❾ ★ **Postsparkasse.** This marvelous example of Secession architecture was designed by Otto Wagner in 1904–6. He won a competition to create a novel structure capable of reflecting the Post Office Savings Bank's innovative procedures, and came up with this extraordinary gray marble facade, held together by 17,000 metal studs and topped by stylized Jugendstil angels. The lofty, light-infused interior (and tiny Wagner museum) can be viewed during bank opening hours. 🕓 *10 min. (30 min. including museum). Georg-Coch-Platz 2.* ☎ *01 599 05-33825. www.ottowagner.com. Museum: €6 adults, €4 concessions, free under 19. Mon–Fri 10am–5pm; Sat 10am–5pm. U-Bahn 1/4 (Schwedenplatz).*

Stop by the Postsparkasse during business hours for a glimpse inside.

10 ★★ **American Bar.** Designed by Adolf Loos in 1908, this closet-sized cocktail bar is an absolute gem, characterized by clever use of mirrors (to create an illusion of space), elegant Art Nouveau glass cabinets, onyx, marble, and—a Loos hallmark—mahogany paneling. Come for early evening drinks, before the tiny space begins to burst at the seams. *Kärntner Durchgang 10.* ☎ *01 512 3283. www.loosbar.at. U-Bahn 1/3 (Stephansplatz). €–€€.*

The Wiener Werkstätte

The Wiener Werkstätte (Viennese Workshop), founded in 1903 by Josef Hoffmann and Koloman Moser as a direct offshoot of the Secession movement, was inspired by the Arts and Crafts movement popular in Britain at the time. The aim was to bring Jugendstil design into homes throughout Vienna. By turning functional, everyday objects such as cutlery, crockery, furniture, and curtains into unique items of great beauty and quality, they sought to transform daily life into a "Gesamtkunstwerk" (total work of art). By 1905, the Wiener Werkstätte had over 100 craftsmen, including Klimt, Loos, and Kokoschka, but it was forced to close in 1932, unable to compete financially with the cheap, mass-produced items made by rival companies. Nowadays, the best collections of Wiener Werkstätte artifacts can be seen in the Leopold Museum and MAK (p 12, ❺). Some upmarket design shops still sell products along similar lines, notably Augarten, Lobmeyr, and Woka (see "The Best Shopping," p 79).

City of Music

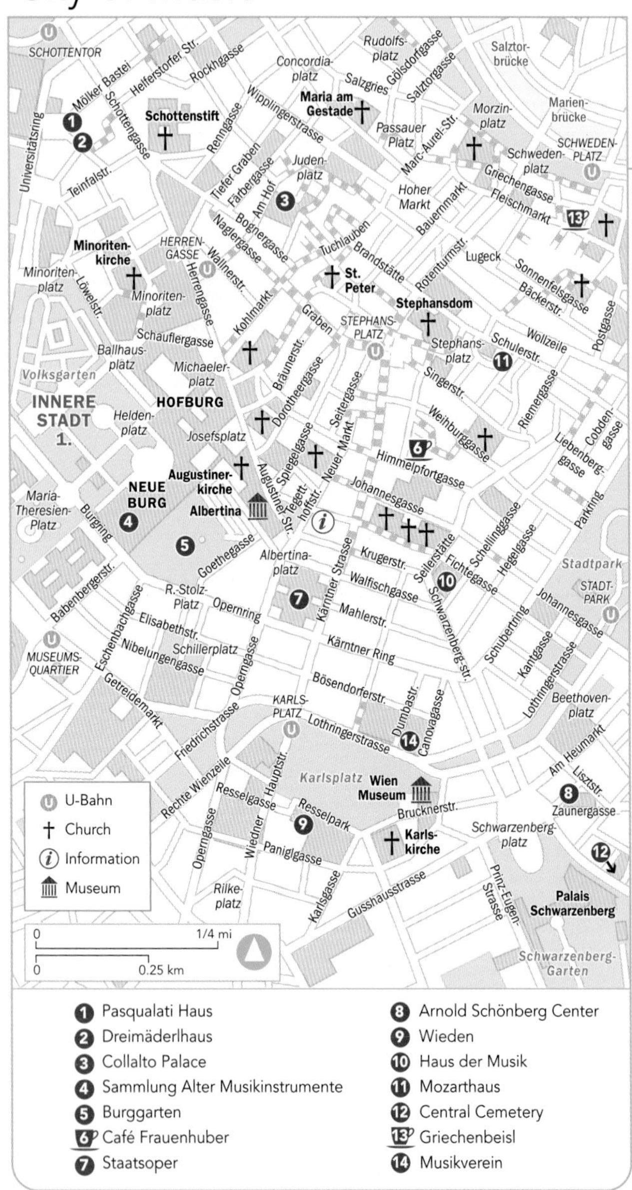

This lengthy but fascinating tour pieces together the extraordinary legacy of one of the world's leading musical cities, from Mozart the musical whiz-kid to the kings of the Viennese waltz. It also includes some lesser-known sights and historic buildings that are closed to the public; you can easily skip them if you are short of time or energy. START: **Pasqualati Haus (U-Bahn 2 Schottentor).**

1 ★★ Pasqualati Haus. The German-born composer Ludwig van Beethoven moved to Vienna at the age of 22 to take lessons with Haydn and Mozart. During his 35 years in the city, he moved house a staggering 68 times. The Pasqualati house on the old city ramparts (named for its longtime owner, Josef von Pasqualati) is the most interesting of three Beethoven houses currently open to the public. The composer lived in this house from 1804 to 1818, and wrote many of his best-loved works here, including the opera *Fidelio*, Symphonies 4, 5, 7, and 8, and his 4th piano concerto. His rooms (on the 4th floor) contain just a handful of mementoes, portraits, scores, and personal belongings, but they are wonderfully evocative. In the back room, enjoy listening to excerpts of his "greatest hits" while gazing over city rooftops. When Beethoven lived here, he would have had sweeping views of the Vienna Woods. ⏲ *45 min. Mölker Bastei 8. ☎ 01 535 8905. www.wienmuseum.at. €5 adults, €4 concessions, free under 19 and first Sun of each month. Tues–Sun 10am–1pm and 2–6pm. U-Bahn 2 (Schottentor), Tram 1/37/38/40/41/42/43/44/71/D.*

2 ★ Dreimäderlhaus. *See p 72, 5.*

3 ★ Collalto Palace. Even though you can't go inside, all Mozart fans make their pilgrimage here to see the simple plaque on the wall of this unremarkable baroque building situated in Vienna's largest enclosed square. It commemorates the site where Mozart made his first public appearance, aged just 6, in 1762. The boy-wonder had recently arrived by boat from his native Salzburg and wowed the audience with his mastery of the clavichord and violin. *Am Hof 13. U-Bahn 3 (Herrengasse).*

The Pasqualati Haus was one of Beethoven's numerous residences.

4 ★ Sammlung Alter Musikinstrumente. It seems fitting that such a musically rich city should have an impressive musical instrument collection; you won't be disappointed by this Collection of Ancient Musical Instruments. Started by Archduke Ferdinand of Tyrol, the collection now contains the finest ensemble of Renaissance instruments in the world, including an extraordinary 16th-century claviorganum, which can reproduce special effects like birdsong; some

A 19th-century Italian mandolin in the Sammlung Alter Musikinstrumente.

early serpents (snake-shaped horns); violins with elaborately carved scrolls; and pianos once owned by Haydn, Beethoven, and Schubert. ⏲ *45 min. Neue Burg, Heldenplatz.* ☎ *01 525 24-4602. www.khm.at. €12 adults, €9 concessions, free under 19; price includes admission to the Ephesus Museum and the Imperial Armory (p 60, ❺), as well as the KHM (p 18, ❻). Wed–Sun 10am–6pm. Tram 1/2/71/D (Burgring).*

❺ ★★ kids **Burggarten.** This informal park in the city center (p 58, ❷) contains a magnificent marble statue of Mozart by Viktor Tilgner (1896), and scenes in bas-relief from his opera *Don Giovanni. Burgring (just inside the main gates, opposite Eschenbachgasse). Tram 1/2/71/D (Burgring).*

6 ★ **Café Frauenhuber.** Fortify yourself with coffee and cake in Vienna's oldest cafe. Mozart once lived in this building, and Beethoven used to perform piano sonatas here. *Himmelpfortgasse 6.* ☎ *01 512 8383. €–€€.*

❼ ★★★ **Staatsoper.** Vienna's reputation as a "City of Music" focuses largely on its prestigious State Opera, which has, for centuries, staged premieres of many leading works. It continues to enjoy a dazzling reputation, with 300 performances annually taken from its vast repertoire of ballets and opera "greats" (including Mozart's *The Magic Flute*, Wagner's *Ring Cycle*, and Beethoven's *Fidelio*). It is also the venue for the annual Opera Ball, the most glittering event in the Austrian social calendar, held on the last Thursday of Vienna's Fasching (Carnival) season celebrations. Stage and stalls are transformed into a gigantic flower-filled ballroom. I thoroughly recommend a guided tour of the interior, for a closer look at its grand staircase and plush red-and-gold auditorium. Tour times vary depending on rehearsal schedules, but they are usually advertised on a billboard near the entrance, which is updated daily. ⏲ *40 min tour. Opernring 2.* ☎ *01 514 44-7810 (box office). www.staatsoper.at. U-Bahn 1/2/4 (Karlsplatz). Tram 1/2/62/17/D (Kärntnerring/ Oper).*

❽ ★★ **Arnold Schönberg Center.** Somewhat off the tourist track, this small archive center is essential viewing for any aficionado of 20th-century classical music (see Jewish Vienna p 48, ❾). Schönberg famously developed a 12-tone compositional

Mozart graces the Burggarten.

The Viennese Waltz

The plodding, triple-time German folk dance known as the Ländler was transformed by the Viennese into a merry, whirling dance during the 1820s. It first became popular in Viennese dance halls thanks to the composer and leader of a small ensemble, Joseph Lanner. Johann Strauss I (also known as "the Elder") was one of his viola players and, in 1825, he broke away to form his own waltz orchestra. The two bandleaders conducted a lengthy "waltz war," performing in the cafes of the Prater, but the rivalry ended amicably when Strauss played waltz tunes (at slow speed) at Lanner's funeral in 1843. After his death, the Strauss family dominated the Viennese waltz scene for over half a century, thanks largely to Johann Strauss II, the second-generation "Waltz King," who composed nearly 400 new dance tunes, including the *Blue Danube* (1867). Today Strauss the Younger's house can be visited at Praterstrasse 54 (Tues–Thurs 2–6pm, Fri–Sun 10am–1pm). His statue graces the Stadtpark (p 95), and his music is performed nightly in venues throughout the city (see "The Best Arts & Entertainment," p 133).

technique, stretching the boundaries of 19th-century tonality to new dimensions. He founded the Second Viennese School of Music along with fellow Viennese composers Alban Berg and Anton von Webern. Their music was not well received at the time, and Schönberg eventually moved to America. Today he is considered one of the most influential and distinguished composers of the 20th century. This fascinating modern center enables you to see the man behind the music—through his photos, brilliant artworks, reconstructed study, and homemade work tools (many from recycled materials)—and to listen to compositions by Schönberg, Webern, and Berg. 🕓 *45 min. Zaunergasse 1–3 (take elevator in inner lobby area up one floor, then ring on the doorbell). ☎ 01 712 1888. www.schoenberg.at. €5 adults, €3 concessions, free for kids under 12. Mon–Fri 10am–5pm. Tram 71 (Am Heumarkt).*

❾ ★★ Wieden. If you have time, explore the bohemian musicians' district of Wieden, just south of another great musical focal-point, the Musikverein (p 13, ❼). Here it is easy to see why Vienna is called the "City of Music," as nearly every street bears a plaque to one musical genius or another. *Start:* Karlsplatz.

❿ ★★★ kids Haus der Musik. In a city full of musical museums, this one is unique amongst them, focusing not only on Vienna's legacy of classical music but also on the science of sound and the listening process. Housed in the former residence of Otto Nicolai, founder of the celebrated Vienna Philharmonic Orchestra, it seems fitting that the museum hosts the orchestra's archives (including sketches, letters, batons, posters, and scores by various composers such as Bruckner, Brahms, and Richard Strauss), and a film of Vienna's illustrious New Year's Day concert. *See p 44,* ❺.

⓫ ★★ kids Mozarthaus. There's no escaping Mozart's association

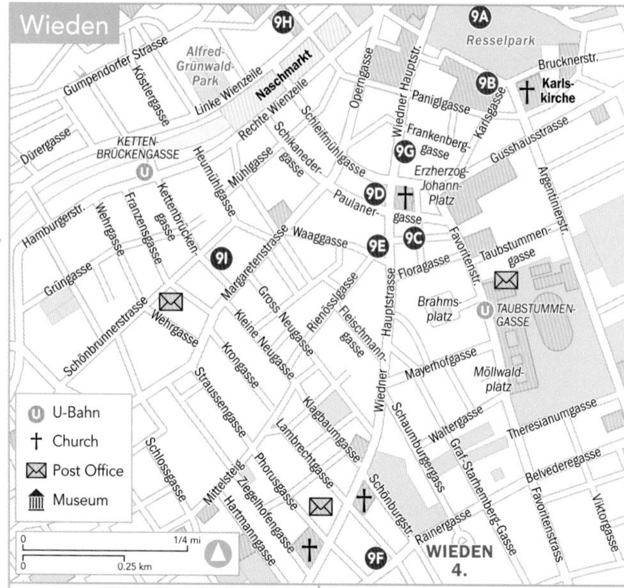

In 9A ★ **Ressel Park,** a statue of the German romantic composer Johannes Brahms faces the Musikverein where he was once director. Brahms lived in nearby Karlsgasse, and was charmed by Vienna, calling it a "village." The Venetian baroque composer Antonio Vivaldi is buried at the 9B ★ **Technische Universität** nearby. Richard Strauss, famed for his symphonic poems, lived at 9C ★★★ **Mozartgasse** from 1919 to 1925. The Jugendstil "Mozart Fountain" outside illustrates scenes from Mozart's opera *The Magic Flute*. German composer Christoph Willibald Gluck (director of Empress Maria Theresa's court orchestra) lived at 9D ★ **Wiedner Hauptstrasse 32.** The Finnish composer Jean Sibelius lived at 9E ★ **Waaggasse 1** from 1890 to 1891. He left Vienna having failed an audition to join the Vienna Philharmonic as a violinist. A plaque at 9F ★ **Johann Strauss Gasse 4** marks the last home of Johann Strauss II. The opening bars of his celebrated *Blue Danube* waltz decorate the wall at number 10. Czech composer Antonín Dvořák frequented the former Hotel Goldenen Lamm at 9G ★ **Wiedner Hauptstrasse 7.** The 9H ★ **Theater an der Wien** (Linke Wienzeile 6) pays homage to Mozart with its Papageno statue (a reference to *The Magic Flute*). It premiered Beethoven's opera *Fidelio* in 1805. Franz Schubert died in 1828 at 9I ★★ **Kettenbrückengasse 6.** Today it contains a small museum with a handful of poignant mementoes. ☎ *01 581 6730. www.wienmuseum.at. €2 adults, €1 concessions, free under 19. Wed–Thurs 10am–1pm and 2–6pm.*

with Vienna—from Mozartkugeln chocolates to ticket touts dressed in his typically flamboyant style. Of his 14 addresses across the city, only the Mozarthaus remains—a most desirable residence even in Mozart's time. On arrival in Vienna in 1781, he wrote to his father, "This is a magnificent place here and the best place in the world for my profession." He lived in this apartment from 1784 to 1787. They were his happiest and most productive years, during which he composed countless chamber works and his opera The Marriage of Figaro. Here, Mozart's career reached its peak, but a taste for the high life, especially gambling, ruined him. Just 4 years later, he died a pauper and was buried in a mass grave in St. Marx Cemetery. It's well worth getting an audio guide here (there's one just for kids, too). Start at the top of the house and work your way down. Although lacking any of the composer's personal possessions, the house vividly portrays his life and times through period furnishings and musical memorabilia.

This elegant fountain, representing Mozart's Magic Flute, *is tucked down a side street in Wieden.*

1 hr. Domgasse 5. ☎ 01 512 1791. www.mozarthausvienna.at. €11 adults, €9 concessions, €9 students, €4.50 kids under 14, €25 family (2 adults, 3 kids under 15), €18/12 adults/kids for a combined ticket with Haus der Musik, see p 12; audio guides for adults and kids are included in the price. Daily 10am–7pm. U-Bahn 1/3 (Stephansplatz).

⓬ ★★ **Central Cemetery.** Visit the final resting places of many of the city's great musicians, including Beethoven, Brahms, Schubert, Schönberg, and all the Strausses at this vast cemetery which contains over 2½ million graves. Look out also for a monument to Mozart (who ended up in a pauper's grave in the evocatively overgrown St. Marx Cemetery). The cemetery's beautiful Jugendstil church was built in 1910 by Max Hegele, a pupil of Otto Wagner. A map near the entrance helps locate the celebrity graves. *Simmeringer Hauptstrasse 232–244. ☎ 01 76041. Free admission. Nov–Feb 8am–5pm; Mar, Oct 7am–6pm; Apr, Sept 7am–7pm; May–Aug 7am–8pm (last admission 30 min before closing) Church: daily 8am–4pm (Mar–Oct until 5pm). Tram 6/71 (Zentralfriedhof).*

13 ★★ kids **Griechenbeisl.** This is perhaps the most clichéd setting in which to dine on Austrian cuisine, in the vaulted dining rooms (or shaded sidewalk terrace) of one of Vienna's oldest inns, but the experience is one of a kind. It's located beside the ornate Greek Orthodox church, and once frequented by Beethoven, Brahms, Schubert, and Mark Twain. *Fleischmarkt 11. ☎ 01 533 1977. €€.*

⓮ ★★ **Musikverein.** A concert here marks the perfect end to a musical day! *See p 13,* ❼.

Vienna with Children

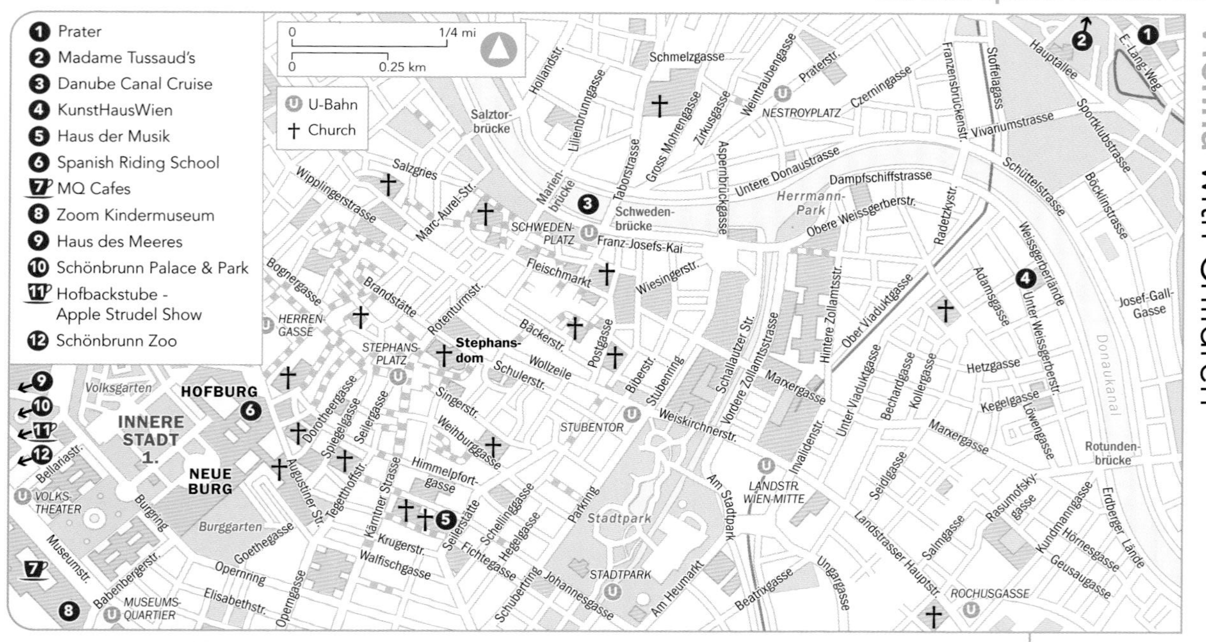

Vienna may not seem the obvious choice for a family break but, ask any local—the city is built around children, cyclists, and dogs. For visiting kids, there is no end to the adventures: Fiakers (horse-drawn carriages), tram rides, boat trips, the Prater Ferris wheel, parks, playgrounds, and a host of child-friendly museums ensure that kids of all ages will find plenty with which to amuse themselves. START: **Prater (U-Bahn 3 Erdberg; U-Bahn 2 Ernst Happel Stadion).**

❶ ★★★ kids **Prater.** A trip to Vienna is not complete without a round on the Riesenrad (giant Ferris wheel), but there is much more fun to be had on the bumper cars and thrill rides at the amusement park, not to mention the park's green open spaces that are great for picnics, playgrounds, and sporting fun. *See p 97.*

❷ ★★ kids **Madame Tussaud's.** *See p 98,* ❹.

❸ ★★ kids **Danube Canal Cruise.** *See p 22,* ❷.

❹ ★★★ kids **KunstHausWien.** Explore the curved and colorful world of the eccentric Austrian artist Friedensreich Hundertwasser. There's a special kids' tour and the cafe is child-friendly too, with a lovely shaded patio garden. *See p 23,* ❹ *and* ❺.

Take a break in KunstHausWien's inviting cafe patio.

The Prater amusement park offers thrill rides and wide open spaces.

Fun and games at the KunstHausWien.

5 ★★★ kids **Haus der Musik.** This eccentric venue describes itself as an "interactive sound museum." As well as the archives of the Vienna Philharmonic Orchestra, and a vivid portrayal of Vienna's classical composers, you can also explore the mechanics of sound and the experience of listening, through hands-on exhibits and instruments, state-of-the-art interactive toys, and touch screens. Test your hearing, compose your own waltz, record your own CD, and, best of all, conduct the Vienna Philharmonic using an electronic baton. The entire museum is like a giant musical theme park—not to be missed for older kids. *1 hr.; make use of the late opening hours and go in the evening. Seilerstätte 30. ☎ 01 513 4850. www.hdm.at. €13 adults, €9 concessions, €6 kids under 12, free under 3, €29 family ticket, €18/€8 adults/kids for a combined ticket with Mozarthaus, see p 39. Daily 10am–10pm. Tram 1/2/62/71/D (Kärntner Ring/Oper).*

6 ★★ kids **Spanish Riding School.** The image of white Lipizzaner stallions performing dazzling dressage steps to waltz music is perhaps Vienna's most powerful marketing tool. A grand performance of these amazing equestrian gymnastics is an unforgettable treat. If you can't get tickets, attend a Privatissimum—a demonstration of their rigorous training routine. Alternatively, watch the dashingly uniformed riders perfect the art of classical horsemanship at the morning exercises. All events take place in the Hofburg's Winter Riding School, the world's oldest indoor riding school built in a stately baroque style. A guided 1-hour tour of the Renaissance stables, tack room, and summer and winter riding schools is a must for horse lovers. *Michaelerplatz 1, Hofburg, Reitschulegasse 2. ☎ 01 533 9031 for Privatissimum and performance dates (most Fri 7pm and Sat 11am; Sept–June also Sun 11am). www.srs.at. Tickets: €25–€217 (available online or from Michaelerplatz 1). Kids under 3 may not attend performances; those aged 3–6 may attend for free if they sit on an adult's lap. Sit in the stalls or Gallery I if possible. Morning exercises: Sept–June Tues–Sat 10am–noon. Tickets €15 adults, €7.50 kids (same day only, at Josefsplatz, Gate 2).Stable tours (in English and German): ☎ 01 533 90 32. Daily 2, 3, and 4pm (reservations recommended). Tickets €18 adults; €9 kids. U-Bahn 3 (Herrengasse).*

7 ★ kids **MQ Cafes.** Of the MuseumsQuartier's many eateries, there are two prime lunch spots for kids. MQ Daily (☎ 01 522 4524, €) allows families to dine al fresco while the kids can can run around outside and burn off energy. Dschungel Wien Café (☎ 01 522 0720, €), outside the Zoom Children's Museum (see below), is used to very young guests and will accommodate strollers and play blankets.

8 ★★★ kids **Zoom Kindermuseum.** This children's museum is brilliant. Designed exclusively for kids, it offers a wide variety of hands-on exhibitions and activities including the "Ocean" play area (ages 8 months–6 years); messy, arty workshops (ages 3–12); and an exciting multimedia "Zoom lab" (ages 8–14). ⏲ *workshops last 1–1½ hr. Museumsplatz 1. ☎ 01 524 7908. www.kindermuseum.at. Check website or phone for times and prices. Reservations essential. Workshop staff speak both German and English. U-Bahn 2 (MuseumsQuartier).*

9 ★★★ kids Haus des Meeres. This aquarium and indoor zoo is housed in one of the Flak Towers left over from World War II. The "House of the Ocean" is loads of fun. From the reptiles and amphibians to the creepy crawlers including an ant farm in plastic tubes that spans the entire structure, curious kids will be in heaven.

10 ★★★ kids Schönbrunn Palace & Park. There's a huge amount for kids at the Schönbrunn Palace, including a puppet theater, a maze, a zany playground, the zoo (p 108, 7), and even a special

Get lost in the maze at Schönbrunn.

Kindermuseum, where kids can experience something of the imperial way of life while playing with toys of the era, laying the table for a banquet, and dressing up in Habsburg costumes. ⏲ *1–4 hr. Kindermuseum. ☎ 01 811 13-239. www.kaiserkinder.at. €8.80 adults, €6.70 concessions and kids (3–18), €24/€46 family. Sat–Sun 10am–5pm (last admission 4pm); daily 10am–5pm during school vacations. U-Bahn 4 (Schönbrunn). See p 106.*

The Kindermuseum is ideal for kids up to age 14.

11 ★★ kids Hofbackstube—Apple Strudel Show. Watch confectioners making traditional apple strudel in the old-fashioned "Court Bakery," then eat one, piping hot, straight from the oven. ⏲ *1 hr. Kavalierstrakt 52. ☎ 01 811 13-239. www.schoenbrunn.at. €3.90. Hourly demonstrations Apr–Oct daily 10am–4pm, Nov–Mar through 5pm. U-Bahn 4 (Schönbrunn).*

12 ★★★ kids Schönbrunn Zoo. *See p 108, 7.*

Jewish Vienna

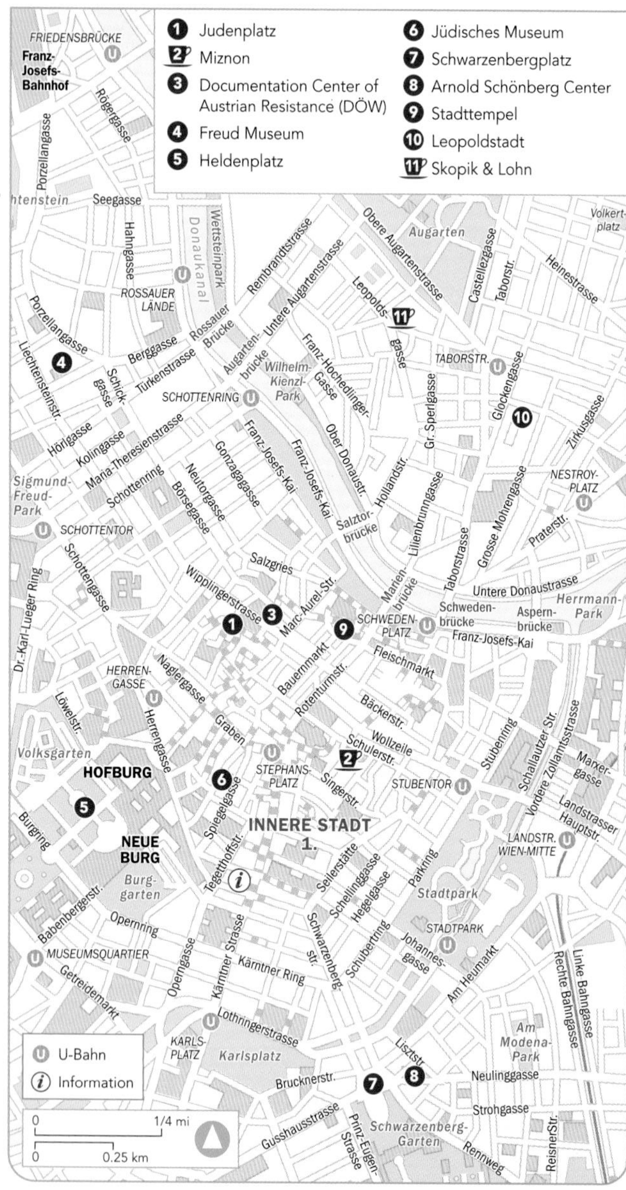

"It is impossible to imagine what it means for one-sixth of the population to be made pariahs overnight, deprived of all human rights . . . " wrote a wartime correspondent in 1938, describing the plight of Viennese Jews. Jews have been persecuted in this city on more than one occasion, despite their outstanding contribution to the arts, science, and politics. Their remarkable story is intrinsic to the history of Vienna. START: **Judenplatz (U-Bahn 1/3 Stephansplatz).**

❶ ★★ **Judenplatz.** This square marks the heart of the medieval Jewish ghetto. The first expulsion of Vienna's Jews took place in 1421. You can learn more about the ghetto during that period at the **Judenplatz Museum,** and visit the remains of one of Europe's largest medieval synagogues, excavated in 1995. In the square, admire the stark poignancy of the modern stone monument devoted to the Holocaust. Designed by British sculptor Rachel Whitbread and erected in 2000, it resembles an inside-out library of nameless books lined up on bookshelves with their spines facing inward, symbolizing the many stories of the victims left untold. 🕒 *30 min. Judenplatz. Museum: Judenplatz 8.* ☎ *01 535 0431. www.jmw.at. Tickets include entrance to both Jewish museums €10 adults, €8 concessions, free for kids under 18. Sun–Thurs 10am–6pm; Fri 10am–2pm. U-Bahn 1/3 (Stephansplatz).*

❷ **Miznon.** This busy and boisterous establishment serves simple and delicious Israeli cuisine. Between smatterings of Hebrew, English, and German, the staff yell out patron's names to pick up one of their mouthwatering sandwiches from the bar. *Schulerstraße 4.* ☎ *01 512 1053. €.*

❸ ★★★ **Documentation Center of Austrian Resistance (DÖW).** Fascinating but inevitably harrowing, this small museum documents the early history of National Socialism and the persecution of its opponents. 🕒 *1 hr. Altes Rathaus, Wipplingerstrasse 6–8.* ☎ *01 228 946 9-319. www.doew.at. Free admission. Mon–Fri 9am–5pm (Thurs until 7pm). U-Bahn 1/3 (Stephansplatz).*

Austria's Tomb of the Unknown Soldier—Castle Gate at Heldenplatz.

❹ ★ **Freud Museum.** *See p 73,* ❾.

❺ ★★ **Heldenplatz.** "Heroes Square," in front of the Neue Burg (p 60, ❺) was built by the Habsburgs as a symbol of imperial strength. It will, however, go down in history as the scene of Hitler's 1938 fateful speech to thousands of cheering Austrians when he announced the infamous *Anschluss* (Annexation), thereby assimilating Austria into the Third Reich. By 1945, Heldenplatz had been ploughed up to plant vegetables to feed Vienna's suffering citizens. Since 1955, the Burgtor (Castle Gate) on the southwestern side of the square has served as Austria's Tomb of the Unknown Soldier. ⏲ *15 min. Heldenplatz. Tram 1/2/71/D (Burgring).*

❻ ★★ **Jüdisches Museum.** The world's first Jewish Museum opened in Vienna in 1895, but the exhibits were confiscated by the Nazis in 1938. Today's museum opened in 1993 and contains an important collection of Judaica and an extraordinary fresco-like "Installation of Remembrance." ⏲ *45 min. Dorotheergasse 11.* ☎ *01 535 0431. www.jmw.at. Tickets include entrance to both Jewish museums €10 adults, €8 concessions, free under 18. Sun–Fri 10am–6pm. U-Bahn 1/3 (Stephansplatz).*

❼ ★ **Schwarzenbergplatz.** This grandiose square was the seat of the military government during World War II, when it was known as "Stalinplatz" and used for military parades. The giant bronze Russen Heldendenkmal (Russian Memorial) was created in 1945. Weighing 15 tons, it was made out of hundreds of melted-down busts of Hitler. *Schwarzenbergplatz. Tram 1/2/71/D (Schwarzenbergplatz).*

❽ ★★ **Arnold Schönberg Center.** This archive center provides a unique insight into the life and music of the Jewish composer, who is now recognized as having had a profound influence on modern classical music. Initially, however, Schönberg's innovative 12-tone compositions received a poor reception in Vienna and in 1933, perturbed by the rise of National Socialism, he emigrated to America. *See p 38,* ❽.

❾ ★ **Stadttempel.** The City Synagogue, designed in 1826 by the renowned local architect Kornhäusel, was the only Viennese

Cartoon depicting Mahler from the Leopold Museum.

synagogue to survive Kristallnacht (see below), thanks largely to its concealed facade. Today it remains at the heart of Vienna's Jewish community. Its impressive elliptical interior features a blue dome, marble columns, and a three-tiered gallery. *Seitenstettengasse 2–4. ☎ 01 535 0431. www.jmw.at. €3 adults, €2 concessions. Visit by guided tour only: Mon–Thurs (except Jewish holidays) 11:30am and 2pm. Bring your passport for ID and arrive 15 min. before tour time. U-Bahn 1/4 (Schwedenplatz).*

⑩ ★ **Leopoldstadt.** The city's ancient Jewish district was created north of the Danube Canal in the Leopoldstadt quarter, following an imperial decree in 1624 that Jews had to live outside the city walls. Half a century later, Emperor Leopold I expelled all Jews from Vienna, and the great synagogue was converted into the Church of St. Leopold. Today, parts of Leopoldstadt retain a Jewish atmosphere, with synagogues, kosher shops, and Jewish schools. *Four slim columns (at Tempelgasse 5) mark the location of the former Great Temple, destroyed on Kristallnacht. U-Bahn 1 (Nestroyplatz).*

These four columns mark the site of Leopoldstadt's former Great Temple.

11 ★ **Skopik & Lohn.** In what is still often called the Jewish Quarter, a charismatic ex–New Yorker of Viennese descent serves up his twin cultures with a nod to his in-laws from Tuscany and Provence. The interior is striking, with wild scribblings of black paint all over the white ceilings. In summer there is intimate outdoor seating. The food is inspired by modern Jewish cuisine, fused with Viennese and artfully served by waiters in white gloves. *Leopoldgasse 17. U-Bahn 2 (Schottenring or Taborstrasse), Tram 2. €€– €€€€.*

Kristallnacht

Many historians date the beginning of the Holocaust to November 9, 1938, when the Nazi government launched a vicious attack on the Jewish community throughout Germany and Austria. This was particularly ruthless in Vienna, where the Jewish population totaled around 200,000 (over 10% of the city's inhabitants). Stormtroopers torched 42 of Vienna's 43 synagogues, looted shops and businesses, and ransacked homes. The event became known as *Kristallnacht*—the "Night of Glass"—because of the shattered glass found on the pavements outside Jewish premises the following day.

"The Third Man" in Vienna

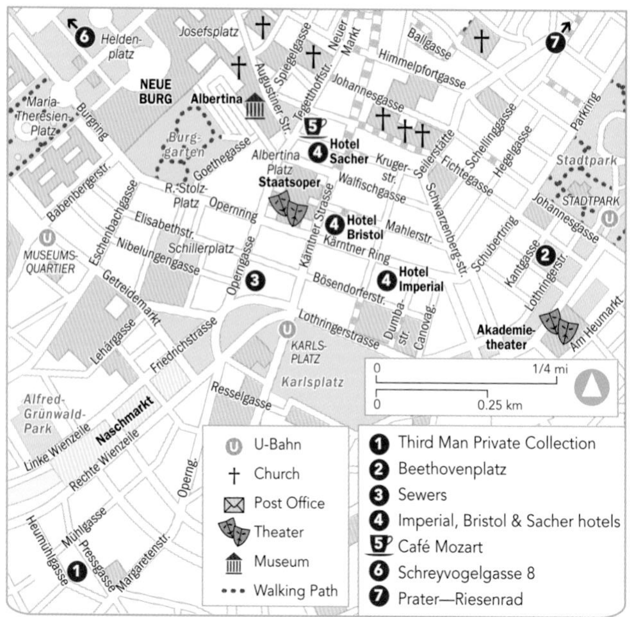

The classic 1949 thriller *The Third Man* is an undisputed masterpiece of British film noir. Scripted by Graham Greene and directed by Carol Reed, it features a legendary performance by Orson Welles, who plays the central character Harry Lime. A multi-layered movie of friendship and betrayal, it provides a unique and authentic testimony of life in the bombed-out ruins of post–World War II Vienna. START: **Third Man Private Collection (U-Bahn 4 Kettenbrückengasse).**

❶ ★★ **Third Man Private Collection.** Any fan of the cult movie should visit this tiny museum, which provides a fascinating insight into the making of *The Third Man*, and post-war Vienna. 🕓 *45 min. Pressgasse 25.* ☎ *01 586 4872. www.3mpc.net. €8.90 adults, €6.90 concessions. Sat 2–6pm. U-Bahn 4 (Kettenbrückengasse).*

❷ ★ **Beethovenplatz.** The Beethoven statue here is featured at the start of the movie. Note the advertising kiosk nearby: during police raids, black-market crooks would disappear into the kiosk and down a manhole into the sewers. *Beethovenplatz. U-Bahn 4 (Stadtpark).*

❸ ★★ kids **Sewers.** The climax of the movie takes place in the sewers, when Lime is eventually cornered by police. The police enter the sewer system via a steel hatch (in Friedrichstrasse). This also

A cult address: Schreyvogelgasse 8.

marks the start of the city's thrilling sewer tour. ⏱ *1 hr. Karlsplatz-Girardipark, across from Café Museum. www.drittemanntour.at* ☎ *01 4000 3033. €7 adults, €5.50 concessions, €3.50 under 18 (minimum age 12). May–Oct Thurs–Sun 10am–8pm (tours every hour). U-Bahn 1/2/4 (Karlsplatz).*

4 ★ Imperial, Bristol & Sacher hotels. From 1945 and for 10 years, Vienna was divided into international zones by the occupying Allied powers. The center was an "international" sector, with American intelligence based at the Hotel Bristol, the Russians at the Imperial, and the British at the Sacher—where Martins stays in the movie, and where Greene conceived the idea from his intelligence cronies in the bar, including his boss the notorious KGB double agent Kim Philby, who was the inspiration for Harry Lime. *Kärtner Ring & Philharmonikerstrasse. U-Bahn 1/2/4 (Karlsplatz), Tram 1/2/62/71/D (Kärntner Ring/Oper).*

5 Café Mozart. Inspired by Greene's favorite cafe, musician Anton Karas composed a "Café Mozart Waltz" for the movie. The cafe scenes were actually shot in a mocked-up set near the Kapuzinerkirche (Capuchin Church), because the square was still full of wartime rubble in 1948. Round the corner is Harry's house, Palais Palavincini (in Josefsplatz). *Albertinaplatz 2.* ☎ *01 241 00-200. €–€€. Tram 1/2/D (Oper).*

6 ★ Schreyvogelgasse 8. This is the site of one of the most dramatic moments in the movie when Harry emerges from the shadows, very much alive, in the doorway here on the Mölker Bastei. *Schreyvogelgasse 8. U-Bahn 2 (Schottentor).*

7 ★★★ kids Prater—Riesenrad. Ride on the 67m (200 ft.) Riesenrad Ferris wheel, one of Vienna's most famous landmarks, immortalized in the movie by the pivotal scene when Martins and Lime eventually meet, and Martins learns the awful truth about his friend. *See p 98,* 5.

Graham Greene's favorite cafe.

Bobo Vienna

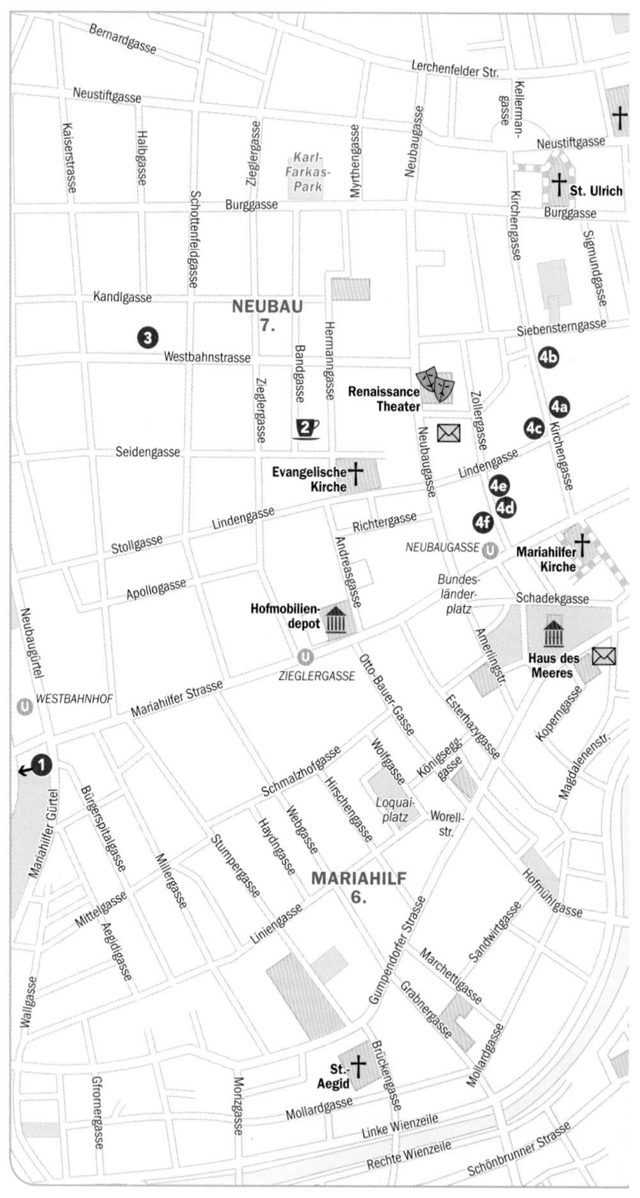
Bernardgasse
Lerchenfelder Str.
Neustiftgasse
Kellerman-gasse
Kaiserstrasse
Halbgasse
Zieglergasse
Karl-Farkas-Park
Myrthengasse
Neubaugasse
Neustiftgasse
St. Ulrich
Schottenfeldgasse
Burggasse
Kirchengasse
Burggasse
Sigmundgasse
Kandlgasse
NEUBAU 7.
Hermanngasse
Siebensterngasse
3
Westbahnstrasse
Bandgasse
Zieglergasse
4b
Renaissance Theater
4a
Zollergasse
4c
Kirchengasse
2
Neubaugasse
Seidengasse
Evangelische Kirche
Lindengasse
4e
4d
Lindengasse
Richtergasse
4f
Stollgasse
NEUBAUGASSE
Mariahilfer Kirche
Andreasgasse
Bundesländerplatz
Apollogasse
Schadekgasse
Hofmobiliendepot
Neubaugürtel
Amerlingstr.
Haus des Meeres
ZIEGLERGASSE
Otto-Bauer-Gasse
WESTBAHNHOF
Mariahilfer Strasse
Esterhazygasse
Koperngasse
Magdalenenstr.
1
Schmalzhofgasse
Wolfgasse
Königsegggasse
Bürgerspitalgasse
Hirschengasse
Loquaiplatz
Worellstr.
Mariahilfer Gürtel
Webgasse
Haydngasse
Stumpergasse
Millergasse
MARIAHILF 6.
Hofmühlgasse
Mittelgasse
Aegidigasse
Liniengasse
Sandwirtgasse
Gumpendorfer Strasse
Marchettigasse
Wallgasse
Grabnergasse
Mollardgasse
Brückengasse
St. Aegid
Gfrornergasse
Morizgasse
Mollardgasse
Linke Wienzeile
Rechte Wienzeile
Schönbrunner Strasse

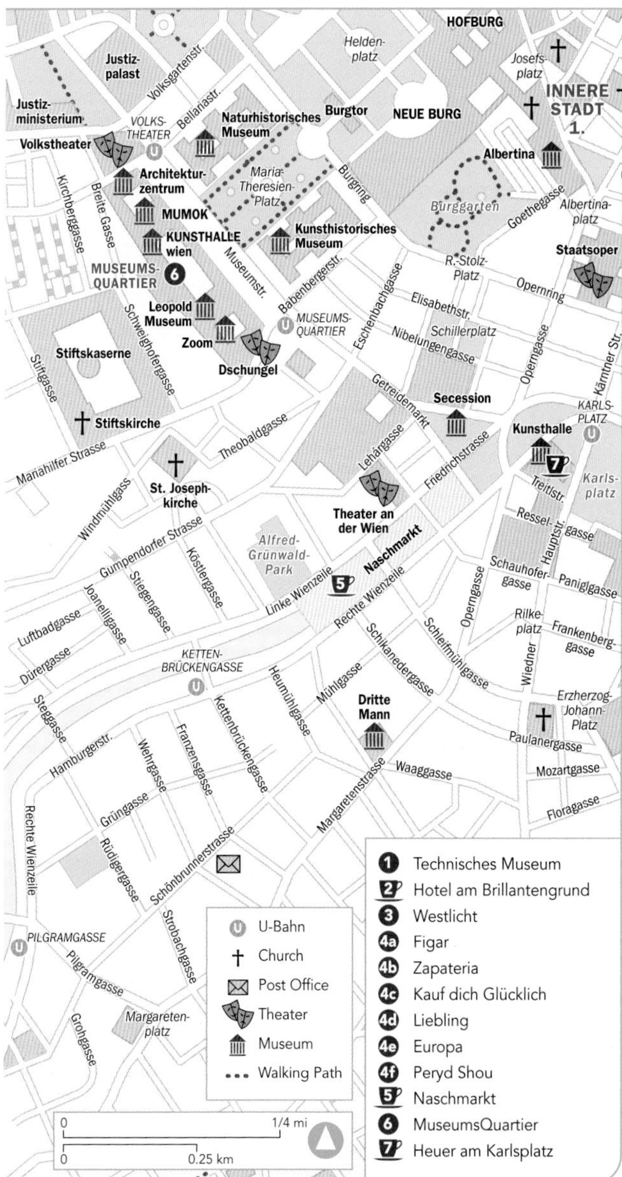
HOFBURG
Helden-platz
Josefs-platz
INNERE STADT 1.
Justiz-palast
Justiz-ministerium
Volksgartenstr.
Bellariastr.
VOLKS-THEATER
Volkstheater
Naturhistorisches Museum
Burgtor
NEUE BURG
Albertina
Architektur-zentrum
MUMOK
KUNSTHALLE wien
MUSEUMS-QUARTIER
Maria-Theresien-Platz
Burgring
Burggarten
Goethegasse
Albertina-platz
Staatsoper
Kunsthistorisches Museum
Museumstr.
Babenbergerstr.
R.-Stolz-Platz
Opernring
Eschenbachgasse
Elisabethstr.
Schillerplatz
Nibelungengasse
Kirchberggasse
Breite Gasse
Leopold Museum
Zoom
Dschungel
MUSEUMS-QUARTIER
Schweighofergasse
Stiftskaserne
Stiftgasse
Stiftskirche
Getreidemarkt
Secession
Operngasse
Kärntner Str.
KARLS-PLATZ
Kunsthalle
Mariahilfer Strasse
Theobaldgasse
Lehárgasse
Friedrichstrasse
Treitlstr.
Karls-platz
St. Joseph-kirche
Windmühlgasse
Theater an der Wien
Ressel-gasse
Hauptstr.
Alfred-Grünwald-Park
Naschmarkt
Gumpendorfer Strasse
Köstlergasse
Stiegengasse
Linke Wienzeile
Rechte Wienzeile
Schauhofer-gasse
Paniglgasse
Operngasse
Joanelligasse
Luftbadgasse
Rilke-platz
Frankenberg-gasse
Schleifmühlgasse
Schikanedergasse
Dürergasse
KETTEN-BRÜCKENGASSE
Heumühlgasse
Mühlgasse
Wiedner
Erzherzog-Johann-Platz
Steggasse
Kettenbrückengasse
Dritte Mann
Paulanergasse
Hamburgerstr.
Wehrgasse
Franzensgasse
Margaretenstrasse
Waaggasse
Mozartgasse
Floragasse
Grüngasse
Rechte Wienzeile
Rüdigergasse
Schönbrunnerstrasse
Strobachgasse
PILGRAMGASSE
Pilgramgasse
Margareten-platz
Grohgasse
U-Bahn
Church
Post Office
Theater
Museum
Walking Path
0
1/4 mi
0
0.25 km
1 Technisches Museum
2 Hotel am Brillantengrund
3 Westlicht
4a Figar
4b Zapateria
4c Kauf dich Glücklich
4d Liebling
4e Europa
4f Peryd Shou
5 Naschmarkt
6 MuseumsQuartier
7 Heuer am Karlsplatz

Vienna's hipsters are a creative crowd: artists, designers, musicians and filmmakers, web designers, and plenty of cool, nerdy types. Identified in 2016 as the world's top city to live in, Vienna is the perfect place to be an independent middle-class creative person—aka bobo. So if that's where you feel at home, get to know today's Vienna, far from Sisi, Klimt, and Mozart. START: **Technisches Museum Wien (Tram 52/58 Penzingerstrasse).**

1 ★★★ kids Technisches Museum Wien. This huge Technical Museum is a bit out of town, but easy to reach by U-Bahn. Start your day here for a crash course on Vienna's everyday history. There are old trams and cars as well as reconstructed kitchens from the post-war period that show how Vienna saw the future of technology in the everyday. There is also a fun exhibit on space travel. *2 hr. Mariahilferstrasse 212. ☎ 01 899 98-6000. www.tmw.at. €8.50 adults, free under 19. Mon–Fri 9am–6pm; Sat–Sun 10am–6pm. Tram 52/58 (Penzingerstrasse) or 10 (Johnstrasse/Linzerstrasse).*

2 ★★ Hotel am Brillantengrund. You know you're a hipster when only secondhand is good enough, and you need concrete walls to feel truly at home. Brillantengrund, at the heart of the boho 7th district, is great for a lunch in the courtyard, where Mama cooks Filipino style. *Bandgasse 4 1. ☎ 01 523 3662. €.* *See p 150.*

3 ★★ WestLicht. The area around Westbahnstrasse has become a mecca for photographers, and the nonprofit WestLicht, part-photo gallery, part-camera museum, fuels their passion. *1 hr. Westbahnstrasse 40. ☎ 01 522 6636-60. www.westlicht.com. €7 adults, €4 concessions free under 6. Check website for opening hours. Tram 49 (Kaiserstrasse).*

4 ★★ Kirchengasse/Zollergasse. The streets of the 7th district are renowned for their hipster flair. On Kirchengasse you'll find a series of cafes with outdoor seating in summer, including **4A ★ Figar.** You can shop for exclusive footwear at **4B Zapateria,** or for the

The WestLicht features all things photography.

An artist-in-residence at quartier 21.

ultimate fashion victim, stop in a 4C ★ **Kauf Dich Glücklich** (translation: Shop yourself happy). If you venture around the corner to Zollergasse, you'll find cafes like 4D ★ **Liebling** or 4E **Europa.** Stop in at 4F **Peryd Shou** for quirky accessories or a T-shirt printed that day with the design of your choice; the perfect souvenir.

5 **Naschmakrt.** This is a great place to do just what the name instructs: "Nosch," or in Yiddish, nibble. Start around Kettenbrückengasse and meander through the many stalls, where you can taste to your hearts content. If you want to purchase something feel free to haggle. *Naschmarkt. Stalls: Mon–Fri 8am–6pm; Sat 6am–1pm. Snack bars: times vary, some open until 10 or 11pm, closed Sun. U-Bahn 1/2/4 (Karlsplatz) or U-Bahn 4 (Kettenbrückengasse). €– €€.*

6 ★★★ MuseumsQuartier. This is the ultimate hangout for creative types or bohemians. The vast complex houses something for everybody but the highlights for hipsters include **quartier 21,** which houses contemporary exhibitions, including work by whatever artist is currently in residence. In addition there are unique shops like **Subotron,** a shop dedicated to gaming history, with consoles and merchandise from over 4 decades of computer gaming. Electric Avenue is home to **The Stash,** and its lovingly crafted giant electric racetrack. In warm weather, entire afternoons can be spent lazily sipping white wine spritzers in one of the quarter's colorful modern lounge chairs, known as Enzis. But we recommended you extract yourself from MQ's trademark loungers and visit both the Leopold Museum (p 76) and contemporary art museum MUMOK (p 76). *2 hr. Museumsplatz 1. 01 523 5881. www.mqw.at. U-Bahn 2 (MuseumsQuartier).*

7 **★★ Heuer am Karlsplatz.** End your day at this glassed-in eatery, smack in the middle of a massive intersection on Karlsplatz. Next to the building is an urban gardening space, where artists stage outdoor exhibitions and musicians lounge on chairs made of wooden Euro-pallets. *Am Karlsplatz Treitlstraße 2. 01 890 0590. www.heuer-amkarlsplatz.com. Mon–Fri 11:30am–2am. U-Bahn 1/2/4 (Karlsplatz). €€.*

The Ringstrasse

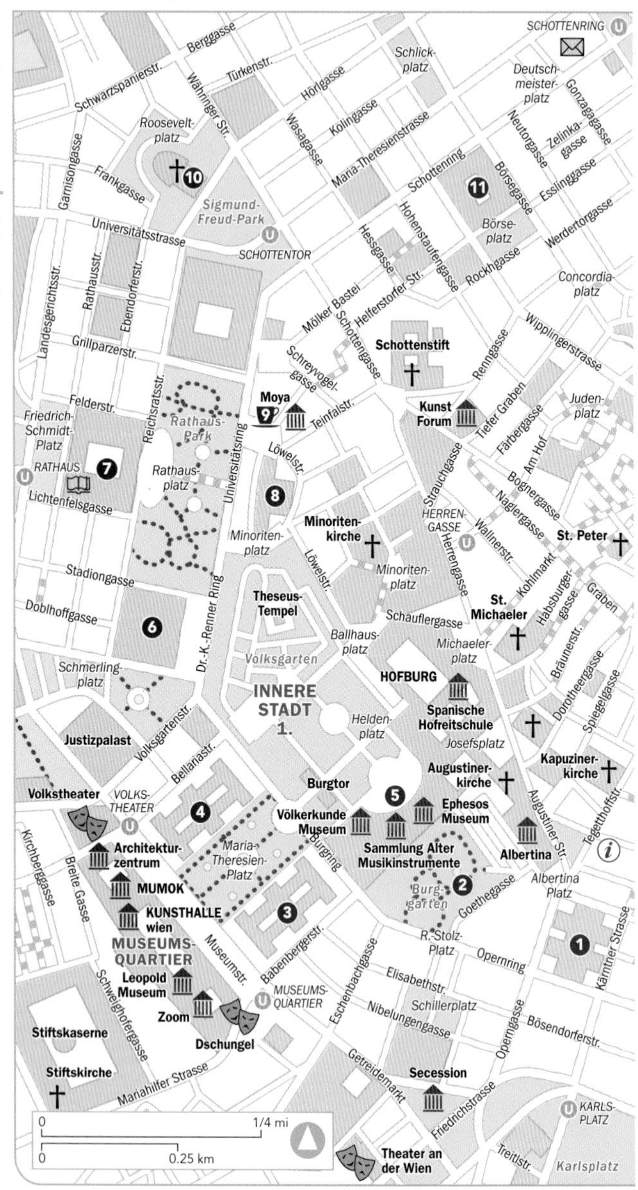

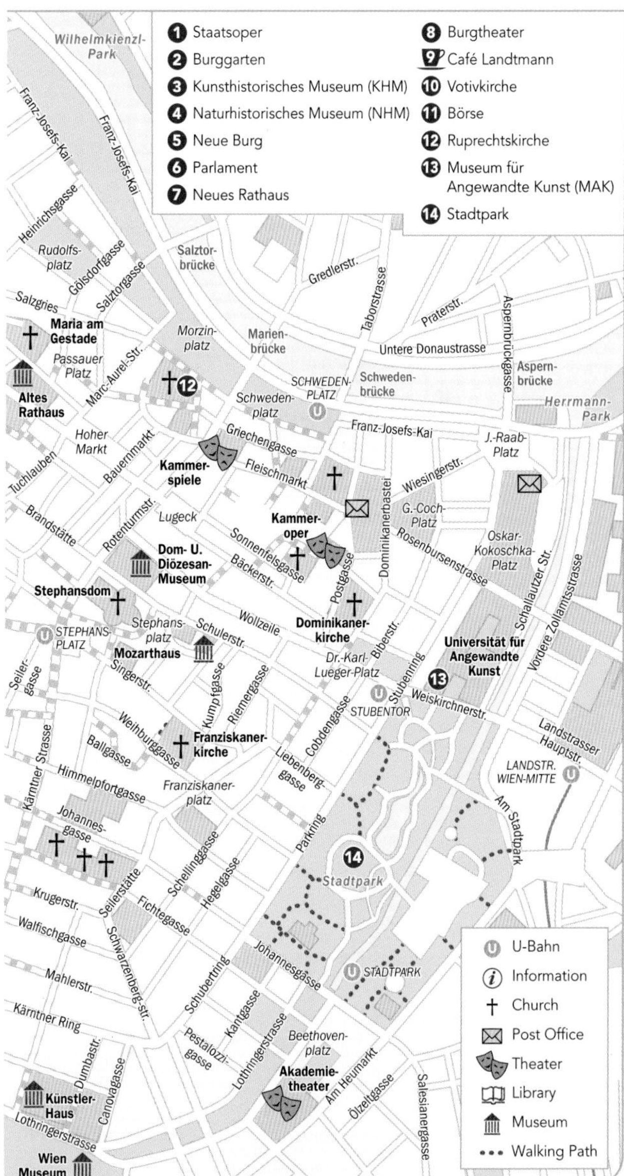
1 Staatsoper
2 Burggarten
3 Kunsthistorisches Museum (KHM)
4 Naturhistorisches Museum (NHM)
5 Neue Burg
6 Parlament
7 Neues Rathaus
8 Burgtheater
9 Café Landtmann
10 Votivkirche
11 Börse
12 Ruprechtskirche
13 Museum für Angewandte Kunst (MAK)
14 Stadtpark
Wilhelmkienzl-Park
Franz-Josefs-Kai
Heinrichsgasse
Rudolfs-platz
Gölsdorfgasse
Salztorgasse
Salztor-brücke
Salzgries
Maria am Gestade
Passauer Platz
Altes Rathaus
Marc-Aurel-Str.
Morzin-platz
Marien-brücke
Gredlerstr.
Taborstrasse
Praterstr.
Aspernbrückgasse
Untere Donaustrasse
Aspern-brücke
Herrmann-Park
SCHWEDEN-PLATZ
Schweden-brücke
Schweden-platz
Hoher Markt
Griechengasse
Kammer-spiele
Fleischmarkt
Wiesingerstr.
J.-Raab-Platz
Tuchlauben
Bauernmarkt
Brandstätte
Rotenturmstr.
Lugeck
Kammer-oper
G.-Coch-Platz
Dominikanerbastei
Rosenbursenstrasse
Oskar-Kokoschka-Platz
Dom- U. Diözesan-Museum
Sonnenfelsgasse
Bäckerstr.
Postgasse
Schallautzer Str.
Vordere Zollamtsstrasse
Stephansdom
Wollzeile
Dominikaner-kirche
STEPHANS-PLATZ
Stephans-platz
Schulerstr.
Mozarthaus
Universität für Angewandte Kunst
Biberstr.
Dr.-Karl-Lueger-Platz
Stubenring
Seiler-gasse
Singerstr.
Kumpfgasse
Riemergasse
Weiskirchnerstr.
STUBENTOR
Cobdengasse
Weihburggasse
Franziskaner-kirche
Landstrasser Hauptstr.
Ballgasse
Liebenberg-gasse
LANDSTR. WIEN-MITTE
Kärntner Strasse
Himmelpfortgasse
Franziskaner-platz
Am Stadtpark
Johannes-gasse
Parkring
Stadtpark
Schellinggasse
Hegelgasse
Krugerstr.
Seilerstätte
Fichtegasse
Walfischgasse
Johannesgasse
Schwarzenberg-str.
Schubertring
STADTPARK
Mahlerstr.
Kärntner Ring
Kantgasse
Lothringerstrasse
Beethoven-platz
Pestalozzi-gasse
Dumbastr.
Canovagasse
Akademie-theater
Am Heumarkt
Ölzeltgasse
Salesianergasse
Künstler-Haus
Lothringerstrasse
Wien Museum
U-Bahn
Information
Church
Post Office
Theater
Library
Museum
Walking Path

A tour of the Ringstrasse is the best way to get oriented to downtown Vienna. Emperor Franz Josef ushered in a new era of grandeur when he expanded the inner city in the 19th century. The old city walls were torn down and the magnificent Ringstrasse was constructed in its place. Today, this circular boulevard still separates the historic city center from the suburbs. It is as grand now as it was then, and it's fun and easy to explore by tram. There's no longer a public tramline that covers the whole Ringstrasse, but the Ring Tram does the circuit every 30 minutes starting at 10am and with the last tour beginning at 5:30pm. Hop aboard at Schwedenplatz. (€8 adults; €4 concessions, free under 6). START: **Schwedenplatz (Tram 1/2, U-Bahn 1/4 Schwedenplatz).**

❶ ★★ **Staatsoper.** The world-famous State Opera was the first of the monumental new public buildings on the Ringstrasse. It was built in the Historicist (neo-Renaissance) style in 1861 to 1869 by architects Nüll and Sicardsburg. Harsh criticism from the public, who thought the opera house looked like a railway station, drove Nüll to commit suicide, and a few weeks later, before the project was completed, a distressed Sicardsburg died from a heart attack. The railway station critiques may have been one of the reasons the building was bombed by allied forces in World War II. The Viennese were keen to restore what had become part of the city's identity to its former glory after the war, and the opera house finally reopened in 1955 with a triumphant performance of Beethoven's *Fidelio*. *See p 38,* ❼.

This sculpture of King Thutmosis III at the KHM dates from around1460 B.C.

❷ ★★ kids **Burggarten.** With its duck pond, butterfly house, fine statuary, and magnificent Jugendstil greenhouse (p 31, 10), this attractive English-style park was originally reserved for the emperor's family. It was opened to the public in 1919 and is now one of the city's most popular open spaces. *Burgring. Daily 6am–10pm. Tram 2 (Burgring).*

❸ ★★★ **Kunsthistorisches Museum (KHM).** *See p 18,* ❻.

❹ ★★★ kids **Naturhistorisches Museum (NHM).** Trace the history

The celebrated Staatsoper.

of the planet and admire a multiplicity of animal species on display at the Natural History Museum. This huge museum is a mirror image of the grand Renaissance-style Kunsthistorisches Museum on the opposite side of the Ringstrasse. Within its majestic display halls lies a bewildering array of archeological, anthropological, mineralogical, zoological, and geological specimens.

Naturhistorisches Museum (NHM)

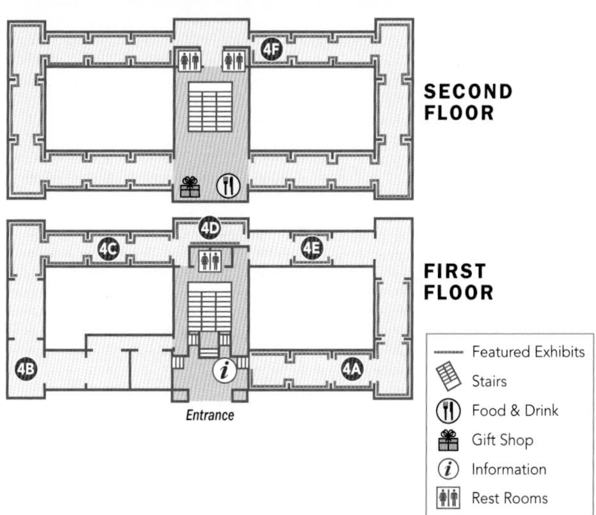

The 4A famous **Venus of Willendorf** is a statuette that dates back to 28,000 B.C. Alongside this piece of ancient art, you'll find other fascinating and unique specimens of natural history. The digital 4B **planetarium** was added in 2015 and features full dome projection technology, with shows ranging from the big bang to dinosaurs and catastrophes in the cosmos. Showings are in both German and English, so check the program. The 4C **prehistory section** contains the world's largest display of human skulls. Kids love the mezzanine floor and especially 4D **Room 10** with its massive dinosaur skeletons, including a Diplodocus—the longest terrestrial vertebrate that has ever lived at 27m (90 ft.). In 4E **Room VII,** a fossil of the **world's largest spider** is not for the squeamish. The upper floor covers ecology, with room after room of every type of 4F **stuffed animal** imaginable, including numerous species now extremely endangered or extinct. *2–3 hr. Maria-Theresien-Platz, Burgring 7. ☎ 01 521 77-0. www.nhm-wien.ac.at. €10 adults, €8 concessions, €5 students and soldiers under 27, free under 19. Wed–Mon 9am–6:30pm (Wed until 9pm). U-Bahn 2/3, (Volkstheater) Tram 1/2/71/46/49 (Dr.-Karl-Renner-Ring).*

5 ★ Neue Burg. Emperor Franz Joseph had plans for two crescent-shaped buildings in his Neue Burg (New Castle), but only one was completed before the Habsburg Empire collapsed in 1918. Today, this vast edifice, with its colonnaded facade, houses several museums. The **Ephesus Museum** (Greek and Roman antiquities), the **Imperial Armory** (Europe's most comprehensive weaponry collection), and the **Old Musical Instruments Collection** (p 37, 4) are all worth a visit. *1–2 hr. Heldenplatz. ☎ 01 525 24-0. www.khm.at. Combined admission for all 3 museums, and for the KHM (see p 18) €15 adults, €11 concessions, free under 19, €4 audio guide. Wed–Sun 10am–6pm. U-Bahn 2/3 (Volkstheater) Tram 1/2/D (Burgring).*

6 ★ Parlament. The Greek-style Parliament building makes a dignified landmark with its classical columns and statues of Greek philosophers. The first Austrian Republic was proclaimed from the Parliament steps in October 1918. *Dr-Karl-Renner-Ring 3. ☎ 01 401 10-0. Free admission to visitor center. Mon–Fri 8:30am–6:30pm; Sat 9:30am–4:30pm. For times of guided tours (€5/€2.50 adults/concessions), see www.parlament.gv.at. Tram 1/2/71/46/49 (Dr-Karl-Renner-Ring).*

7 ★★ kids Neues Rathaus. Festooned with ornamental tracery, loggias, and spires, the neo-Gothic New Town Hall is the showiest building on the Ringstrasse. Atop the main tower is a statue of a knight holding a lance, affectionately called the *Rathausmann.* There is a flag attached to the lance, with a star at the top, which also serves as a lightning conductor. The large square in front of the town hall always seems to be hosting some sort of festivity: open-air cinema or food festivals in summer; ice-skating in winter; and the best-known Christmas market in town (*Christkindlmarkt*). *Rathausplatz. ☎ 01 52550. Free admission. Guided tours Mon, Wed, Fri 1pm. U-Bahn 2 (Rathaus).*

8 ★★ Burgtheater. The most prestigious theater venue in the German-speaking world is known not only for drama but also for its grand staircases and frescoes by Gustav Klimt. Constructed in Italian Renaissance style in 1888, the theater was rebuilt following severe damage sustained during World War II. *Universitätsring 2. ☎ 01 514 444 140. www.burgtheater.at. 50 min. tours in English and German, Sept–June Fri–Sun 3pm. €7 adults, €6 concessions, €3.50 students and kids. Tram 1/71/D (Burgtheater).*

9 Café Landtmann. Pass through the entrance encased in a modern sun terrace, and step indoors to see the *fin-de-siècle* decor of ornate mirrors and paneled wood. While locals know this place as a favorite for low-key business meetings, the cafe's past is full of celebrities. It seems that everyone from Marlene Dietrich to Gustav Mahler enjoyed coffee and cake here. It was also Sigmund Freud's favorite cafe. *Dr-Karl-Lueger-Ring 4. ☎ 01 24100-100. Daily 7:30am–midnight. Entrees €– €€.*

10 ★ Votivkirche. *See p 72, 6.*

11 ★ Börse. *See p 72, 8.*

12 ★★★ Ruprechtskirche. *See p 65, 9.*

13 ★★ Museum für Angewandte Kunst (MAK). *See p 12, 5.*

14 ★★ kids Stadtpark. *See p 95.*

3 The Best Neighborhood Walks

Stephansdom Quarter

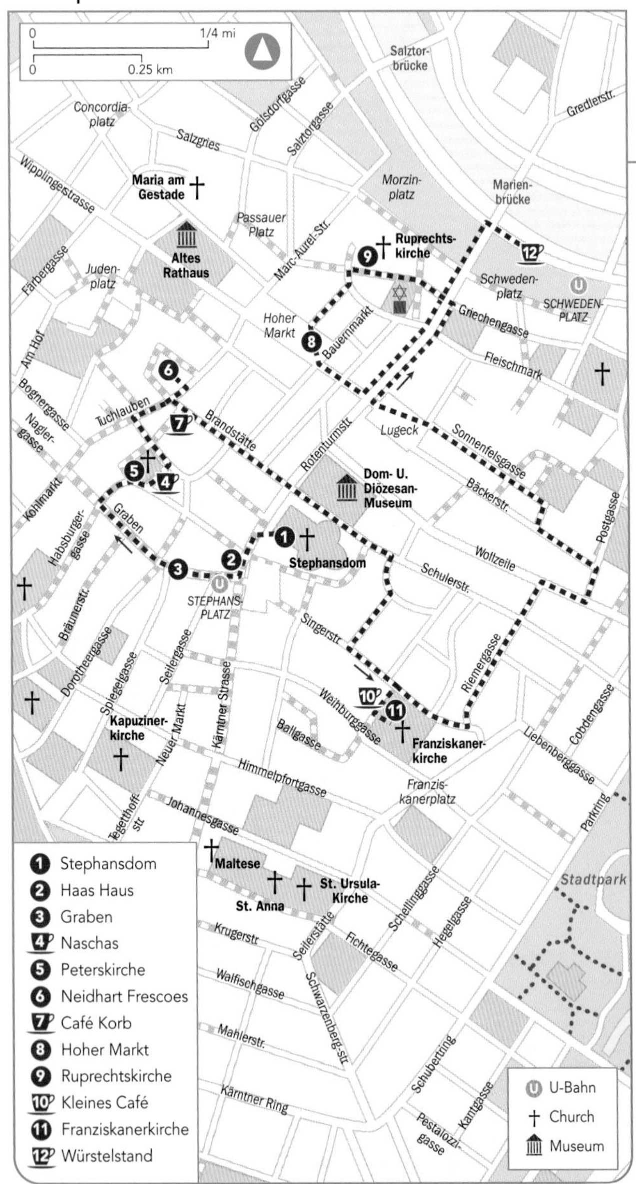

Previous page: The controversial Haas Haus, in the heart of the UNESCO–protected old city.

This is a walk to suit the whole family. It takes you right to the historic heart of Vienna, to the foundations of ancient Roman Vindobona, and to some of the city's oldest inns and churches. Explore the atmospheric maze of medieval alleyways surrounding Stephansdom, and enjoy the chichi shops of the Graben—as well as the best apple strudel in town. START: **Stephansdom (U-Bahn 1/3 Stephansplatz).**

❶ ★★★ **Stephansdom.** *See p 11,* ❸.

❷ ★★ **Haas Haus.** Created by Hans Hollein in the 1980s, this curvaceous building of polished granite, concrete, and glass, which houses a boutique hotel on the 6th and 7th floors, is one of Vienna's most controversial pieces of modern architecture. Love it or hate it, it offers tremendous views of the Stephansdom from the rooftop bar (6th floor) and restaurant (7th floor). *Stock-im-Eisenplatz. U-Bahn 1/3 (Stephansplatz).*

❸ ★★ **Graben.** This broad, pedestrianized shopping street was once the town moat, hence the name Graben (ditch). It later became a marketplace and is now one of the city's finest boulevards. All the buildings date from the baroque, 19th-century, or Belle Epoque eras, and many still bear their K.u.K. (Kaiserlich und Königlich—Imperial and Royal) warrant. The exuberant baroque Pestsäule (Plague Column) in the middle of the street was erected to commemorate Vienna's deliverance from the plague of 1679. *Graben. U-Bahn 1/3 (Stephansplatz).*

4 ★★★ **Naschas.** This Petersplatz eatery is dedicated to modern European cuisine and design. The breakfast is delectable and at lunchtime the menu ranges from oysters to duck breast, and they offer a fine array of European cheeses. The outdoors seating is cozy and quiet. *Petersplatz 11.* ☎ *01 925 5636. €–€€.*

❺ ★★ **Peterskirche.** St. Peter's is my favorite baroque church. Full of pomp and grandeur, yet intimate at the same time, its superb acoustics make it a marvelous concert venue. I love the graceful oval nave and the pews, each decorated with three carved angels' heads, but the artistic *pièce de résistance* is undoubtedly the spectacular fresco on the domed ceiling—*The Martyrdom of St. Sebastian*, by Michael Rottmayr. 🕓 *30 min. Petersplatz.*

The Plague Column on the Graben.

☎ *01 533 6433. www.peterskirche.at. Mon–Fri 7am–8pm; Sat–Sun 9am–9pm. Occasional free concerts (including organ recitals in summer Mon–Fri 3pm). U-Bahn 1/3 (Stephansplatz).*

6 ★★ Neidhart Frescoes. One of Vienna's best-kept secrets, these richly colored wall paintings are the oldest secular frescoes in the city. Commissioned by a cloth merchant around the year 1407, their scenes of love and revelry (depicting the four seasons) were inspired by the songs of the lyrical poet Neidhart von Reuenthal, who revived the courtly love song in the early Middle Ages. Fun and frivolous, they give a lively and humorous insight into medieval life. ⏲ *30 min. Tuchlauben 19.* ☎ *01 535 9065. www.wienmuseum.at. €5 adults, €4 concessions, free under 19, free first Sun of each month. Tues–Sun 10am–1pm and 2–6pm. U-Bahn 1/3 (Stephansplatz).*

7 ★★★ Café Korb. This deliciously run-down cafe is a favorite for actors and journalists. Their *apfelstrudel* (apple strudel) is fantastic, and the sidewalk terrace with its tiny fountain is a pleasant place to sit and write postcards. *Brandstätte 9.* ☎ *01 533 7215. €–€€.*

The Anker clock at Hoher Markt.

8 ★★★ Hoher Markt. Most visitors head toward Vienna's oldest square, site of a medieval fish market, to see the splendid Jugendstil clock known as the Ankeruhr. Every hour on the hour, historical figures (including the Roman emperor Marcus Aurelius and Duke Rudolf IV) parade across the golden clock face. It's best viewed at noon, when all the figures emerge. Beneath the square, you can see the city's best-preserved Roman remains in the small but fascinating **Römermuseum,** where the legionary fortress of Vindobona stood nearly 2,000 years ago. ⏲ *45 min. Hoher Markt 3.* ☎ *01 535 5606. www.wienmuseum.at. €4 adults, €3 concessions, free under 19, free first Sun of each month. Tues–Sun 9am–6pm. U-Bahn 1/3 (Stephansplatz).*

Peterskirche is hidden just off the Graben.

9 ★★★ Ruprechtskirche. Set in a quiet, cobbled square off the beaten tourist track, this is Vienna's oldest church, first referenced in the year 1200. It's dedicated to St. Rupert, the patron saint of salt merchants and the first Bishop of Salzburg. Salt barges would once have passed by this church on the banks of the Danube. A statue of St. Rupert, clutching a barrel of salt, can be found half-hidden among bushes behind the church. Visit in the morning when the ancient stained-glass windows bathe the interior in brightly colored light. *20 min. Ruprechtsplatz. ☎ 01 535 6003. Free admission. Mon, Wed, Fri 10am–noon; Tues, Thurs 2–4pm; Fri 9pm–midnight. U-Bahn 1/4 (Schwedenplatz).*

You're never far from a Würstelstand in Vienna.

10 ★★ Kleines Café. This adorable hole in the wall is a legendary haunt for actors and famous visitors to Vienna. The cozy interior is snug as can be, and there's outdoor seating on charming cobblestone square. *Franziskanerplatz 3. No phone. €–€€.*

Ruprechtskirche dates to the year 1200.

11 ★ Franziskanerkirche. The Franciscan Church is the only church in Vienna with a Renaissance facade. The interior is a striking blend of Gothic and northern Renaissance style, with numerous later-baroque features. The square outside contains a copy of an 18th-century Moses fountain (the original was melted down by the Nazis) and the charming pint-sized Kleines Café. *20 min. Franziskanerplatz. ☎ 01 512 4578. Daily 8am–6pm. U-Bahn 1/3 (Stephansplatz).*

12 ★★ Würstelstand. Night owls meet early birds (open 8am–4am) for coffee, refreshments, or a snack—sausages, kebabs, pizza, and so on. After an evening partying in the bars of the nearby "Bermuda Triangle" bar zone (around Rotenturmstrasse), I recommend the hearty Käsekrainer sausages, oozing with cheese. *Schwedenplatz. No phone. €.*

The Belvedere

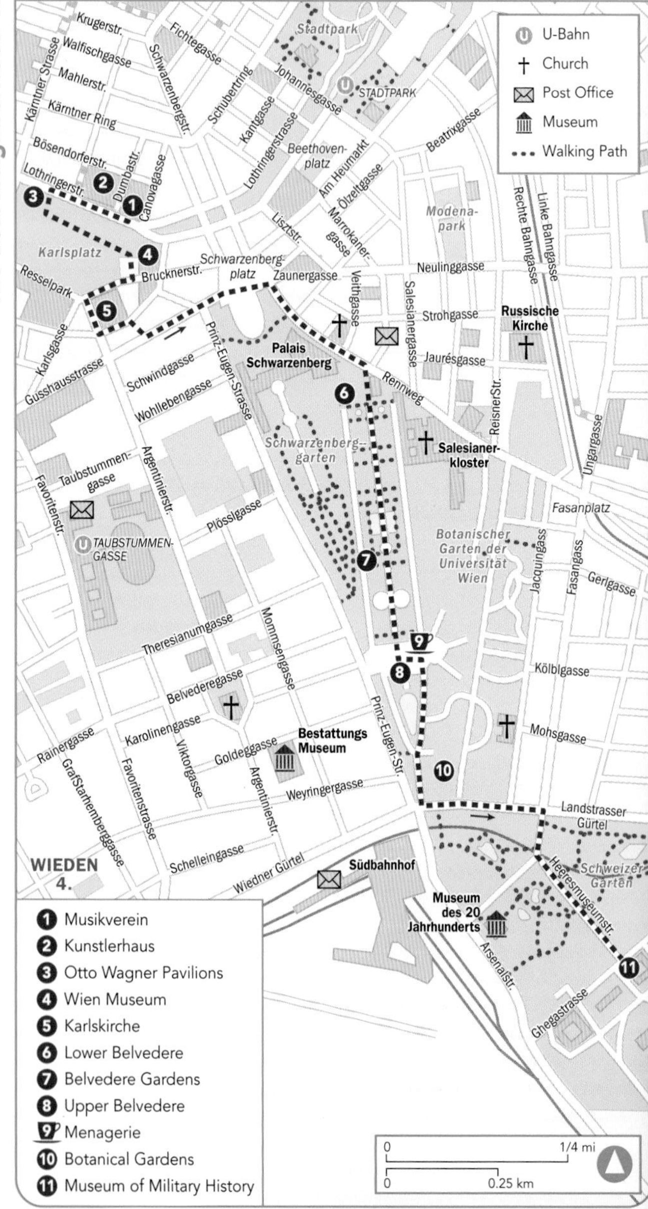

The extravagance of the Belvedere neighborhood is breathtaking. Vienna's aristocracy built their lavish summer residences in the countryside here during the 18th and 19th centuries. Today, this charming quarter of palaces and parks takes life at a sedate pace, despite being so close to the city center. **START: Musikverein (U-Bahn 1/2/4 Karlsplatz).**

❶ ★★ **Musikverein.** *See p 13,* ❼.

❷ ★ **Künstlerhaus.** The Artists' House was commissioned in 1868 by the Austrian Artists' Association as an exhibition hall for its members and is still a popular venue for fashion events and temporary exhibitions. Its architecture is a typical example of the Ringstrasse's pompous historical style. *Karlsplatz 5. ☎ 01 587 9663. www.k-haus.at. Daily 10am–6pm (Thurs until 9pm). U-Bahn 1/2/4 (Karlsplatz).*

❸ ★★ **Otto Wagner Pavilions.** *See p 33,* ❷.

❹ ★★★ **Wien Museum.** *See p 16,* ❶.

❺ ★★★ **Karlskirche.** The colossal dome of this high-baroque church dominates the square of Karlsplatz on which it stands. Designed in 1716 by Fischer von Erlach, the Karlskirche showcases the work of the most important architects and artists of the time. It was originally commissioned by Emperor Karl VI, who made a solemn vow to build a great church during a virulent outbreak of plague in 1713. It is dedicated to the emperor's namesake, St. Carlo Borromeo, the patron saint of plagues. Its remarkable architectural complexity pays homage to St. Peter's Basilica in Rome, to the Roman emperors Augustus and Trajan, and to the Temple of Solomon in Jerusalem. St. Carlo sits happily on top of the portico alongside statues of Religion, Mercy, Repentance, and Piety, flanked by two angels representing the Old and New testaments. The triumphal pillars (modeled on Trajan's Column in Rome and crowned by imperial eagles) show scenes from Borromeo's life. Unlike some baroque churches, the oval interior is light and airy, and its decoration is

It's hard to beat Karlskirche for Baroque architectural extravagance.

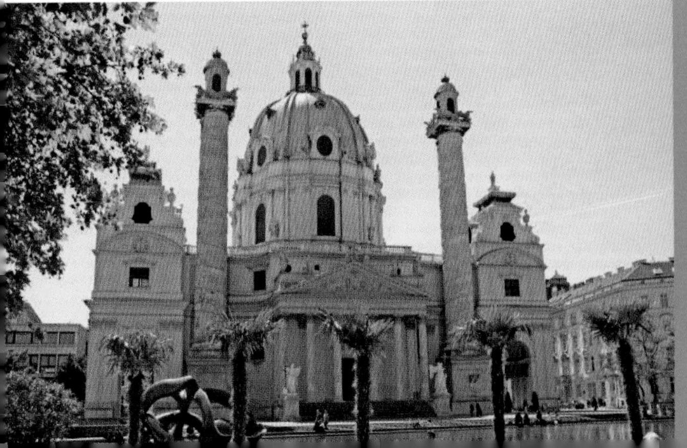

agreeably restrained. The frescoes by Michael Rottmayr are especially fine. *Karlsplatz. ☎ 01 504 6187. www.karlskirche.at. €8 adults, €4 students and kids, free under 10. Mon–Sat 9am–6pm; Sun noon–7pm. Holy Mass Mon–Sat 6pm; Sun 11am and 6pm. U-Bahn 1/2/4 (Karlsplatz).*

6 ★ Lower Belvedere. Prince Eugene of Savoy, the most important military commander of his day, had not one but two grandiose baroque summer residences built by Johann Lukas von Hildebrandt on a low hill with exceptional views over the city center. The state rooms of the lower palace provide a fascinating insight into baroque interior design, and create an impressive backdrop for temporary exhibitions. *45 min.; lunchtime is the quietest time to visit. Rennweg 6. ☎ 01 795 57 200. www.belvedere.at. €12 adults, €9 concessions, free under 19 (combined tickets with the Upper Belvedere are also available). Daily 10am–6pm (Wed until 9pm). Tram 71 (Unteres Belvedere).*

7 ★★ kids Belvedere Gardens. The two Belvedere palaces are linked together by a strictly symmetrical French-style garden laid out on a gently sloping hill. Look for the white marble fountains, stone sphinxes (symbols of strength and intelligence), and 12 charming *putti* (cherubic statues) on the steps (representing months of the year). On the upper terrace, the spectacular cityscape has barely changed over the centuries and is especially dramatic at sunset. Little wonder the palace is called "Belvedere" (Beautiful View). *30 min. Rennweg 6/Prinz-Eugen-Strasse 27. ☎ 01 7984 1120. Free admission. Apr, Oct 6am–6pm; May–June 6am–8pm; July–Aug 6am–9pm; Nov–Mar 6:30am–6pm. Tram 71 (Unteres Belvedere) or Tram D (Schloss Belvedere).*

8 ★★★ Upper Belvedere. The finer of Prince Eugene's two summer palaces now contains the Austrian Gallery, with art dating from the Middle Ages to the present day. Medieval and baroque art is found at street level, with neoclassicism, Romanticism, and Viennese Biedermeier on the top floor. The real crowd-puller, however, is Austrian art from the 19th and 20th centuries, which includes the world's largest collection of works by Klimt. *See map at the right.*

9 ★★ Menagerie. The Upper Belvedere's bistro is the perfect spot to enjoy a drink and a gooey cream-cake, or a light lunch after viewing the galleries. There is a small garden, which is open in summer. *Prinz-Eugen-Strasse 27. ☎ 01 320 111 113. €€–€€€.*

10 ★★ Botanical Gardens. Vienna's Botanical Gardens were created in the 18th century to cultivate medicinal herbs. Few people discover the tiny adjoining Alpine Garden. It's a beautiful spot to sit and relax in summer. *45 min. Rennweg 14/Landstrasser Gürtel 3. ☎ 01 4277-54100. www.botanik.univie.ac.at/hbv. Free admission. Opens daily at 10am; closing varies by season, but generally late fall/winter until 4pm; early spring/early fall until 5pm; late spring/summer until 6pm. Tram D (Schloss Belvedere).*

Statue from the Upper Belvedere—Prince Eugene's grand summer palace.

Upper Belvedere

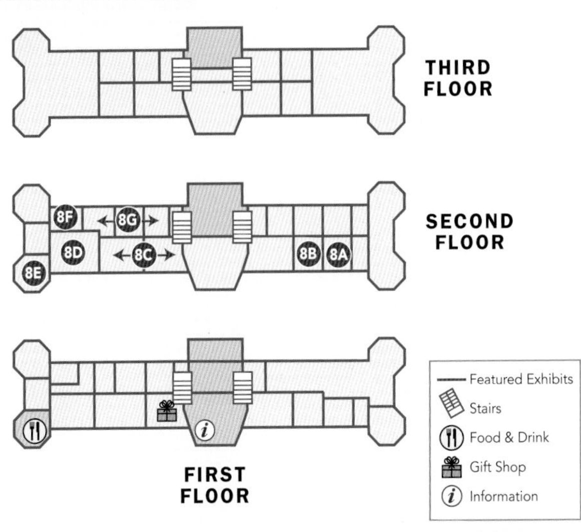

Start in the "Vienna 1880–1900" section to admire an early Klimt portrait of 8A **Sonja Knips** (1898) in an Impressionistic style, and 8B **Spring at the Prater by Tina Blau** (1882). The next section—"Vienna around 1900"—marks a shift from historicism to modernity, through a series of 8C **Impressionist paintings** by Monet, Renoir, and Van Gogh. The highlights of the museum's Jugendstil collection are in Room 3, with Klimt's two famous "golden phase" pictures: 8D ***The Kiss*** (1907–8), and ***Judith*** (1901). Further noteworthy works by Klimt include 8E ***Adam and Eve*** (1917–18, Room 4) and the unfinished 8F ***Bride*** (1918, Room 5). The remaining rooms move toward Expressionism with important works by 8G **Schiele, Gerstl, Oppenheimer, Boeckl, and Munch.** *1 hr. Prinz-Eugen-Strasse 27. 01 795 57-0. www.belvedere.at. €14 adults, €12 concessions, free under 19 (combined tickets with the Lower Belvedere are also available), €4 audio guide, 30 min. guided tours cost extra. Daily 10am–6pm. Tram D (Schloss Belvedere).*

⓫ ★★ kids **Museum of Military History.** Housed within the impressive, fortress-style Arsenal building, this superb museum presents the nation's military prowess from the 16th century to the present. *1 hr. Arsenal: Objekt 1, Ghegastrasse. 01 795 61-0. www.hgm.or.at. €6 adults, €4 concessions, free under 19, free first Sun of each month, €2 audio guide. Daily 9am–5pm; tank garden 9am–4:45pm. Tram 18/0 (Fasangasse) or Tram D (Südbahnhof).*

Schottenring & Alsergrund

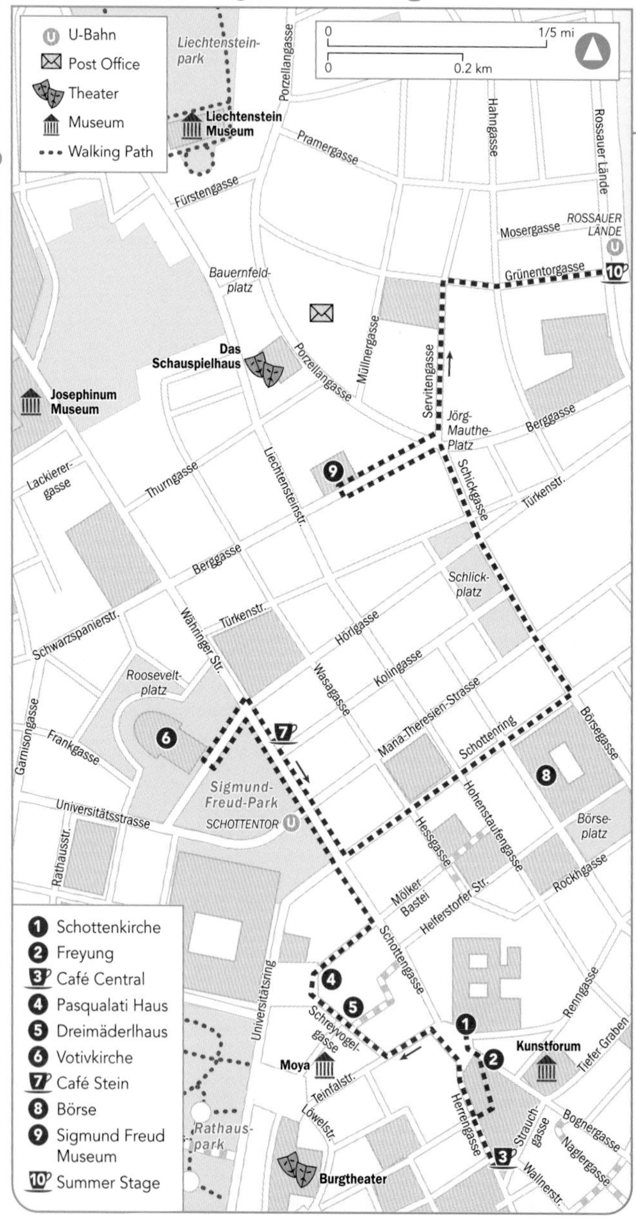

These intimate districts just north of the city center claim a surprising variety of sights, from the Freyung's handsome palaces to the laid-back university district of Alsergrund. The Serviten quarter is especially picturesque: Its cobbled streets, boutiques, and sidewalk cafes are Vienna's answer to Paris's St-Germain-des-Prés. START: **Schottenkirche (U-Bahn 2 Schottentor).**

❶ ★ **Schottenkirche.** Vienna's "Scottish Church" has nothing to do with Scotland. It was founded in 1155 by Duke Heinrich II who brought monks to Vienna from Ireland (which was then known as Scotia Maior). The adjoining monastery (Schottenkloster) remained independent of ducal authority, and had the right to shelter asylum seekers, hence the name of the square here—Freyung (from *frey*, an old spelling of the German word for "free"). The church was remodeled during the baroque period, and it's worth a peep inside to see the rich, if somewhat gloomy, interior. *🕔 10 min. Freyung 6. ☎ 01 5349 8200. www.schottenpfarre.at. Daily 9am–8pm. U-Bahn 2 (Schottentor).*

The Freyung's Austrian Fountain.

❷ ★★★ **Freyung.** This spacious, triangular, cobbled square is essential viewing for architecture fans. Dominated by the Schottenkirche, it was once the city's main rubbish dump. Now, together with adjoining Herrengasse (Lord's Lane), it is lined with imposing baroque palaces formerly owned by the Viennese aristocracy. Many of these are currently used as government offices and embassies. They include the beautifully restored Palais Kinsky, Palais Harrach (where Joseph Haydn's mother was the family cook), and Italianate-style Palais Ferstel, which housed the Vienna Stock Exchange until 1877. The quaint covered alleyways and courtyards of this district contain alluring boutiques and upmarket restaurants. Freyung Passage, leading to the famous Café Central (see below), is particularly elegant. In the middle of the square is the celebrated Austria Fountain, whose four bronze figures symbolize the principal rivers of Austria–Hungary (the

The Schottenkirche's tower dominates the Freyung square.

Elbe, Vistula, Danube, and Po), crowned by an allegorical statue of Austria. On alternate weekends the square is transformed into a farmers market (☎ 0664 531 7301 for details), providing a chance to taste delicious organic produce from Lower Austria. *Freyung. U-Bahn 2 (Schottentor).*

3 ★★ **Café Central.** This splendid coffeehouse was once Vienna's most important literary rendezvous point frequented by eminent local writers such as Kraus, Bahr, and Altenberg. Trotsky used to play chess with Stalin under the vaulted arches. Now popular with tourists, it serves reliable (if pricey) cafe cuisine. *Herrengasse 14/corner Strauchgasse. ☎ 01 533 3764-26. €€.*

4 ★★★ **Pasqualati Haus.** *See p 37,* **1**.

5 ★ **Dreimäderlhaus.** Just round the corner from the Pasqualati Haus, you'll find one of Vienna's most appealing Biedermeier houses. Legend has it that three sweethearts (*drei Mäderl*) of Franz Schubert once lived here, as recounted in the 1920s operetta of the same name, which contains the Viennese composer's melodies. *Schreyvogelgasse 10. U-Bahn 2 (Schottentor).*

Café Central—a celebrated tourist attraction.

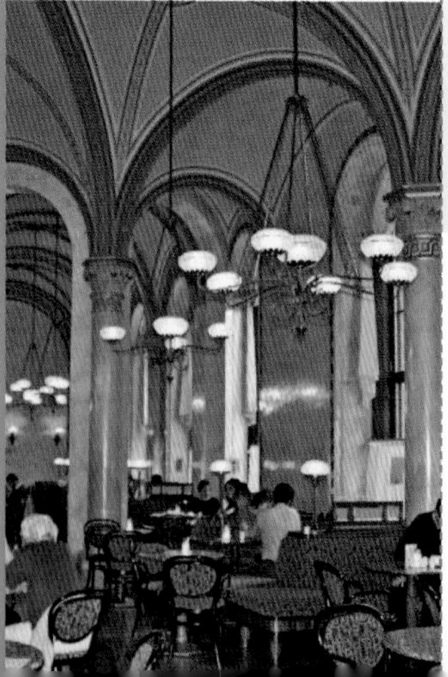

6 ★ **Votivkirche.** The striking white sandstone Votive Church, designed by Heinrich von Ferstel, was erected as a thanksgiving after a failed attempt on the life of Emperor Franz Joseph in 1853. It was one of the first buildings constructed on the new Ringstrasse, and is Vienna's most important example of the neo-Gothic style, distinguished by its patterned roof and lacy twin spires. The interior is rather impersonal, but it does contain some notable frescoes and a carved altar depicting the Passion of Christ. *Rooseveltplatz 8. ☎ 01 406 1192. www.votivkirche.at. Sun 9am–1pm; Tues–Sat 9am–1pm and 4–6pm. U-Bahn 2 (Schottentor).*

7 ★ **Café Stein.** This cafe is the stuff of post-modern legend. Having been owned by a famous club owner in the 1980s, it developed cult status. It's not especially beautiful, but it is a great place to people-watch and hang with the student and workaday crowd. They have good salads, and it is one of the best places to sip a Weiß gespritzt. *Währingerstraße 6–8. ☎ 01 319 72 41. U-Bahn 2 (Schottentor). €–€€.*

8 ★ **Börse.** Vienna's Stock Exchange is one of the most elegant buildings on the Ringstrasse. Constructed in 1877 by the acclaimed architect Theophil Hansen (who also built the Parlament and Burgtheater), it is noteworthy for its handsome red brickwork (known locally as *Hansenrot*). Don't miss Ledrleitner, the intoxicating flower shop in the cellar, and

Dine al fresco at the Summer Stage.

there's a fantastic (yet pricey) restaurant next to it, Hansen. *Schottenring 20. ☎ 01 531 650. www.wienerborse.at. Closed to visitors. U-Bahn 2 (Schottentor).*

9 ★ Sigmund Freud Museum. One of Vienna's most famous citizens, the physician Sigmund Freud (1856–1939) lived in this apartment for most of his life. The museum has few original artifacts or furnishings, but a fascinating photo gallery casts a revealing light on the father of psychoanalysis. For decades, Freud was regarded as a leading figure in the world of medicine, but his Jewish background prevented him from becoming a professor of Vienna's university until 1902. He was eventually driven from the city by the Nazis in 1937. ⏲ *30 min. Berggasse 19. ☎ 01 319 1596. www.freud-museum.at. €7 adults, €5.50/€4.50 concessions, €2.50 kids, €2 audio guide. Daily 9am–5pm (July–Sept until 6pm). U-Bahn 2 (Schottentor).*

Votivkirche—easy to confuse in appearance with Stephansdom.

10 ★★★ kids Summer Stage. A holiday atmosphere spreads along the Danube Canal during the summer months. This lively alfresco bar and restaurant zone is open May through September. Tempting eateries and cool cocktail bars line the canal banks, providing live music and entertainment most nights. Try Pizzeria Riva (☎ 01 310 20 88, €) for Italian food; Shebeen (☎ 0650 3551447, €) for fish 'n' chips, or Pancho (☎ 01 319 0576, €–€€) for Tex-Mex cuisine. There's also trampolining, boules, beach volleyball, and a kids' club at weekends. *Rossauer Lände. ☎ 01 315 5202. www.summerstage.co.at. Mon–Sat 5pm–1am; Sun 3pm–1am. U-Bahn 4 (Rossauer Lände).*

The MuseumsQuartier (MQ)

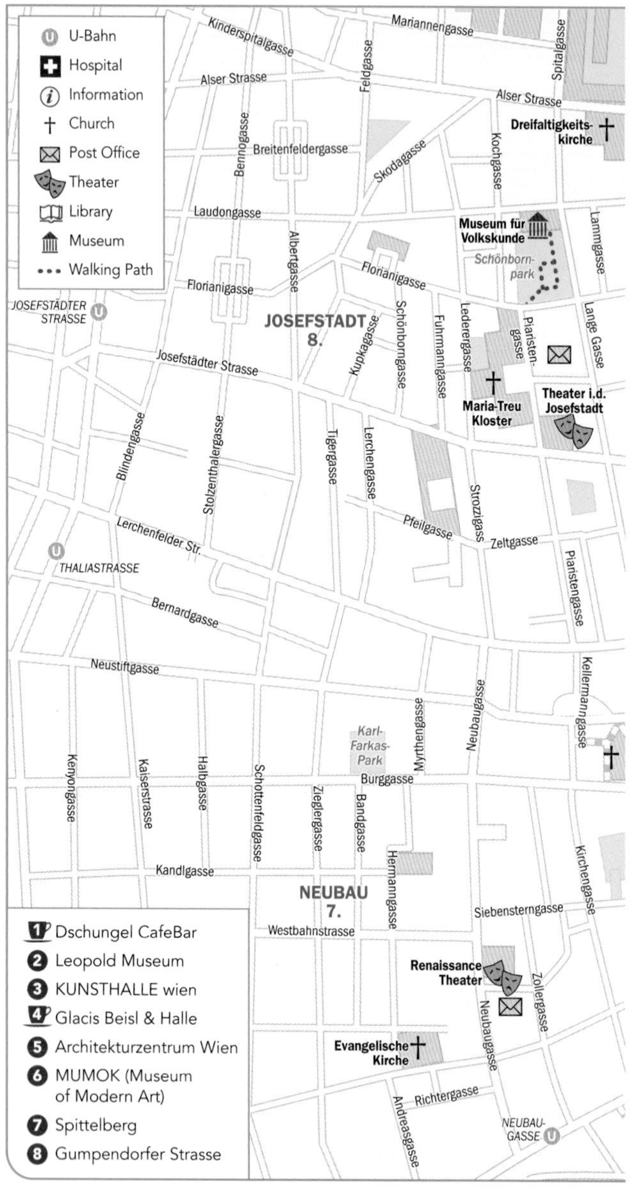

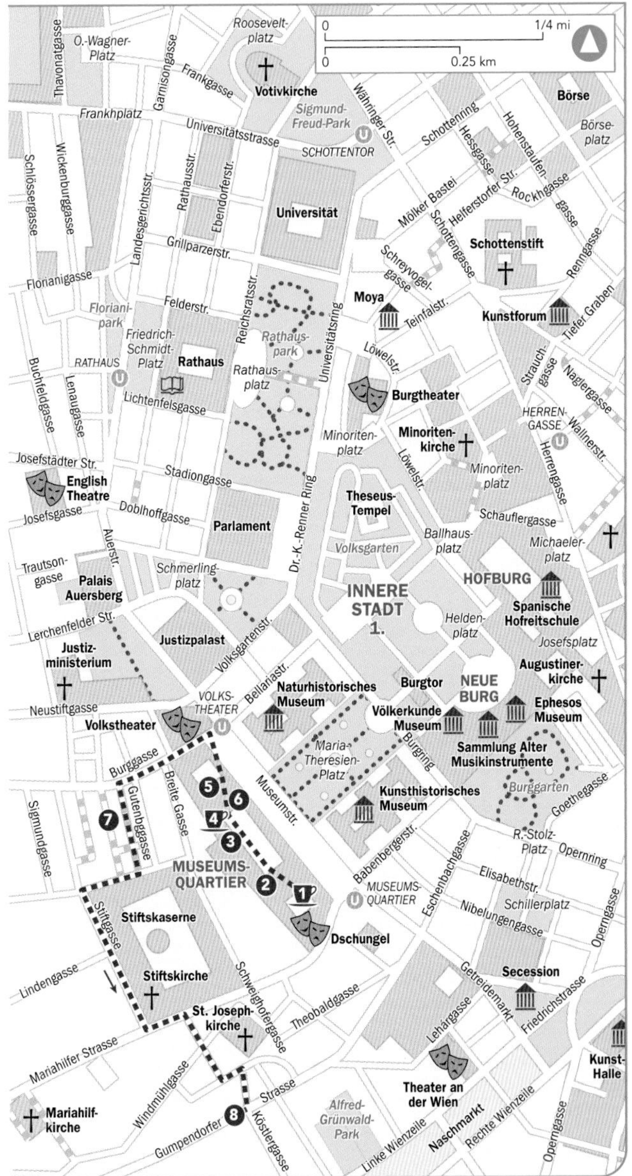

0
1/4 mi
0
0.25 km
Votivkirche
Roosevelt-platz
Sigmund-Freud-Park
SCHOTTENTOR
Universität
Börse
Börse-platz
Schottenstift
Kunstforum
Moya
Rathaus
Rathaus-park
Rathaus-platz
Burgtheater
Minoriten-kirche
English Theatre
Parlament
Theseus-Tempel
Volksgarten
HOFBURG
Spanische Hofreitschule
INNERE STADT 1.
Palais Auersberg
Justizpalast
Justiz-ministerium
Naturhistorisches Museum
Burgtor
NEUE BURG
Völkerkunde Museum
Ephesos Museum
Augustiner-kirche
Sammlung Alter Musikinstrumente
Volkstheater
Maria-Theresien-Platz
Kunsthistorisches Museum
Burggarten
MUSEUMS-QUARTIER
Dschungel
Stiftskaserne
Stiftskirche
St. Joseph-kirche
Secession
Theater an der Wien
Kunst-Halle
Mariahilf-kirche
Alfred-Grünwald-Park
Naschmarkt

#2

It's easy to spend all day at the MuseumsQuartier (Museum Quarter). One of Vienna's most popular areas, it offers a superb mix of modern architecture, world-class galleries, and family attractions. However, just round the corner, two of the city's most attractive and beguiling quarters also await your discovery—Spittelberg and Gumpendorf—with their cobbled streets and enticing bars and restaurants. START: **ZOOM Kindermuseum (U-Bahn 2, MuseumsQuartier).**

1 ★★★ kids **Dschungel Cafe-Bar.** A great way to start your stroll and a superb choice for breakfast, this café is family friendly and has delicious baked good as well as Middle Eastern breakfast with hummus, olives, and feta. *€–€€.* *See p 140.*

2 ★★★ **Leopold Museum.** This major gallery hosts a leading collection of 19th- and 20th-century Austrian art, belonging to Viennese aficionados Rudolf and Elizabeth Leopold. The main Jugendstil and Secessionist collections are on Level 0, alongside some important canvases by Klimt, Gerstl, and Moser, but the main draw is the world's largest assembly of works by Egon Schiele. *See map at the right.*

3 ★ **KUNSTHALLE wien.** The temporary exhibitions of modern art staged here enjoy international repute, despite their location within an architecturally unremarkable building. This is also the location of the city's premiere modern dance venue, Tanzquartier Wien (p 138). *Museumsplatz 1. ☎ 01 521 8933. www.kunsthallewien.at. €8 adults, €6 concessions. Daily 11am–7pm (Thurs until 9pm). U-Bahn 2 (MuseumsQuartier).*

4 ★★ My two favorite lunch spots here are the modern, wood-paneled **Glacis Beisl** (Museumsplatz 1, ☎ 01 526 5660, €€) with its beautiful garden seating and mouthwatering Austrian menu; and the more laid-back **Halle** (Museumsplatz 1, ☎ 01 523 70 01, €€), which serves tempting soups, salads, and excellent value set lunch menus on its sunny terrace.

5 ★ **Architekturzentrum Wien.** This small Architecture Center provides a vivid account of 20th- and 21st-century Austrian architecture, through models, interactive displays, and photographs. The only controversial omission is Hundertwasser (p 22), who is apparently considered to be more of an artist than an architect. *45 min. Museumsplatz 1. ☎ 01 522 3115. www.azw.at. €9 adults, €7 concessions. Daily 10am–7pm. U-Bahn 2/3 (Volkstheater).*

6 ★★ **MUMOK (Museum of Modern Art).** The dramatic cuboid exterior this museum is undeniably impressive, clad in sleek gray basalt. The interior contains a significant collection of modern and contemporary art, covering a broad spectrum of genres from Cubism and Expressionism to Photo Realism, Fluxus, and Nouveau Réalisme. Its acclaimed Pop Art section contains representative works by Warhol, Jasper Johns, Liechtenstein, and Rauschenberg. Its Viennese Actionism collection—one of the most extreme of all modern-art movements—is the largest in the world. However, only

Leopold Museum

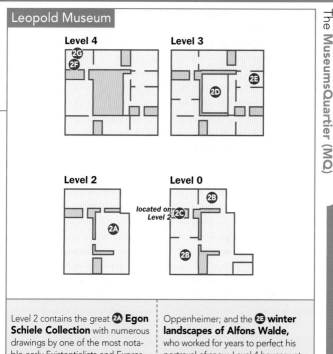

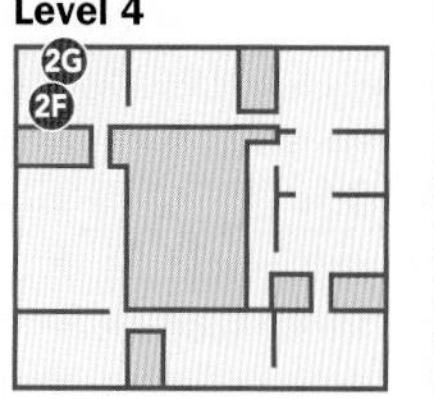

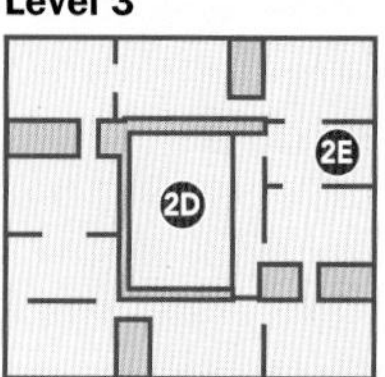

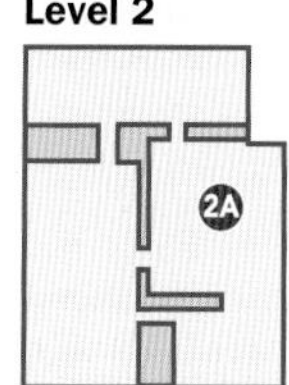

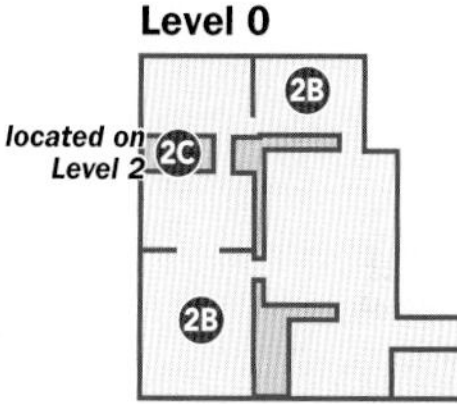

Level 2 contains the great 2A **Egon Schiele Collection** with numerous drawings by one of the most notable early Existentialists and Expressionists, including the poignant ***Mother and Daughter*** (1913) and ***Edith Schiele in a Striped Dress*** (1915). On Level 0, the 2B **Jugendstil and Secessionist paintings** include canvases by Schiele, Gerstl, and Klimt. The 2C **cafe** on Level 2 is worth a stop, before moving on to the brilliant collection of 2D **Expressionist and inter-war paintings** on Level 3. The real gems here are works by Schiele (including ***Self-Portrait***—1910), Kokoschka, Huber, Boeckl, and Oppenheimer; and the 2E **winter landscapes of Alfons Walde,** who worked for years to perfect his portrayal of snow. Level 4 houses yet more impressive paintings by Klimt, including ***Attersee*** (1901), and the celebrated 2F ***Death and Life*** (1911–15). Some exquisite 2G ***Wiener Werkstätte furniture*** and decorative items by Moser, Loos, and Hoffmann can also be seen on this floor. *2 hr. Museumsplatz. 01 525 70-0. www.leopoldmuseum.org. €13 adults, €8 concessions, €4 audio guide. Wed–Mon 10am–6pm (Thurs until 9pm). U-Bahn 2 (MuseumsQuartier).*

a small selection of the overall collection is on display at any one time. *1 hr. Museumsplatz 1. 01 52500. www.mumok.at. €11 adults, €8 concessions, €7 students, free under 19. Mon 2–7pm, Tues–Sun 10am–7pm (Sat until 9pm) U-Bahn 2/3 (Volkstheater).*

7 ★★★ Spittelberg. Just behind the MQ (between Breitegasse, Siebensterngasse, Sigmundgasse, and Burggasse), this

Relaxing in the MQ complex.

romantic, pedestrianized district of narrow cobbled streets, with pretty Biedermeier houses and fountain-splashed squares, epitomizes old-world Vienna at its most approachable. Formerly a red-light district servicing the nearby barracks, Spittelberg became a fashionable place to live in the 1970s and is now one of the city's most desirable addresses: an enclave of galleries, *beisls* (traditional Austrian country-style inns), and sidewalk cafes. The Christmas market held here is one of Vienna's best. *www.spittelberg.at. U-Bahn 2/3 (Volkstheater).*

8 ★★★ Gumpendorferstrasse. One of the less frequented areas for tourists boasts some of the best food and most adorable cafes in town. Head down the charming stairway by Rahlgasse to the multifaceted **Aux Gazelles,** which serves Middle Eastern food and offers a fantastic Hamam spa by day and a popular dance club by night. At the corner, the English-language cinema **Top Kino** has a cozy cafe attached. As you turn onto Gumpendorferstrasse, you'll encounter the statue of **St. Augustin,** a symbol of hope for the Viennese people. Further down, **Café Sperl** is an old-style cafe made famous by the 1990s film *Before Sunrise.* Continue to **St. Charles Apotheke,** a beautiful old pharmacy turned cosmetics boutique. Stay on that street until you reach a park containing one of the flak towers from WWII. Enter for the wonderful **Haus des Meeres** indoor zoo, which concentrates on fish and sea creatures, but also features charming monkeys, exotic birds, and more. If you have a stomach for it next door is the blood-curdling **Foltermuseum** (Torture museum). *Mariahilf. Haus des Meeres für Volkskunde: Fritz-Grünbaum-Platz 1. ☎ 01 406 8905. www.haus-des-meeres.at. €17 adults, €7.60 under 15, €5.10 ages 3–5. Daily 9am–6pm. U-Bahn 3 (Neubaugasse), or Bus 13A (Haus des Meeres).* ●

The distinctive grey basalt facade at the Museum of Modern Art (MUMOK).

4 The Best Shopping

Shopping Best Bets

Most **Trendy Interior Design**
★★★ Stilwerk, *Praterstrasse 1 (p 86)*

Best for **Gourmands**
★★★ Meinl am Graben, *Graben 19 (p 88)*

Best **Austrian Designs**
★★ Lila, *Kirchengasse 7 (p 87)*

Best **Boutique for Fashionistas**
★★ Mode Mühlbauer, *Seilergasse 5 & 10 (p 87)*

Best **Hot-Date Lingerie**
★★ Lingerie at Steffl, *Kärntner Strasse 19 (p 87)*

Best for **Chocoholics**
★★★ Xocolat, *Freyung 2 (Im Passage) (p 89)*

Best **Quirky Gifts**
★★★ MAK Design Shop, *Stubenring 5 (p 92)*

Best **Picnic Supplies**
★★★ Naschmarkt, *Naschmarkt (p 88)*

Most **Unusual Shop**
★★★ phil, *Gumpendorferstrasse 10–12 (p 86)*

Most **Trendy Concept Store**
★★ Kauf Dich Glücklich, *Kirchengasse 09 (p 88)*

Best for **Sleek Porcelain**
★★★ Feine Dinge, *Margaretenstrasse 35 (p 86)*

Best for **Maps & Travel Guides**
★★ Freytag & Berndt, *Kohlmarkt 9 (p 85)*

Best **Deconstructed sandwiches**
★ Trzesniewski, *Dorotheergasse 1 (p 89)*

Mozart gets around—here he is selling chocolates.

Best for **Treasure-Hunting**
★★ Dorotheum, *Dorotheergasse 17 (p 85)*

Best for **Classical Music**
★★ Arcadia, *Kärtnerstrasse 40 (p 92)*

Best **Lederhosen—for him**
★★★ Tostmann Trachten, *Schottengasse 3a (p 87)*

Most **Eccentric Dirndls—for her**
★★★ Lena Hoschek, *Gutenberggasse 17 (p 87)*

Best **Hipster Gifts**
★★ Die Sellerie, *Burggasse 21 (p 90)*

Best **Cakes**
★★★ Sacher Confiserie, *Philharmonikerstrasse 4 (p 89)*; ★★★ Demel, *Kohlmarkt 14 (p 88)*

Best to **Placate the Kids**
★★★ Der Kleine Salon, *Linke Wienzeile 40 (p 90)*

Previous page: Postcards from Hundertwasserhaus.

Around Kärtnerstrasse Shopping

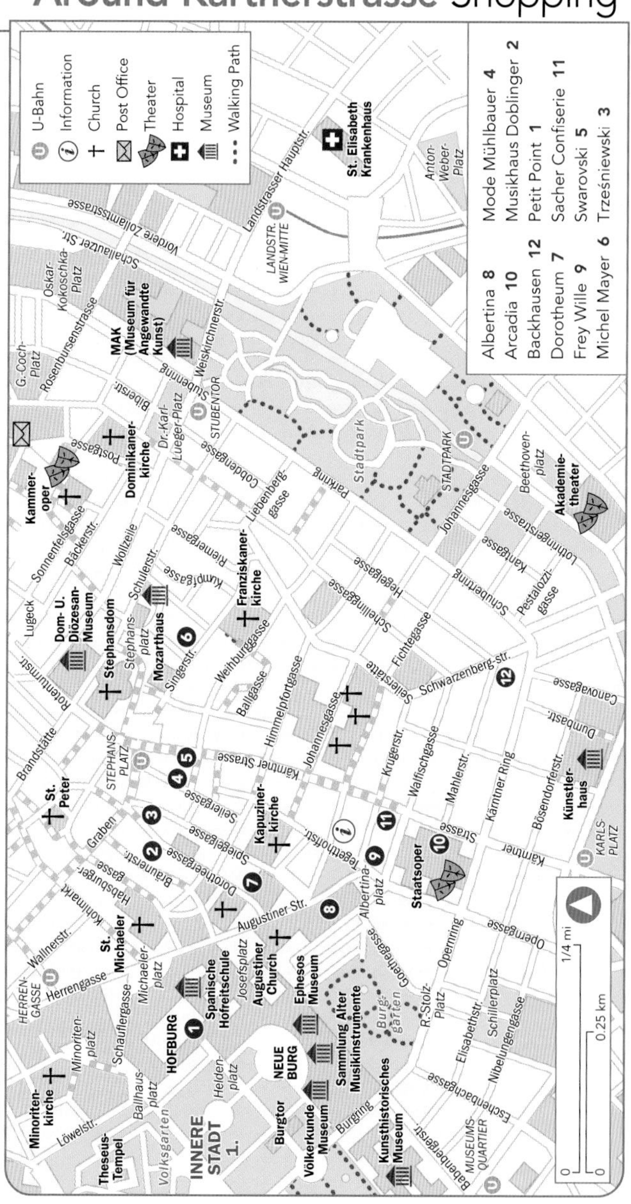

City Center North Shopping

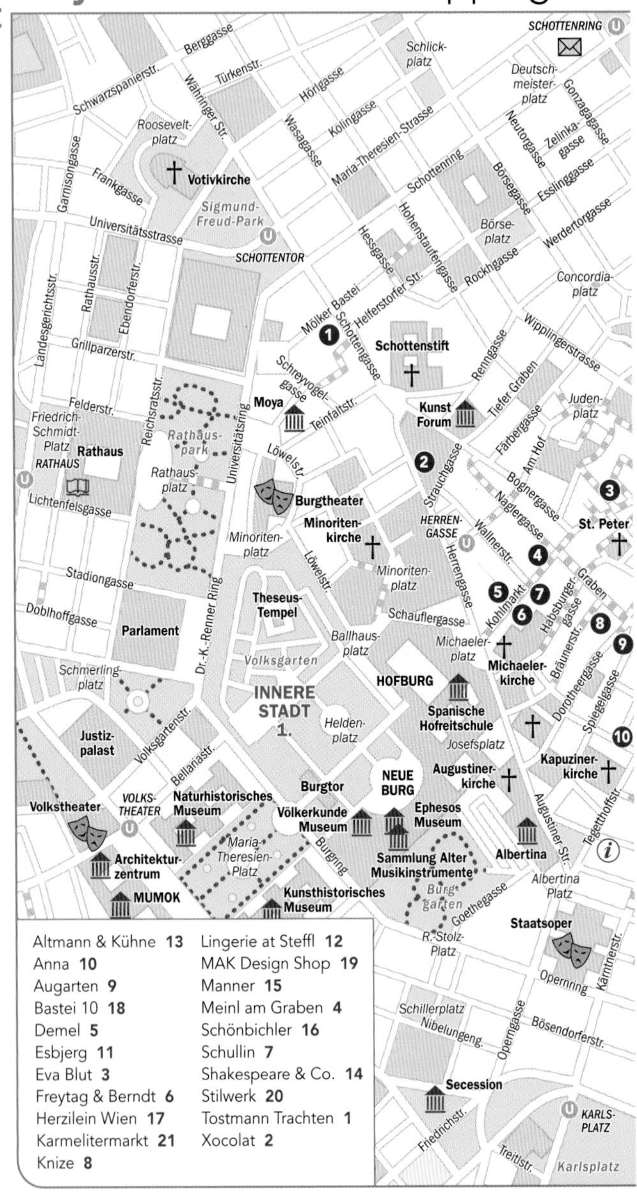

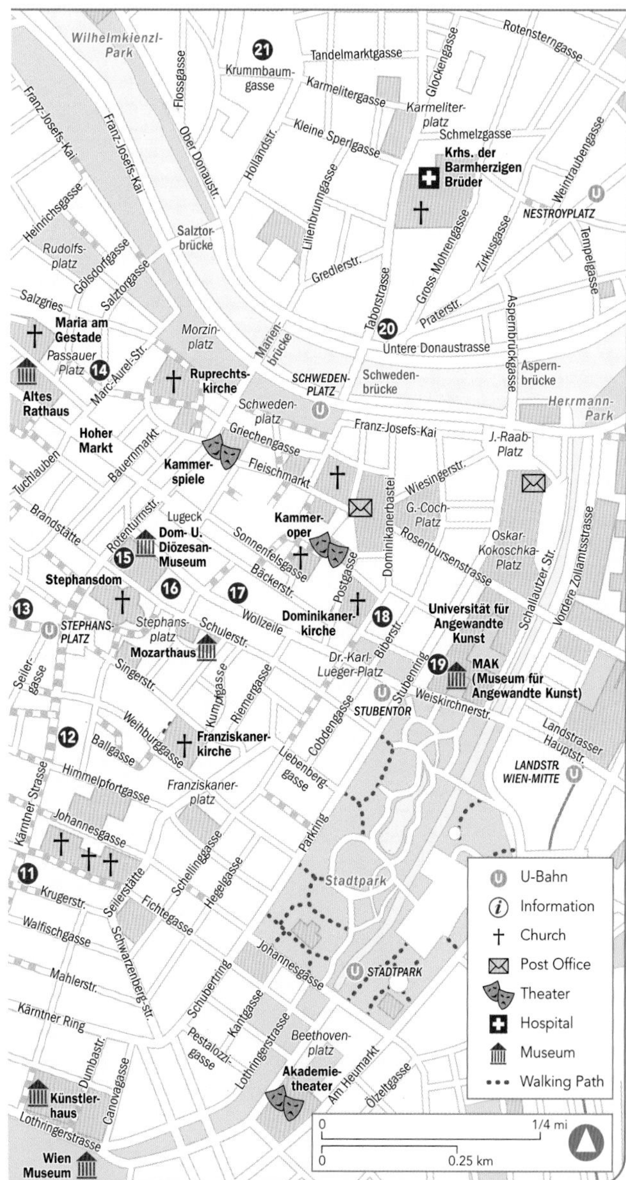
Wilhelmkienzl-Park
Rotensterngasse
Tandelmarktgasse
Krummbaumgasse
Flossgasse
Glockengasse
Karmelitergasse
Karmeliterplatz
Schmelzgasse
Kleine Sperlgasse
Krhs. der Barmherzigen Brüder
Franz-Josefs-Kai
Ober Donaustr.
Hollandstr.
Lilienbrunngasse
Weintraubengasse
NESTROYPLATZ
Heinrichsgasse
Salztorbrücke
Gross Mohrengasse
Zirkusgasse
Tempelgasse
Rudolfsplatz
Gölsdorfgasse
Salztorgasse
Gredlerstr.
Taborstrasse
Praterstr.
Salzgries
Maria am Gestade
Morzinplatz
Marienbrücke
Aspernbrückengasse
Untere Donaustrasse
Passauer Platz
Marc-Aurel-Str.
Ruprechtskirche
SCHWEDENPLATZ
Schwedenbrücke
Aspernbrücke
Altes Rathaus
Schwedenplatz
Herrmann-Park
Hoher Markt
Griechengasse
Franz-Josefs-Kai
J.-Raab-Platz
Bauernmarkt
Kammerspiele
Fleischmarkt
Wiesingerstr.
Tuchlauben
Dominikanerbastei
G.-Coch-Platz
Brandstätte
Lugeck
Kammeroper
Rotenturmstr.
Dom- U. Diözesan-Museum
Sonnenfelsgasse
Rosenbursenstrasse
Oskar-Kokoschka-Platz
Vordere Zollamtsstrasse
Schallautzer Str.
Stephansdom
Bäckerstr.
Postgasse
Universität für Angewandte Kunst
Dominikanerkirche
Wollzeile
STEPHANSPLATZ
Stephansplatz
Schulerstr.
Biberstr.
Mozarthaus
Dr.-Karl-Lueger-Platz
Stubenring
MAK (Museum für Angewandte Kunst)
Seilergasse
Singerstr.
Kumpfgasse
Riemergasse
Weiskirchnerstr.
STUBENTOR
Cobdengasse
Weihburggasse
Franziskanerkirche
Landstrasser Hauptstr.
Ballgasse
Liebenberggasse
LANDSTR WIEN-MITTE
Himmelpfortgasse
Franziskanerplatz
Kärntner Strasse
Johannesgasse
Parkring
Schellinggasse
Hegelgasse
Stadtpark
Krugerstr.
Seilerstätte
Fichtegasse
Walfischgasse
Schwarzenberg-str.
Johannesgasse
STADTPARK
Mahlerstr.
Schubertring
Kärntner Ring
Kantgasse
Pestalozzigasse
Lothringerstrasse
Beethovenplatz
Dumbastr.
Canovagasse
Akademietheater
Am Heumarkt
Ölzeltgasse
Künstlerhaus
Lothringerstrasse
Wien Museum
U-Bahn
Information
Church
Post Office
Theater
Hospital
Museum
Walking Path
0
1/4 mi
0
0.25 km

Mariahilf & Neubau Shopping

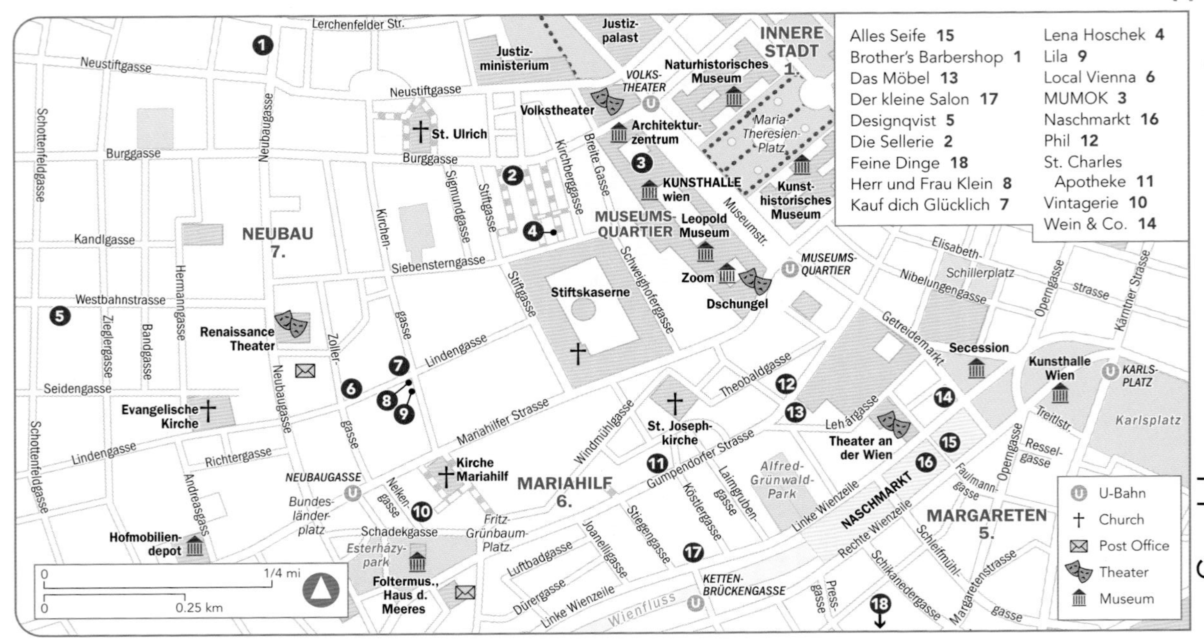

Vienna Shopping A to Z

Art & Antiques

★★ Dorotheum CITY CENTER Pick up some unusual and authentic treasures at this world-renowned auction house, which holds regular sales of paintings, furniture, jewelry, decorative objects, and toys. *Dorotheergasse 17. ☎ 01 515 60-0. www.dorotheum.at. U-Bahn 1/3 (Stephansplatz). Map p 81.*

★★ Vintagerie NASCHMARKT They call themselves "the modernist showroom" and carry everything from dishware to chandeliers, concentrating on the aesthetic value of the pieces. You may find kitsch here, but it's tasteful and each piece has a story. *Nelkengasse 4. ☎ 01 581 28 50. www.vintagerie.at. U-Bahn 3 (Neubaugasse). Map p 84.*

Beauty Products

★ Alles Seife NASCHMARKT Gorgeous, almost good-enough-to-eat soaps in an astonishing array of aromas—from honey and marzipan to mandarin and coffee. *Naschmarkt 54. ☎ 06991 161 1291. U-Bahn 1/2/4 (Karlsplatz). Map p 84.*

★★ Brother's Barbershop SPITTELBERG Brother's is dripping with hipster chic. While Vienna used to be void of traditional barbershops, the beard trend has resulted a few contenders of which this is the best. They also carry all the product a self-respecting beardsman could need. *Neubaugasse 81. ☎ 01 990 8304. www.barbershop.wien. U-Bahn 3 (Neubaugasse). Map p 84.*

★ Esbjerg CITY CENTER This is heaven for high-end beard and skin care accessories and tools. From beautiful shaving set to exclusive skin and body care solutions. Great for gifting. *Krugerstrasse 7. ☎ 01 513 1936. www.esbjerg.com. U-Bahn 1/2/4 (Karlsplatz). Map p 82.*

★★ St. Charles Apotheke MQ Alongside their own organic skin and body solutions, this stylish shop carries brands like Aesop and NEOM. There's a spa and restaurant attached. *Gumpendorferstrasse 30. ☎ 01 586 1363. U-Bahn 2 (MuseumsQuartier). Map p 84.*

Books & Maps

★★ Freytag & Berndt CITY CENTER A staggering collection of maps and travel guides (many in English) on Vienna, the Wienerwald, Austria, and the rest of the world, housed in a magnificent Jugendstil house. *Kohlmarkt 9. ☎ 01 533 8685. www.freytagberndt.at. U-Bahn 3 (Herrengasse). Map p 82.*

★★ Shakespeare & Company CITY CENTER I could spend hours browsing in this overstuffed, old-fashioned bookshop, containing a fantastic selection of English-language books (including Austrian authors in translation). *Sterngasse 2. ☎ 01 535 5053. www.shakespeare.co.at. U-Bahn 1/4 (Schwedenplatz). Map p 82.*

Design & Interiors

★★★ Augarten CITY CENTER Some of the exquisite patterns of the former imperial porcelain manufacturer are centuries old, including hand-decorated rose chinaware, designed in the 18th century for Empress Maria Theresa. *Spiegelgasse 3. ☎ 01 512 1494. www.augarten.at. U-Bahn 1/3 (Stephansplatz). Map p 82.*

★ **Backhausen** CITY CENTER Once supplier to the famous Wiener Werkstätte, this seventh-generation textile manufacturer still creates fabrics and accessories based on their original designs. There's also a museum and textile archive. *Mahlerstrasse/corner Schwarzenbergstrasse. ☎ 01 514 04-0. www.backhausen.com. Tram 1/2/71/D (Schwarzenbergplatz). Map p 81.*

★★ **das möbel > das geschäft** MQ This spacious store, laid out like an exclusive apartment, is *the* place for seriously cool furniture and innovative accessories by young, up-and-coming Austrian designers. *Gumpendorferstrasse 11. ☎ 01 924 3834. www.dasmoebel.at. U-Bahn 2 (MuseumsQuartier). Map p 84.*

★ **Designqvist** SPITTELBERG This place concentrates on Scandinavian mid-century design and while it's tiny, this style is extremely popular among the Viennese. Smaller pieces include gorgeous wooden salt-and-pepper shakers and charming candle holders. *Singerstrasse 16. ☎ 0680 504 70 00. http://designqvist.at. U-Bahn 3 (Zieglergasse). Map p 84.*

★★★ **Feine Dinge** NASCHMARKT This store is a joy to enter. They carry tableware, lamps, vases, and jewelry crafted from the finest porcelain. The style is modern and calm, mostly in subdued pastels and whites. *Margaretenstrasse 35. ☎ 01 954 0918. www.feinedinge.at. U-Bahn 4 (Kettenbrückengasse). Map p 84.*

★★★ **phil** MQ No two chairs or tables are alike in this unusual cafe/shop, where guests come not just to eat and drink but also to buy the constantly changing retro furniture. *Gumpendorferstrasse 10–12. ☎ 01 581 0489. www.phil.info. U-Bahn 2 (MQ). Map p 84.*

★★★ **Stilwerk** KARMELITER A shopping center featuring exclusively state-of-the-art design shops: behan + thurm for office and home furnishings; Ma Maison for tableware and accessories; Klimo for modish lighting; and Verdarium for garden furnishings. *Praterstrasse 1. ☎ 01 212 06 10 50. www.stilwerk.at. U-Bahn 1/4 (Schwedenplatz). Map p 82.*

Fashion & Accessories

★★ **Eva Blut** CITY CENTER You will struggle to find accessories this versatile anywhere else. Blut uses only premium material to create

phil's—not just a shop, but a cafe too.

everything from clutches to shoppers. *Kühfussgasse 2.* ☎ *01 890 6560-15. www.evablut.com. U-Bahn 1/3 (Stephansplatz). Map p 82.*

★★ **Knize** CITY CENTER This old-fashioned, wood-paneled shop, created by interior-design genius Adolf Loos, offers classy, tailor-made, and *prêt-à-porter* menswear, with traditional service at its finest. *Graben 13.* ☎ *01 512 2119. www.knize.at. U-Bahn 1/3 (Stephansplatz). Map p 82.*

★★★ **Lena Hoschek** SPITTELBERG Access your inner pinup girl in this world-famous designer boutique where traditional Austrian meets rockabilly. The shop specializes in vintage dresses and *dirndls* with attitude. *Gutenberggasse 17.* ☎ *01 293 2203. www.lenahoschek.com. U-Bahn 2/3 (Volkstheater). Map p 84.*

★★ **Lila** SPITTELBERG This young local designer's collections are very feminine without being revealing. Expect casual, evening, and swimwear for women as well as a small men's collection. *Kirchengasse 7.* ☎ *0699 11696012. www.lila.cx. U-Bahn 3 (Neubaugasse). Map p 84.*

★★ **Lingerie at Steffl** CITY CENTER The entire first floor of the Steffl department store is dedicated to women's undergarments. Ladies can enjoy champagne service while trying on brands like Agent Provocateur, Stella McCartney, or Austria's own hosiery brand, Wolford. *Kärntner Strasse 19.* ☎ *01 930 56-0. www.steffl-vienna.com. U-Bahn 1/3 (Stephansplatz). Map p 82.*

★★ **Local Vienna** SPITTELBERG This adorable minimalist boutique offers a perfectly curated selection of designer brands, but only those whose fashion is manufactured in the same country as it was designed. You'll find the latest in clothing, bags, accessories, and jewelry. *Zollergasse 12.* ☎ *01 522 0353. www.localvienna.com. U-Bahn 3 (Neubaugasse). Map p 84.*

★★★ **Michel Mayer** CITY CENTER Mix and match daytime separates with floaty feminine designs in extravagant fabrics at the bijou boutique of this sought-after Austrian designer. *Singerstrasse 7.* ☎ *01 967 4055. www.michelmayer.at. U-Bahn 1/3 (Stephansplatz). Map p 81.*

★★ **Mode Mühlbauer** CITY CENTER The labels here should set any keen fashionista's pulse racing. Stemming from the high-end hat brand, it stocks creations by local and international designers. Eye-catching modern millinery and sophisticated accessories in a sister store across the street add the finishing touches to any outfit. *Seilergasse 5 & 10.* ☎ *01 513 7070. www.muehlbauer.at and www.modemuehlbauer.at. U-Bahn 1/3 (Stephansplatz). Map p 81.*

★★★ **Tostmann Trachten** SCHOTTENRING Come here for traditional Austrian fashions and hand-embroidered *dirndls, lederhosen,* felt slippers, and beautiful patchwork in a genial rustic setting. *Schottengasse 3a.* ☎ *01 533 5331. www.tostmann.at. U-Bahn 2 (Schottentor). Map p 82.*

Concept Stores

★★★ **Bastei 10** CITY CENTER This high-end deli-cum-gift-shop carries fresh sandwiches and baked goods; its own brand of conserves, nuts, candies, and dried fruits; as well as design objects, books, and other small and charming gift ideas. *Dominikanerbastei 10.* ☎ *01 512 2010. www.marcosimonis.com. U-Bahn 1/4 (Schwedenplatz). Map p 82.*

★★ **Kauf dich Glücklich** SPITTELBERG The hippest of the hip in womens- and menswear alongside interior design objects and cosmetics. A millennial fashion lover's paradise. *Kirchenngasse 09. ☎ 01 9247755. www.kaufdichgluecklich-shop.de. U-Bahn 3 (Neubaugasse). Map p 84.*

Food & Wine

★★ **Altmann & Kühne** CITY CENTER The trademark mini-chocolates sold by this old-fashioned confectioner make perfect gifts, attractively packaged in tiny handmade boxes decorated with traditional Viennese scenes. *Am Graben 30. ☎ 01 533 0927. www.altmann-kuehne.at. U-Bahn 1/3 (Stephansplatz). Map p 82.*

★★★ **Demel** CITY CENTER The imperial confectioners have baked cakes and sweets for the rich and famous for several centuries, and the proof is in the eating. These traditional tearooms are pricey but popular. *Kohlmarkt 14. ☎ 01 535 1717-0. www.demel.at. U-Bahn 3 (Herrengasse). Map p 82.*

There's always a mouthwatering display at the former Imperial confectionery, Demel.

★★★ **Karmelitermarkt** CITY CENTER A brief walk across the Danube Canal from downtown, this market attracts everyone from bobos to gourmands. Saturdays are especially busy, when the farmers market offers everything from giant walnut breads to organic spreads and pumpkin seed oil. The market is also a fabulous place to spend an afternoon sipping coffee in the sunshine at Zimmer 37 (37–39), or grab one of the famed pizzas from Pizza Quartier (96). Cheese lovers should take an extended visit to Kaas am Markt (33–36), where you can sample regional cheeses and their daily warm menu. Or sample some delicious hummus and Mediterranean dishes at Tewa (26–32) *Karmelitermarkt Stalls: Mon–Fri 6am–9:30pm; Sat 6am–5pm. U-Bahn 2 (Schottenring), exit Herminengasse. Map p 82.*

★★ **Manner** CITY CENTER Vienna's favorite wafer—a delicious blend of hazelnut cream—makes an ideal snack to keep you going between museums and galleries. *Stephansplatz 7. ☎ 01 513 7018. www.manner.com. U-Bahn 1/3 (Stephansplatz). Map p 82.*

★★★ **Meinl am Graben** CITY CENTER Vienna's top delicatessen is known for its superb coffee, tea, chocolates, wines, and its impressive array of top-notch produce from Austria and around the world. *Graben 19. ☎ 01 532 3334. www.meinlamgraben.at. U-Bahn 3 (Herrengasse). Map p 82.*

★★★ **Naschmarkt** NASCHMARKT Vienna's best and liveliest produce market is the perfect place to shop for a picnic, but with such a bewildering choice of food stalls it's difficult to know where to start. Appealing stands to look out for

Head to Meinl am Graben for the best coffee in town.

include Strmiska (248) for superb sauerkraut and pickled gherkins; Käseland (172) or Der Urbanek (46) for cheese and cold cuts; Poehl (158) for breads and olive oil; Gegenbauer (111–114) for unusual, flavored vinegars; and Oberlaa (175) for cakes and confectionery. *Naschmarkt. Stalls: Mon–Fri 8am–6pm; Sat 6am–1pm. U-Bahn 1/2/4 (Karlsplatz) or U-Bahn 4 (Kettenbrückengasse). Map p 84.*

★★★ **Sacher Confiserie** CITY CENTER Indulge yourself with Vienna's most celebrated cake—the rich, chocolate *Sachertorte*. You can even ship them home beautifully packaged in wooden boxes. *Philharmonikerstrasse 4. ☎ 01 514 56-734. www.sacher.com. Tram 1/2/D (Oper). Map p 81.*

★★ **Schönbichler** CITY CENTER A fragrant, wood-paneled shop, selling over 150 varieties of teas, teapots, storage jars, and other tea accessories. *Wollzeile 4. ☎ 01 512 1816. www.schoenbichler.at. U-Bahn 1/3 (Stephansplatz). Map p 82.*

★ **Trzesniewski** CITY CENTER This cash-only tiny, old-fashioned bar/shop sells the most delicious, bite-sized open sandwiches, just right for preventing hunger pangs during shopping or sightseeing. *Dorotheergasse 1. ☎ 01 512 3291. www.speckmitei.at. U-Bahn 1/3 (Stephansplatz). Map p 81.*

★★ **Wein & Co** NASCHMARKT This wine supermarket offers a comprehensive selection of wines from around the globe, including some excellent Austrian wines at affordable prices. Try before you buy in the adjoining wine bar. *Getreidemarkt 1. ☎ 01 585 7257. www.weinco.at. U-Bahn 1/2/4 (Karlsplatz). Map p 84.*

★★★ **Xocolat** SCHOTTENRING Essential viewing for chocoholics, this little shop displays an eye-popping selection of bar chocolate, flavored cocoa powders, sauces,

Käseland—a cheese lover's paradise at the Naschmarkt.

and fondue mixtures. *Freyung 2 (Im Passage).* ☎ *01 535 4363. www. xocolat.at. U-Bahn 3 (Herrengasse). Map p 82.*

For Kids

★★★ Der Kleine Salon NASCHMARKT High-end clothes, toys, and accessories for kids, from newborns to pre-teens. *Linke Wienzeile 40.* ☎ *0676 964 16 16. derkleinesalon.at. U-Bahn 4 (Kettenbrückengasse). Map p 84.*

★★ Herr und Frau Klein SPITTELBERG Adorn your kids up to age 6 here in fair trade European designer labels. The shop also carries adorable and practical kiddie dishware as well as buggies, toys, and children's design objects. *Kirchengasse 7.* ☎ *01 9904394. www. herrundfrauklein.com. U-Bahn 3 (Neubaugasse). Map p 84.*

★★ Herzilein Wien CITY CENTER A pretty pastel-colored shop containing adorable clothing for boys and girls (under 9), plus shoes, tasteful toys and teddy bears, and gorgeous appliquéd bed linens. *Wollzeile 17.* ☎ *0676 657 7106. www.herzilein-wien.at. U-Bahn 3 (Stubentor). Map p 82.*

Gifts & Viennese Souvenirs

★★ Die Sellerie SPITTELBERG Beautiful, sophisticated design and paper items inhabit an appealing one-room shop. This place is great for gifting young intellectuals or creative professionals. *Burggasse 21.* ☎ *0699 121 09 304. diesellerie. com. U-Bahn 2/3 (Volkstheater). Map p 84.*

★ Petit Point CITY CENTER Fine *petit point* inspired by the embroidery of Viennese court ladies during the rococo era. Delicate evening bags and brooches make classic souvenirs. *Hofburg Passage 2.* ☎ *01 533 6098. www. maria-stransky.at. U-Bahn 3 (Herrengasse). Map p 81.*

★★ Swarovski CITY CENTER The glittering crystal vases, jewelry, and accessories produced by this celebrated Tyrolean glassmaker

Vienna's traditional wooden toys make special presents.

Vienna's Favorite Shopping Street

In 2015 Mariahilferstrasse, the bustling boulevard separating Vienna's 6th and 7th districts finished its transformation into a pedestrian zone. In years prior, the Viennese were divided on the concept; the opposition fearing heavy traffic congestion in the surrounding areas. But despite the controversy, the construction is complete and the shopping street is livelier than ever. Mariahilferstrasse is home to international giants like H&M, Zara, Berska, and Forever 21, but you'll also find plenty of unique local shops and full-on departments stores like Gerngross. There are cafes, ice cream parlors, and multiple rooftop eateries, offering everything from schnitzel to sushi. Shops are open Monday to Wednesday from 9am to 7pm, Thursday and Friday 9:30am to 8pm, and Saturday from 9:30am to 6pm. Take U-Bahn 3 to Neubaugasse.

enjoy an international reputation. Kids especially love the distinctive miniature animals. *Kärtnerstrasse 24.* ☎ *01 324 0000. www.swarovski.com. U-Bahn 1/3 (Stephansplatz). Map p 81.*

Jewelry

★★★ **Anna** CITY CENTER Fine lines and clear shapes are at the core of this designer's style. Fans of minimalist accessories will love the two-finger rings and delicate necklaces. *Kohlmarkt 11.* ☎ *01 5322050. www.annaij.com. U-Bahn 3 (Herrengasse). Map p 82.*

★ **Frey Wille** CITY CENTER Distinctive gold jewelry, scarves, ties, and cufflinks with striking designs in luminous enamel colors, inspired by artists such as Monet, Klimt, and Hundertwasser. *Lobkowitzplatz 1.* ☎ *01 513 8009-14. www.frey-wille.com. Tram 1/2/D (Oper). Map p 81.*

★★ **Schullin** CITY CENTER The unusual modern wood-and-marble facade of this family-run jeweler reflects the contemporary design and quality craftsmanship on display inside. *Kohlmarkt 7.* ☎ *01 533 9007. www.schullin.com. U-Bahn 3 (Herrengasse). Map p 82.*

Shullin's unusual facade was designed by Hans Hollein.

You'll find your fill of music-themed souvenirs.

Museum Shops

★★★ **Albertina** CITY CENTER This expansive museum shop stocks an artistic A–Z of quality Viennese souvenirs plus a superb choice of art history and coffee-table books. *Albertinaplatz 1. ☎ 01 534 83-552. www.albertina.at. Tram 1/2/D (Oper). Map p 81.*

★★★ **MAK Design Shop** CITY CENTER Even if you don't visit the museum, it's worth coming here for the latest Austrian lifestyle trends and to pick up some special-edition pieces by local designers. *Stubenring 5. ☎ 01 711 36-228. www.makdesignshop.at. U-Bahn 3 (Stubentor). Map p 82.*

★★ **MUMOK** MQ This shop is crammed with eccentric goodies and amusing presents for the whole family—such as paper vases, mobiles, puzzles, and doodle books—as befits a trendy, modern-art gallery. *Museumsplatz 1. ☎ 01 52500. www.mumok.at. U-Bahn 2 (MuseumsQuartier). Map p 84.*

Music

★★ **Arcadia** RINGSTRASSE Under the arcades of the State Opera House, this music store sells an assortment of quality opera, ballet, and classical recordings, as well as books and musical memorabilia. *Kärtnerstrasse 40. ☎ 01 513 9568. www.arcadia.at. Tram 1/2/D (Oper). Map p 81.*

★★ **Musikhaus Doblinger** CITY CENTER One of Europe's largest shops for sheet music, specialist books, and magazines covering all musical genres from classical to rock and pop. *Dorotheergasse 10. ☎ 515 03-0. www.doblinger.at. U-Bahn 1/3 (Stephansplatz). Map p 81.* ●

5 The **Great Outdoors**

Stadtpark

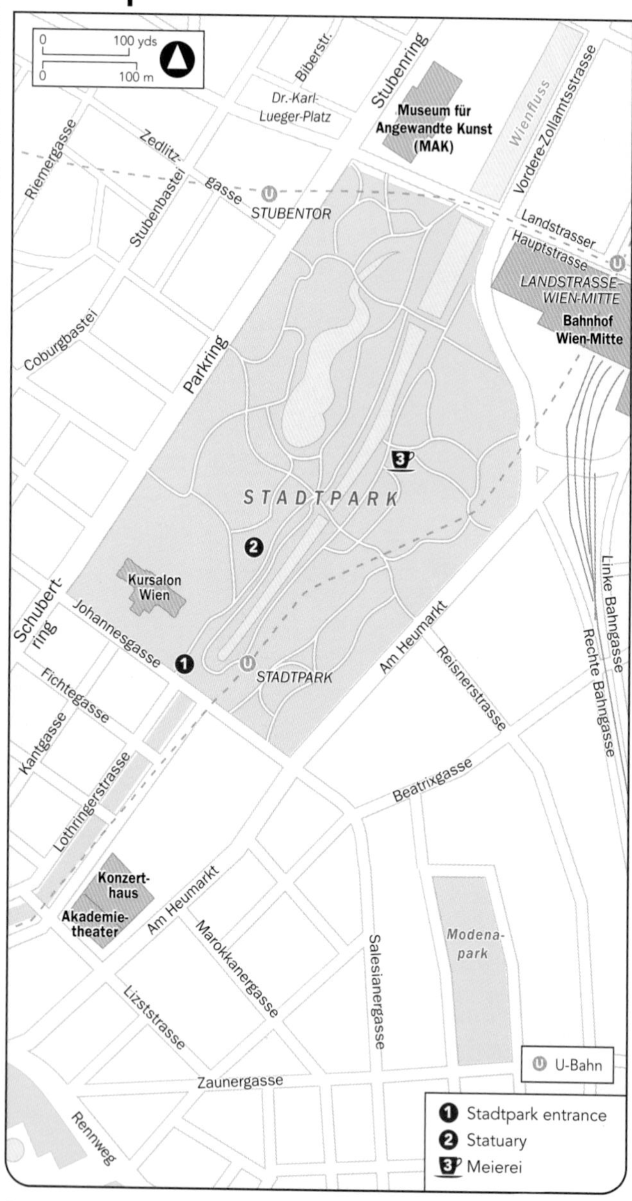

Previous page: Cooling off near the Karlsplatz fountain.

Just outside the Ringstrasse, the "City Park" was once open ground outside the city walls. Flanking the Vienna River (Wienfluss), it was laid out in English landscape style in 1862. With expansive lawns, shaded areas, a playground, and a duck pond, it is a popular and tranquil destination just on the fringe of the inner city, for both tourists and locals. START: **Stadtpark entrance (U-Bahn 4, Stadtpark).**

The Kursalon is the place to hear Strauss waltzes.

❶ ★★★ kids **Stadtpark entrance.** The main entrance (off Johannesgasse) is flanked by magnificent Jugendstil portals of carved stone. The chase scene through the sewers at the end of *The Third Man* movie—one of the most famous in the history of cinema—was produced along the Wienfluss under the bridge here. *See p 50.*

❷ ★ **Statuary.** Scattered around the park you'll find busts commemorating some of the many musicians and artists associated with Vienna—Schubert, Bruckner, and Lehár are here, together with landscape painter Emil Schindler (1842–92) and the hugely influential artist, designer, and "magician of colors," Hans Makart (1840–84). The park's most famous tenant, however, is Johann Strauss II. The rather gaudy, gilded statue of the "King of the Waltz" playing his violin near the Kursalon is, without doubt, Vienna's most famous (and much photographed) statue.

❸ ★★★ **Meierei im Stadtpark.** This low-key cafe, with a trendy white-on-white decor (and adjoining the celebrated Steirereck restaurant), serves superb breakfasts, light snacks, 120 different cheeses, and traditional Austrian desserts. *Am Heumarkt 2A. ☎ 01 713 3168. €€.*

Kids' Playgrounds

Viennese playgrounds are generally excellent, featuring plenty of sturdy swings, slides, sandpits, and tree houses. The Stadtpark has one of the best. Others can be found beside Karlskirche in the Rathauspark, at Börseplatz, and farther afield at Schlickplatz (in Alsergrund) and Schönborn Park (in Josefstadt). The Prater has several wonderful playgrounds too (p 97). The Schönbrunn Park's Irrgarten (Maze, p 108, ❺) is the most eccentric, but parents will especially appreciate the one at the university campus (Altes AKH) best, as it's right next to a great tavern with shaded outdoor seating.

Prater

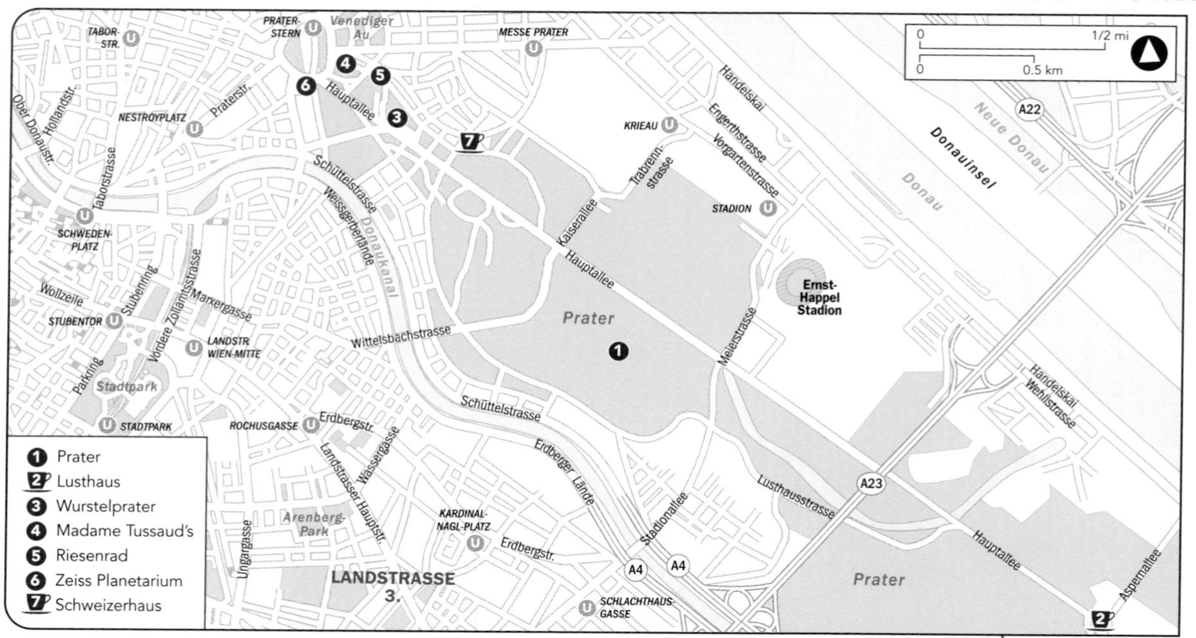

TABOR-STR.
PRATER-STERN
Venediger Au
MESSE PRATER
0
1/2 mi
0
0.5 km
A22
Neue Donau
Donauinsel
Donau
Handelskai
Engerthstrasse
Vorgartenstrasse
KRIEAU
Trabrenn-strasse
STADION
Ernst-Happel Stadion
Ober Donaustr.
Hollandstr.
NESTROYPLATZ
Praterstr.
Hauptallee
Schüttelstrasse
Weissgerberlände
Donaukanal
Taborstrasse
SCHWEDEN-PLATZ
Kaiserallee
Hauptallee
Wollzeile
Stubenring
Vordere Zollamtsstrasse
Marxergasse
STUBENTOR
LANDSTR WIEN-MITTE
Wittelsbachstrasse
Prater
Meierstrasse
Parkring
Stadtpark
STADTPARK
Schüttelstrasse
ROCHUSGASSE
Erdbergstr.
Wassergasse
Landstrasser Hauptstr.
Erdberger Lände
Handelskai
Wehlistrasse
A23
Lusthausstrasse
Stadionallee
KARDINAL-NAGL-PLATZ
Erdbergstr.
Arenberg-Park
Ungargasse
LANDSTRASSE
3.
A4
A4
SCHLACHTHAUS-GASSE
Hauptallee
Prater
Aspernallee
1 Prater
2 Lusthaus
3 Wurstelprater
4 Madame Tussaud's
5 Riesenrad
6 Zeiss Planetarium
7 Schweizerhaus

On sunny days, all year round, there's nothing quite like an idle day strolling the tree-lined roads and paths of the Prater. Here you can visit the Wurstelprater amusement park with its famous giant Ferris wheel and countless rides and games, through woodland and vast sunbathing meadows to one of its fine taverns with garden seating. This is one of the best places in the city to watch the Viennese at play. START: **Prater (U-Bahn 3 Erdberg; U-Bahn 2, Ernst Happel Stadion).**

1 ★★★ kids **Prater.** In 1766, Josef II opened the old imperial hunting grounds to the public, creating a huge tract of recreational parkland. Today, the Prater is Vienna's most popular park and one of its main "green lungs," crisscrossed by a maze of quiet paths and streams meandering through open fields and mixed woodland. It is a major sporting venue, containing the Ernst Happel football stadium, and a trotting track. Its golf course, tennis courts, and swimming pool appeal to sports enthusiasts, while kids love the vast open spaces for picnics, games, and tree-climbing. It has well-equipped playgrounds, skateboard and BMX courses for older children, pony and horse stables, and even a mini-train (the Liliput-Bahn) which tours the park every 30 minutes from 10am to 7pm (from the Riesenrad). You can hire a bike or some rollerblades (see Bike Rentals, p 162) or take a small boat on the Heustadlwasser. A broad avenue (the Hauptallee), planted with ancient chestnut trees, represents the park's backbone, stretching 5km (3 miles) from the idyllic Green Prater to the Wurstelprater funfair zone. *U-Bahn 2 (Messe Prater, Krieau or Stadion). www.prater.at.*

The Lusthaus restaurant was once an imperial hunting lodge.

2 ★★ **Lusthaus.** This unusual 18th-century octagonal pavilion at the heart of the Prater woods was originally built as a hunting lodge. Now converted to a restaurant, it retains its imperial dignity and is a popular choice with locals for weddings and special events of all sorts. Try the game dishes in season—the venison with fresh herbs and cranberries is especially tasty. *Freudenau 254. ☎ 01 728 9565. €€–€€€.*

3 ★ kids **Wurstelprater.** At the western end of the Prater, you can travel on a ghost train, ride a traditional merry-go-round, or drive bumper cars in the world's oldest amusement park. In the 19th century, it consisted of a few inns, coffeehouses, badminton courts, a bowling alley, and a Ferris wheel, which was built to amuse the Viennese working classes. Now, with over 250 hi-tech rides, sideshows, and fast-food stands, it's one of Vienna's top leisure attractions—a colorful, noisy spectacle for the whole family. Don't miss the watery Aqua-Gaudi; the revolving Break Dance; or the high-octane Volare rollercoaster for the ultimate adrenalin rush. The Vienna Airlines ride takes you on a breathtaking whistle-stop tour over the rooftops of Vienna in a 5D flight simulator that uses motion, fan, and scent devices. ☎ *01 728 0516. www.prater.at. Free admission; rides cost €1–€10. Mid-Mar to Oct daily 10am–1am. U-Bahn 1/2 (Praterstern).*

4 ★★ kids Madame Tussaud's. Rub shoulders with the rich and famous at this branch of the famous waxworks. Expect to see life-sized (and remarkably lifelike) wax models of Barack Obama, Johnny Depp, and Michael Jackson alongside such Austrian celebrities as Falco, Gustav Klimt, Franz Schubert, Empress Sisi (p 11), Arnold Schwarzenegger, and Sigmund Freud. They also have interactive installations where you can test your intelligence against Albert Einstein, or conduct the Blue Danube Waltz with Johann Strauß. *Riesenradplatz.* ☎ *01 890 33 66. www.madametussauds.com/wien. €23 adults, €19 kids, €77 family ticket. Daily 10am–6pm (last entry at 5pm). U-Bahn 1/2 (Praterstern).*

5 ★★★ kids Riesenrad. My favorite ride at the Wurstelprater funfair is this world-famous Ferris wheel, Riesenrad. Gliding slowly to a height of 67m (200 ft.) above the rooftops, you catch awesome views of Vienna, the "UNO City" (p 101, 6), and Kahlenberg beyond. The giant structure was built in 1897 by an Englishman named Walter Basset. It is one of the city's great

Display inside the Vienna Airlines ride at Wurstelprater.

Wiener Prater is one of Vienna's top leisure attractions.

landmarks, immortalized in the movie *The Third Man.* It takes 30 minutes to complete one circuit and is especially magical at night. As well as the ride there's also a charming small museum in the entrance area, which illustrates the history of the wheel and the city in miniature. For a really special occasion, you can hire out a cabin for a romantic dinner or drinks. *Wurstelprater. ☎ 01 729 5430. www.wienerriesenrad.com. €9.50 adults, €4 kids, €24 family ticket. Jan–Feb 10am–7pm; Mar–Apr 24, Oct 10am–9:45pm; Apr 25–Sept 9am–11:45pm; Nov–Dec 10am–7:45pm. U-Bahn 1/2 (Praterstern).*

6 ★ kids Zeiss Planetarium. The state-of-the-art Zeiss projector enables budding astronomers to stargaze into the skies above the Prater—over 9,000 stars are visible on a clear night—or to enjoy one of the exciting film shows, which are geared toward a young audience. *Oswald-Thomas-Platz 1. ☎ 01 891 7415 0000. www.astronomie-wien.at. €9 adults, €6.50 kids. Call for show times. U-Bahn 1/2 (Praterstern).*

7 ★★★ kids Schweizerhaus. There's always a lively crowd in this enormous beer garden, which seats 1,300. Try the specialty crispy Stelzen (pigs' trotters) or one of several other authentic Bohemian specialties, all washed down with the best Czech Budvar beer in town. *Strasse des ersten Mai 116. ☎ 01 728 0152-13. Mid-Mar to Oct Mon–Fri 11am–11pm; Sat–Sun 10am–11:30pm. €€.*

There's plenty to amuse the children at the Prater.

The **Danube**

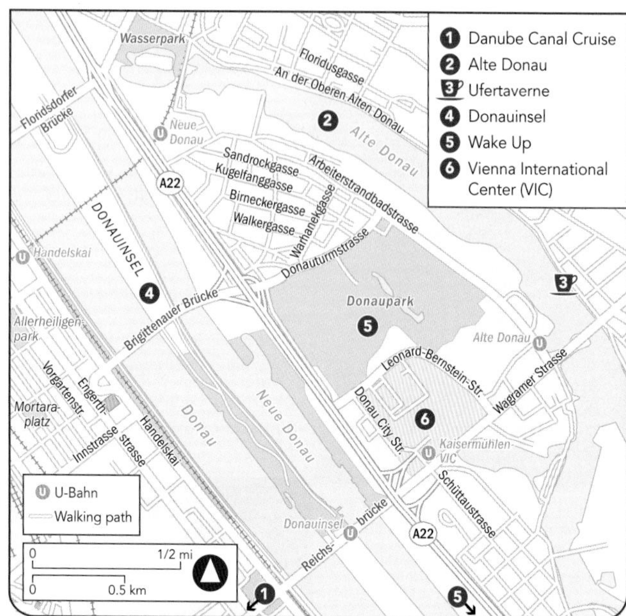

Today more than ever, Vienna takes advantage of its waterfront—along both the Danube Canal and the banks of the Danube River itself—as a full-fledged leisure zone. The vast Danube River (known as Donau in Vienna) flows 2,860km (1,777 miles) from Germany's Black Forest through Austria to the Black Sea. Yet in Vienna it simply offers a huge recreational area in which to relax, sunbathe, sail, and swim—all just a stone's throw from the city center. START: **Danube Canal at Schwedenplatz (U-Bahn 1/4 Schwedenplatz).**

❶ ★★★ **Danube Canal.** On a hot summer day there is no location more central for a midday dip than at the **Badeschiff,** a pool, sun deck, and underwater hotel, docked canal-side, right near Schwedenplatz. After your swim, you can recline on beach chairs at one of several nearby bars and eateries. Some of my faves include **Motto am Fluss** in a modern boat-like structure, **Pub Klemo am Wasser** for a wine and snack to go, **Slow Tacos** for Mexican food, and **Strandbar Hermann** for fresh cocktails. Across the water there's Asian street food at **Adria Wien** and Israeli cuisine and DJs at the ever-popular **Tel Aviv Beach.** *U-Bahn 1/4 (Schwedeplatz) or U-Bahn 2/4 (Schottenring).*

1A ★ kids **Danube Canal Cruise.** *See p 22,* ❷.

2 ★★★ kids **Alte Donau.** The "Old Danube" carried the main flow of the river until 1875 when its course was changed to prevent flooding, turning it into a vast, landlocked expanse of water. Ever since, it has been a favorite destination for Viennese bathers and boating enthusiasts. Boats (electric motorboats, sailboats, and paddle boats) can be hired at a number of renters, including Eppel Boote (Wagramer Strasse 48a).

The largest and most popular of several beach complexes here is Gänsehäufel (Goose Island), which has kiddie pools, water slides, beach volleyball, cafes, playgrounds, and minigolf. *Alte Donau: 2 hr. U-Bahn 1 (Alte Donau). Gänsehäufel: Moissigasse 21. ☎ 01 269 9016. www.gaensehaeufel.at. May–Sept Mon–Fri 9am–7pm; Sat–Sun 8am–7pm. €4.70 adults (€3.70 for half-day), €1.60 kids. U-Bahn 1 (Kaisermühlen-VIC) or U-Bahn 2 (Donaustadtbrücke) then Bus 92a to Schüttauplatz or Mendelssohngasse.*

3 ★★ **Ufertaverne.** This beautiful restaurant directly on the marina serves a great selection of wines as well as solid Mediterranean fare. *An der Oberen Alten Donau 186. www.ufertaverne.at. ☎ 01 204 3953. €€.*

4 ★★ kids **Donauinsel.** The Danube Island was created in the 1980s when the Neue Donau (New Danube) was constructed parallel to the main river to prevent flooding. With more than 40km (25 miles) of *schotterstrände* (gravel beaches) and crisscrossed by paths, this tiny sliver of land is a paradise for cyclists, walkers, swimmers, and sunbathers. Bikes, inline skates, and boats are available for hire. In late June, the island hosts the hugely popular (we're talking 3 million fans) Donauinselfest—a 3-day festival of rock, pop, and folk music. *1 hr. www.donauinsel.at. U-Bahn 1 (Donauinsel).*

5 kids ★★★ **Wake Up.** Not only is this a great beach bar and casual eatery, but it's connected to Vienna's only wakeboard lift. *Am Wehr 1, Neue Donau. wakeup.at. ☎ 01 202 51 23. €€.*

6 ★ **Vienna International Center (VIC).** This 1970s cluster of Y-shaped skyscrapers is home to numerous international organizations. It serves as one of the United Nations' four headquarters, hence its local nickname, "UNO City." *tours last 1 hr; a passport is required for entry. Wagramerstrasse 5. ☎ 01 260 60-3328. www.unvienna.org. €5 adults, €3 concessions. Mon–Fri 11am and 2pm. U-Bahn 1 (Kaisermühlen-VIC).*

Swimming in the Danube

The banks of the Danube, especially the segments called "Old" and "New" Danube (Alte Donau and Neue Donau), are home to some of the most popular swimming and sunbathing retreats in the city. Since these parts of the river are disconnected from the main flow of the river, the high-water quality is unaffected by the pollution or contamination that affects other parts of the Danube. Note that nudist areas are identified as FKK. Try the beaches at the Gäsehäufel, or the charming wooden docks by Untere Alte Donau. *U-Bahn 2 (Donau Stadtbrücke), or U-Bahn 1 (Donauinsel/Alte Donau).*

Grinzing

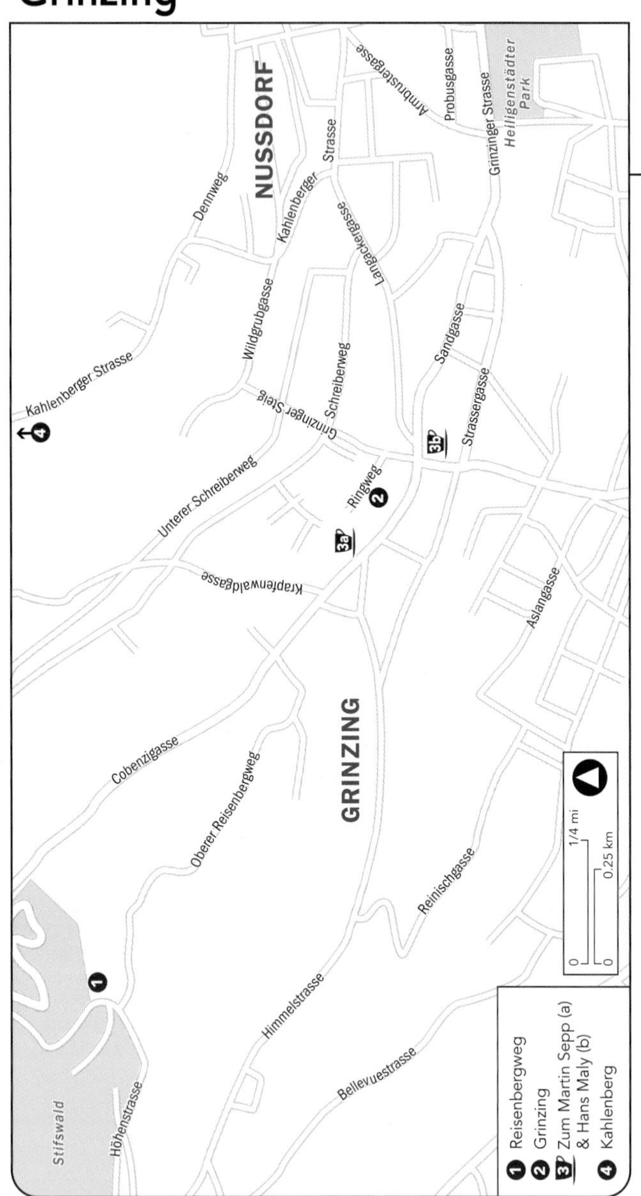
NUSSDORF
GRINZING
Stifswald
Heiligenstädter Park
Kahlenberger Strasse
Dennweg
Wildgrubgasse
Armbrustergasse
Probusgasse
Grinzinger Strasse
Langackergasse
Schreiberweg
Grinzinger Steig
Sandgasse
Strassergasse
Unterer Schreiberweg
Ringweg
Krapfenwaldgasse
Aslangasse
Cobenzlgasse
Oberer Reisenbergweg
Reinischgasse
Himmelstrasse
Bellevuestrasse
Höhenstrasse
0 1/4 mi
0 0.25 km
1 Reisenbergweg
2 Grinzing
3 Zum Martin Sepp (a) & Hans Maly (b)
4 Kahlenberg

In the northwestern outskirts of Vienna lies a region of picturesque old wine villages and vineyard-covered hills. This is where Vienna's prestigious Grüner Veltliner white wines are produced. Grinzing is one of the best-known and popular wine villages, noted for its quaint old houses and *gemütlich* (cozy) wine taverns, or *Heurigen*, usually marked by a bunch or wreath of pine sprigs. START: **Cobenzl Parkplatz (U-Bahn 4 Heiligenstadt, then bus 38a Cobentzl Parkplatz).**

❶ ★★★ kids **Reisenbergweg.** On arrival at Cobenzl (450m/1476 ft.), pause awhile to admire the breathtaking views over Vienna (there's a coffeehouse and petting farm here, too). Cross the road and descend a narrow country lane (Oberer Reisenbergweg) through the vineyards to the village of Grinzing, stopping for your first tipple of local wine at Weingut am Reisenberg (Thurs–Sat 5–11pm, Sun 1–11pm; until 9pm in winter) halfway down. This establishment boasts a comfortable lounge area from which to admire the breathtaking views of the city. *Bus 38a (Cobenzl Parkplatz).*

Each Heurigen *has its own crest.*

❷ ★★★ **Grinzing.** This village has preserved its charming country character, despite the large number of tourists who frequent its numerous *Heurigen*. Most of the romantic old vintners' houses date from the 16th and 17th centuries. Grinzing has many associations with historical celebrities: Schubert wrote some of his songs on local outings, and Strauss composed his *Tales from the Vienna Woods* nearby. The secret of dreams was revealed to Freud here, and Mahler is buried in the village cemetery. *Bus 38a (Grinzing).*

❸ ★ The bulk of the *Heurigen* are in close proximity to one another and are quite touristy. For something more peaceful try Sirbu (below) or **Zum Martin Sepp** (Cobenzlgasse 34, ☎ 01 320 3233, €€) with its jolly courtyard garden and nourishing bar meals. **Hans Maly** (Sandgasse 8, ☎ 01 320 1384, €) also has a picturesque garden, but serves simpler fare. Like many *Heurigen*, both often offer live music.

❹ ★★ kids **Kahlenberg.** Unlike the establishments in "downtown" Grinzing the places further up the mountain are less touristy and more rustic. Take the bus up the winding Höhenstraße to one of the local favorites, **Sirbu.** It is perhaps the *Heurigen* with the most breathtaking views over the adjacent vineyards and the city. (Kahlenberger Str. 210; ☎ 01 320 59 28). *Bus 38A (Kahlenberg) and walk 15 minutes.*

The view from the Reisenbergweg.

Schönbrunn

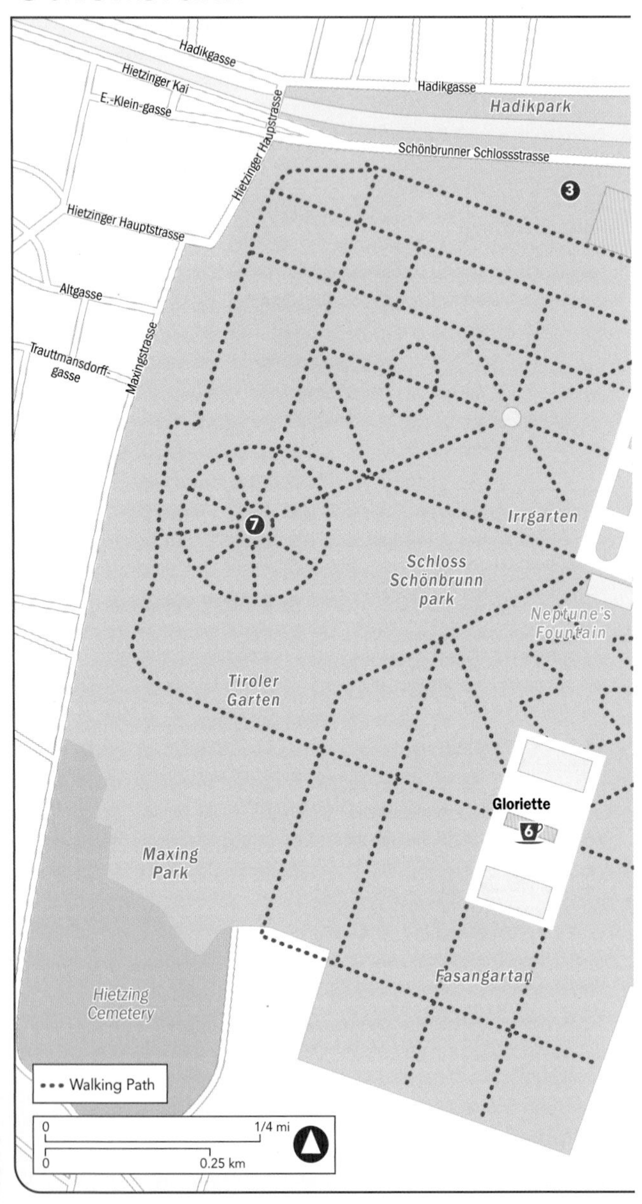
Hadikgasse
Hietzinger Kai
E.-Klein-gasse
Hietzinger Hauptstrasse
Hadikgasse
Hadikpark
Schönbrunner Schlossstrasse
3
Hietzinger Hauptstrasse
Altgasse
Trauttmansdorff-gasse
Maxingstrasse
7
Irrgarten
Schloss Schönbrunn park
Neptune's Fountain
Tiroler Garten
Gloriette
6
Maxing Park
Fasangartan
Hietzing Cemetery
Walking Path
0
1/4 mi
0
0.25 km

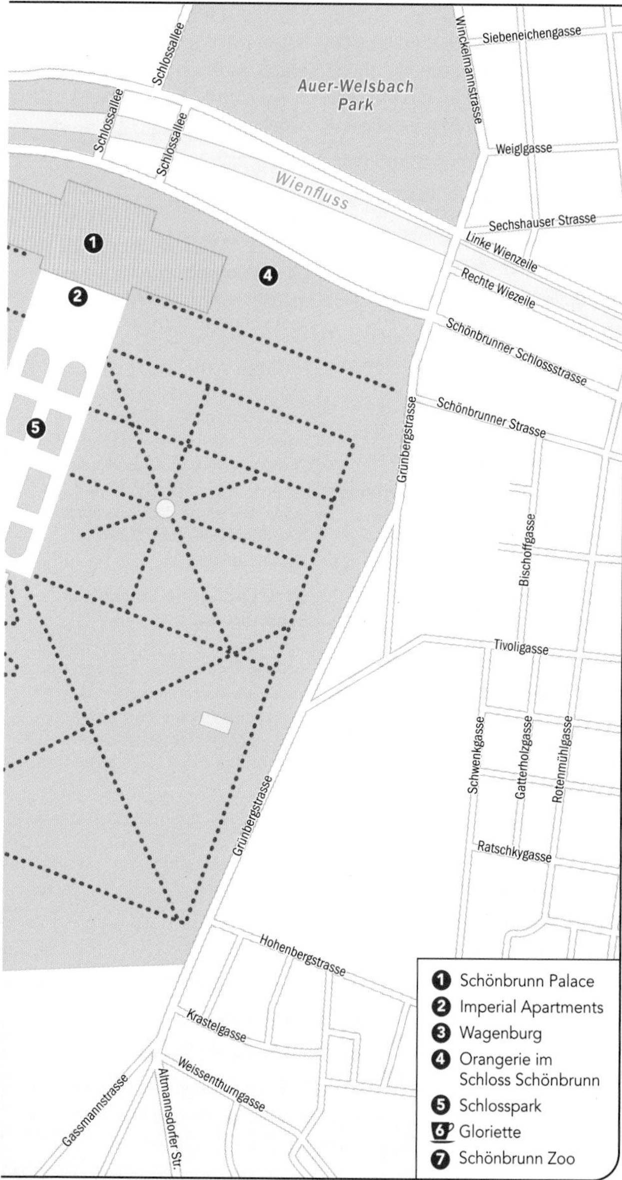
Schlossallee
Schlossallee
Schlossallee
Auer-Welsbach Park
Winckelmannstrasse
Siebeneichengasse
Weiglgasse
Wienfluss
Sechshauser Strasse
Linke Wienzeile
Rechte Wiezeile
Schönbrunner Schlossstrasse
Schönbrunner Strasse
Grünbergstrasse
Bischoffgasse
Tivoligasse
Schwenkgasse
Gatterholzgasse
Rotenmühlgasse
Ratschkygasse
Grünbergstrasse
Hohenbergstrasse
Krastelgasse
Weissenthurngasse
Gassmannstrasse
Altmannsdorfer Str.
1 Schönbrunn Palace
2 Imperial Apartments
3 Wagenburg
4 Orangerie im Schloss Schönbrunn
5 Schlosspark
6 Gloriette
7 Schönbrunn Zoo

What Versailles is to France, Schönbrunn is to Austria. This grandiose baroque palace was once the summer residence of the imperial family. It is hard to believe that it began life as a simple hunting lodge, built by Maximilian II in 1569, taking its name from the "beautiful spring" found here. Now listed as a UNESCO World Heritage Site, it is Vienna's most-visited historic building. START: **Schönbrunn Palace (U-Bahn 4, Schönbrunn).**

❶ ★★★ kids Schönbrunn Palace. Leopold I commissioned the great architect Fischer von Erlach to build a monumental palace here for his son in the 17th century. It remained incomplete until Empress Maria Theresa added another floor to accommodate her 16 children, supervised the interior design and the layout of the grounds, and painted it her favorite color—*Schönbrunnergelb* (Schönbrunn yellow).

❷ ★★★ Imperial Apartments. Maria Theresa is the monarch most closely associated with the palace. She lived here with her entourage of 1,500 staff and courtiers. The state rooms with their extravagant rococo decor give an evocative insight into her lifestyle. Of the two guided tours on offer, choose the "Grand Tour," which visits 40 rooms (out of nearly 2,000 in total)—the Imperial Tour covers only 22 rooms, not including the impressive west wing. *See map at right.*

❸ ★ Wagenburg. It is fun to wind the clocks back to olden times at the Imperial Carriage Collection, with its magnificent horse-drawn carriages, sedan chairs, and fairy-tale sleighs housed in the Winter Riding School. *30 min. Schönbrunner Schlossstrasse. ☎ 01 525 24-0. www.khm.at. €8 adults, €6 concessions, free under 19, €2 audio guide. Daily May–Oct 9am–6pm; Nov–Apr 10am–4pm. U-Bahn 4 (Schönbrunn).*

❹ ★ Orangerie im Schloss Schönbrunn. This grand 18th-century edifice is the world's second-largest baroque orangery after Versailles. Part of it is still used to keep citrus trees over the winter. The other section hosts nightly

Schönbrunn Palace—Vienna's most-visited attraction.

Imperial Apartments

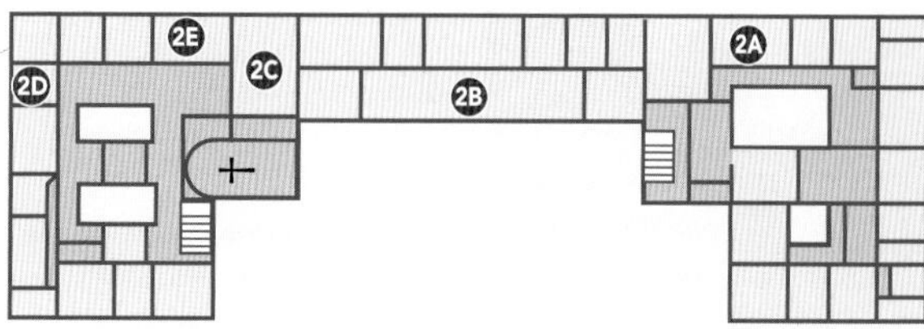

The tour starts in the private rooms of Elisabeth (Sisi) and Franz Josef. A highlight of the state apartments is the 2A ★★ **Hall of Mirrors,** where the 6-year-old Mozart first played the clavichord to Maria Theresa in 1762. His virtuoso performance was soon the talk of the town, laying the foundations for his meteoric rise to fame. The 2B ★★ **Great Gallery** is dominated by three enormous ceiling frescoes celebrating the glory of the Habsburgs and illuminated by magnificent chandeliers. In the painting of Isabella's wedding procession in 2C ★ **Hall of Ceremonies,** each of the 98 coaches belonging to the aristocracy of Europe is identifiable by its family insignia. Maria Theresa clearly had expensive tastes; she spent a million silver florins on the rosewood paneling and priceless miniatures in the 2D ★★★ **Million Room.** Finally, don't miss the 2E ★★ **Blue Chinese Room** where Karl I abdicated in 1918, ending a remarkable 6 centuries of Habsburg rule. *2 hr.; early morning is very busy, lunchtime is the quietest time to visit. Schönbrunner Schlossstrasse. ☎ 01 811 13-239. www.schoenbrunn.at. Grand Tour (40 rooms)/Imperial Tour (22 rooms): €17/€13 adults, €15/€9.80 concessions, €11/€9.80 kids (6–18). Apr–June, Sept–Mar 8:30am–5pm; July–Aug 8:30am–6pm. U-Bahn 4 (Schönbrunn).*

Mozart and Strauss concerts, performed by the Schönbrunn Palace Orchestra. In this setting in 1785, Mozart and his lifelong adversary Antonio Salieri vied for supremacy in a composers' competition (one of the most memorable scenes in the movie *Amadeus*). In case you're wondering . . . Salieri won. *Schönbrunner Schlossstrasse.* ☎ *01 812*

Kids just love the Palace's Irrgarten (Crazy Garden).

5004-0. www.imagevienna.com. Tickets €42–€126; available online. U-Bahn 4 (Schönbrunn).

5 ★★★ kids **Schlosspark.** It's hard not to feel rather superior as you stroll among the statues, fountains, immaculately clipped hedging, and bright flower-filled beds of the vast and beautiful Palace Park. Laid out by Maria Theresa's son, Joseph II (a keen gardener), in the strict symmetry of French-style gardens of the era, it's a great place to watch the Viennese at leisure. Highlights include the Schöner Brunnen, complete with grotto and nymph in true baroque style; the Fountain of Neptune facing the palace; and the majestic Gloriette—a neoclassical arcade. The magnificent iron-and-glass Palm House (a replica of the one in London's Kew Gardens), is full of exotic plants collected over centuries. Kids large and small will enjoy the Maze and the adjoining **Irrgarten** (Crazy Garden)—an eccentric kids' playground full of unusual wooden toys, crazy mirrors, sandpits, and wacky climbing frames. ⏲ *2 hr. Schlosspark. No phone. www.schoenbrunn.at. Free admission. Apr–Oct 6am–dusk; Nov–Mar 6:30am–dusk, see website for exact times. Palm House: free admission. Daily Oct–Apr 9:30am–5pm; May–Sept 9:30am–6pm. Maze/Irrgarten: €3.50 adults, €2.20 kids, €7.50 family ticket. Apr–June, Sept 9am–6pm; July–Aug 9am–7pm; Oct 9am–5pm. U-Bahn 4 (Schönbrunn).*

6 ★★ **Gloriette.** This immense neoclassical arcade was built to commemorate the Austro-Hungarian victory over the Prussians in 1775. Sited high on a hill overlooking the palace and gardens, with the city as a distant backdrop, its upmarket cafe affords sensational views, especially at sunset. The weekend brunch, aka Sisi Buffet (€33), is excellent. *Schlosspark.* ☎ *01 879 1311. €€.*

7 ★★★ kids **Schönbrunn Zoo.** Take a break from all the art, music, and culture, and visit the zoo—Vienna's most-visited attraction after Schönbrunn Palace. It's the oldest zoo in the world, founded in 1752 by Emperor Franz I. Some of the 750-plus animals are housed in original baroque buildings. You can travel round the enclosures by mini-train. Current crowd-pullers include polar bear twins, Tuluba (Big Ears) the elephant (b. 2010) and the first giant pandas ever to reproduce naturally in Europe. ⏲ *2 hr.; avoid Sat–Sun and school holidays if possible. Maxingstrasse 13b.* ☎ *01 877 9294. www.zoovienna.at. €19 adults, €9 concessions and kids, free under 6. Daily Feb 9am–5pm; Mar 9am–5:30pm; Apr–Sept 9am–6:30pm; Oct–Jan 9am–4:30pm. U-Bahn 4 (Hietzing).* ●

6 The Best Dining

Dining Best Bets

Café Sperl is one of the oldest and most popular coffeehouses in town.

Most **Eccentric Loos**
★★★ Steirereck im Stadtpark, *Am Stadtpark (p 121)*

Best for **Carnivores**
★★ The Brickmakers Pub & Kitchen, *Zieglergasse 42 (p 116)*

Best for **Afternoon Tea & Cake**
★★★ Demel, *Kohlmarkt 14 (p 117)*

Best **Tafelspitz**
★★ Plachutta, *Wollzeile 38 (p 121)*

Best **Neighborhood Italian**
★ Disco Volante, *Gumpendorferstrasse 98 (p 117)*

Best **Boho Cafe**
★★★ Hawelka, *Dorotheergasse 6 (p 118)*

Best **Meal with a View**
★★★ Le Loft, Sofitel Hotel, *Praterstrasse 1 (p 119)*

Most **Traditional Coffeehouse**
★★★ Café Sperl, *Gumpendorferstrasse 11 (p 117)*

Best **Fish**
★★ Umarfisch, *Naschmarkt 76–79 (p 122)*

Best **Ice Cream**
★★★ Eis Greissler, *Rotenturmstrasse 14 (p 117)*

Best **Asian Cuisine**
★★★ Mochi, *Praterstrasse 15 (p 120)*

Best **Brunch**
★ burg.ring1, *Burgring 1 (p 116)*

Best **Pizza**
★★ Pizza Quartier, *Karmelitermarkt 96 (p 120)*

Best **Noodle Bar**
★★★ Kuishimbo, *Linke Wienzeile 40 (p 119)*

The **Coolest Cafe in Town**
★ Café Francais, *Währingerstrasse 6–8 (p 116)*

Best **Alfresco Meal**
★★★ Glacis Beisl, *Breite Gasse 4 (MQ) (p 118)*

Best **Vegetarian**
★★ Tian, *Himmelpfortgasse 23 (p 121)*

Previous page: The swanky, modern Steirereck im Stadtpark.

Naschmarkt & Margareten Dining

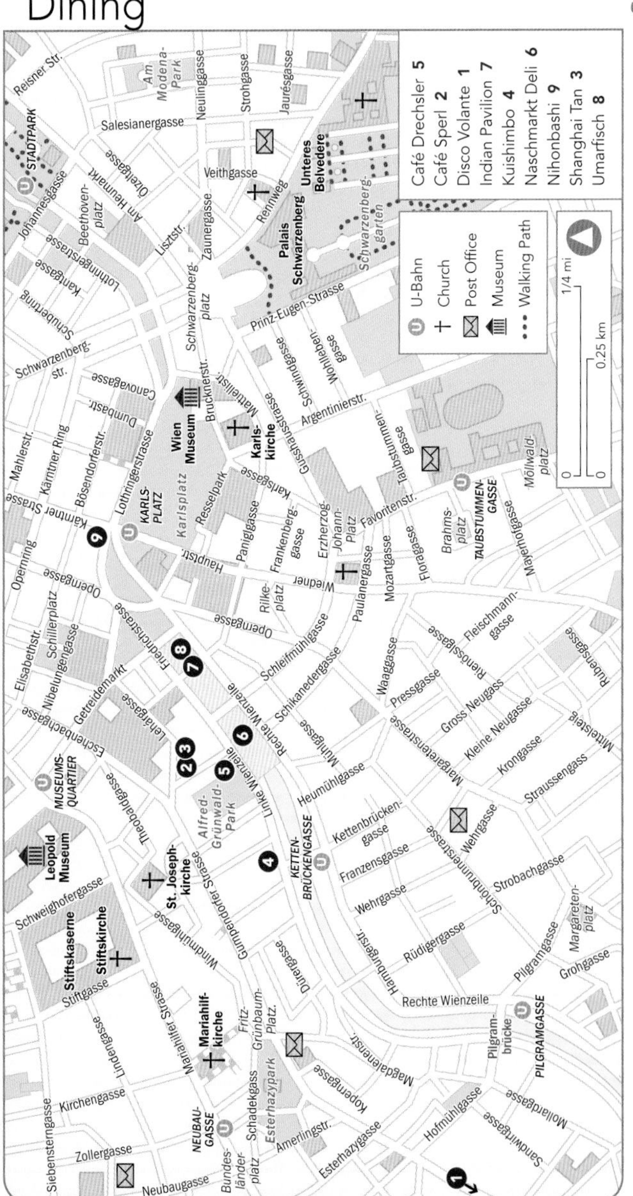

City Center Dining

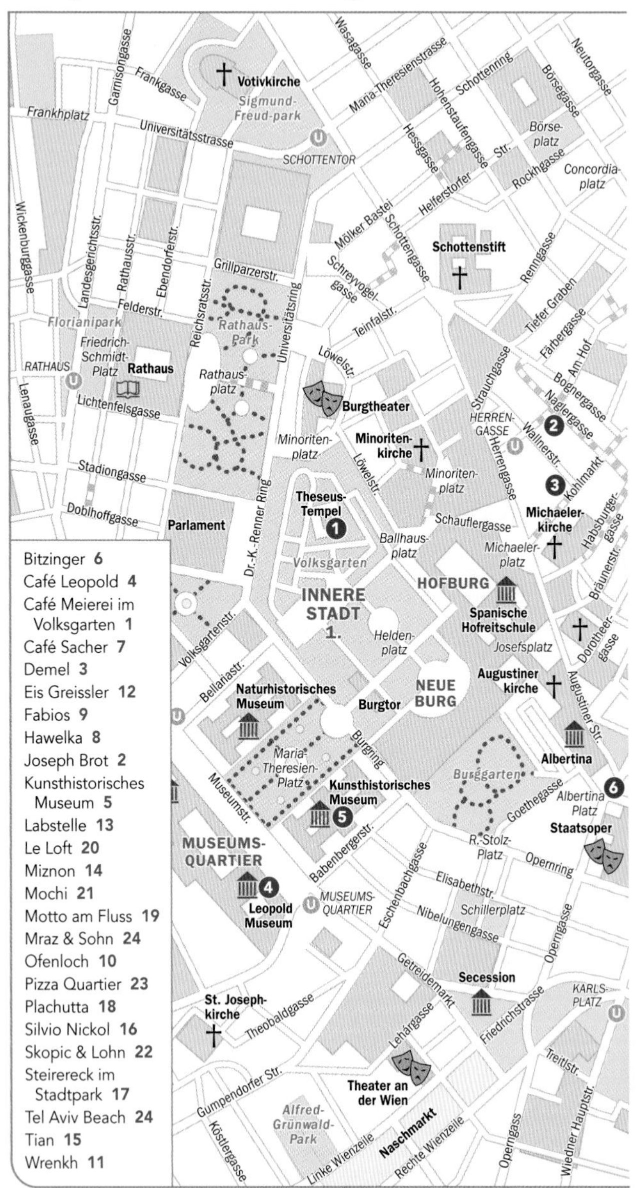

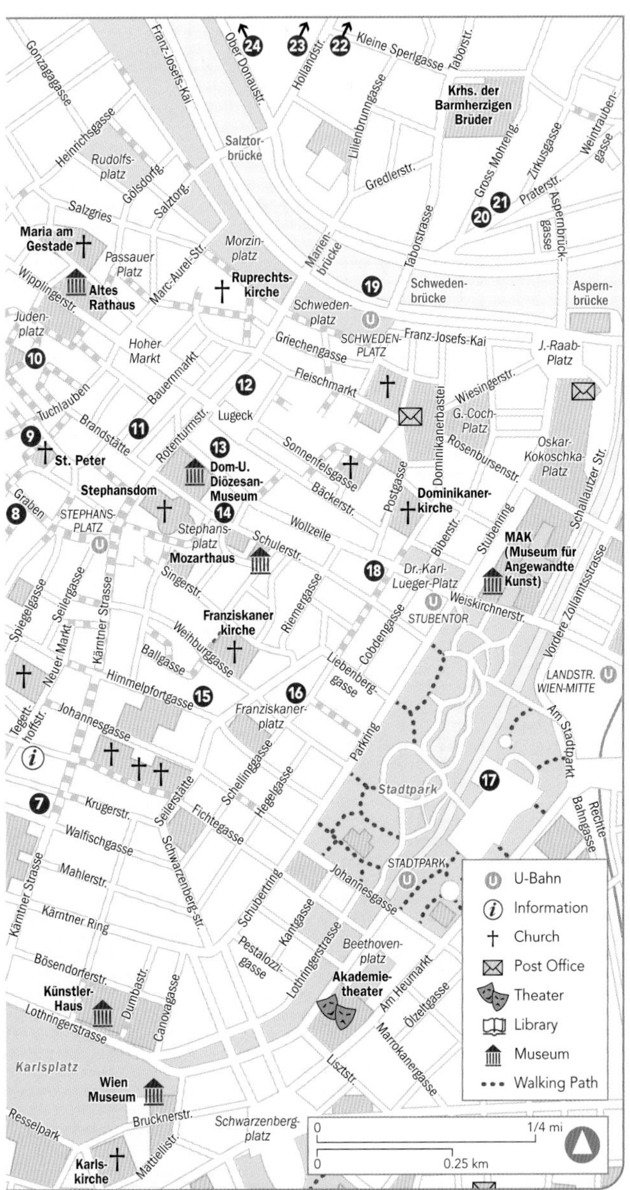
Kleine Sperlgasse
Taborstr.
Krhs. der Barmherzigen Brüder
Franz-Josefs-Kai
Ober Donaustr.
Hollandstr.
Gonzagagasse
Lilienbrunngasse
Heinrichsgasse
Rudolfs-platz
Salztor-brücke
Gölsdorfg.
Salztorg.
Salzgries
Gredlerstr.
Gross Mohreng.
Zirkusgasse
Weintrauben-gasse
Praterstr.
Aspernbrück-gasse
Taborstrasse
Maria am Gestade
Passauer Platz
Marc-Aurel-Str.
Morzin-platz
Marien-brücke
Ruprechts-kirche
Schweden-brücke
Aspern-brücke
Wipplingerstr.
Altes Rathaus
Juden-platz
Schweden-platz
SCHWEDEN-PLATZ
Franz-Josefs-Kai
J.-Raab-Platz
Hoher Markt
Griechengasse
Fleischmarkt
Bauernmarkt
Wiesingerstr.
Tuchlauben
Lugeck
Dominikanerbastei
G.-Coch-Platz
Brandstätte
Rotenturmstr.
Rosenbursenstr.
Oskar-Kokoschka-Platz
St. Peter
Sonnenfelsgasse
Dom-U. Diözesan-Museum
Stephansdom
Postgasse
Dominikaner-kirche
Schallautzer Str.
Graben
STEPHANS-PLATZ
Bäckerstr.
Stephans-platz
Wollzeile
Biberstr.
Stubenring
MAK (Museum für Angewandte Kunst)
Schulerstr.
Mozarthaus
Dr.-Karl-Lueger-Platz
Spiegelgasse
Seilergasse
Singerstr.
Riemergasse
Weiskirchnerstr.
Kärntner Strasse
Franziskaner kirche
Cobdengasse
STUBENTOR
Vordere Zollamtsstrasse
Neuer Markt
Weihburggasse
Ballgasse
Liebenberg-gasse
LANDSTR. WIEN-MITTE
Himmelpfortgasse
Franziskaner-platz
Tegett-hoffstr.
Johannesgasse
Parkring
Am Stadtpark
Schellinggasse
Stadtpark
Krugerstr.
Seilerstätte
Hegelgasse
Rechte Bahngasse
Walfischgasse
Fichtegasse
Mahlerstr.
Schwarzenberg-str.
STADTPARK
Johannesgasse
Kärntner Strasse
Schubertring
Kärntner Ring
Kantgasse
Beethoven-platz
Pestalozzi-gasse
Lothringerstrasse
Bösendorferstr.
Akademie-theater
Am Heumarkt
Künstler-Haus
Dumbastr.
Canovagasse
Ölzeltgasse
Lothringerstrasse
Marrokanergasse
Karlsplatz
Lisztstr.
Wien Museum
Resselpark
Brucknerstr.
Schwarzenberg-platz
Mattiellistr.
Karls-kirche
U-Bahn
Information
Church
Post Office
Theater
Library
Museum
Walking Path
0
1/4 mi
0
0.25 km
7
8
9
10
11
12
13
14
15
16
17
18
19
20
21
22
23
24

Neubau & Josefstadt Dining

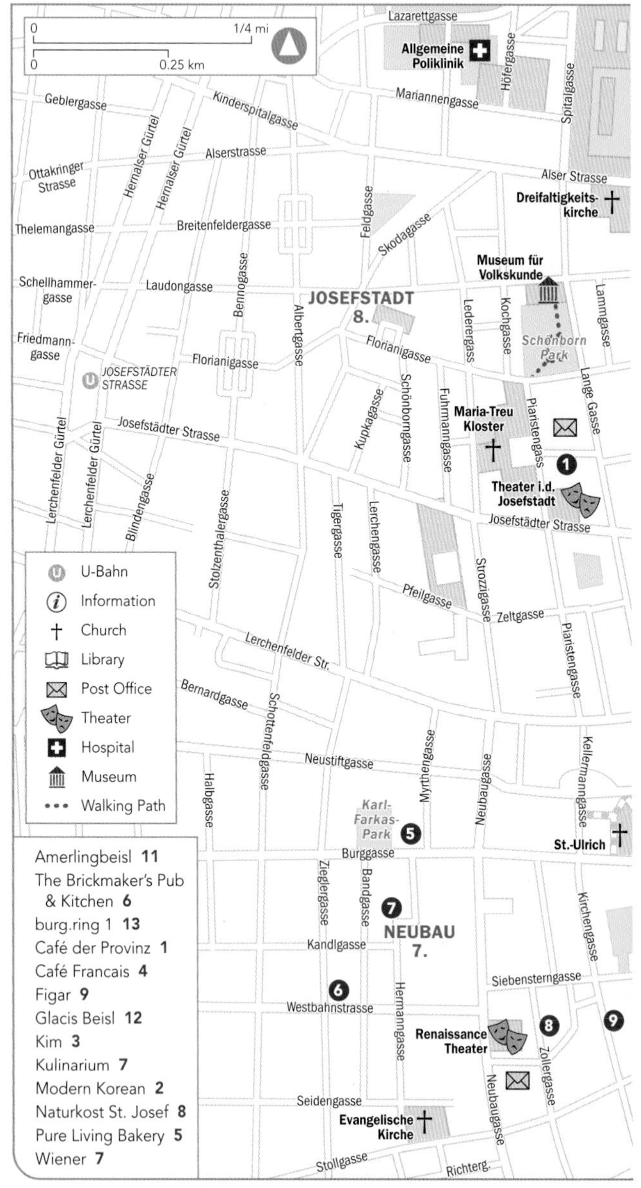

Amerlingbeisl **11**
The Brickmaker's Pub & Kitchen **6**
burg.ring 1 **13**
Café der Provinz **1**
Café Francais **4**
Figar **9**
Glacis Beisl **12**
Kim **3**
Kulinarium **7**
Modern Korean **2**
Naturkost St. Josef **8**
Pure Living Bakery **5**
Wiener **7**

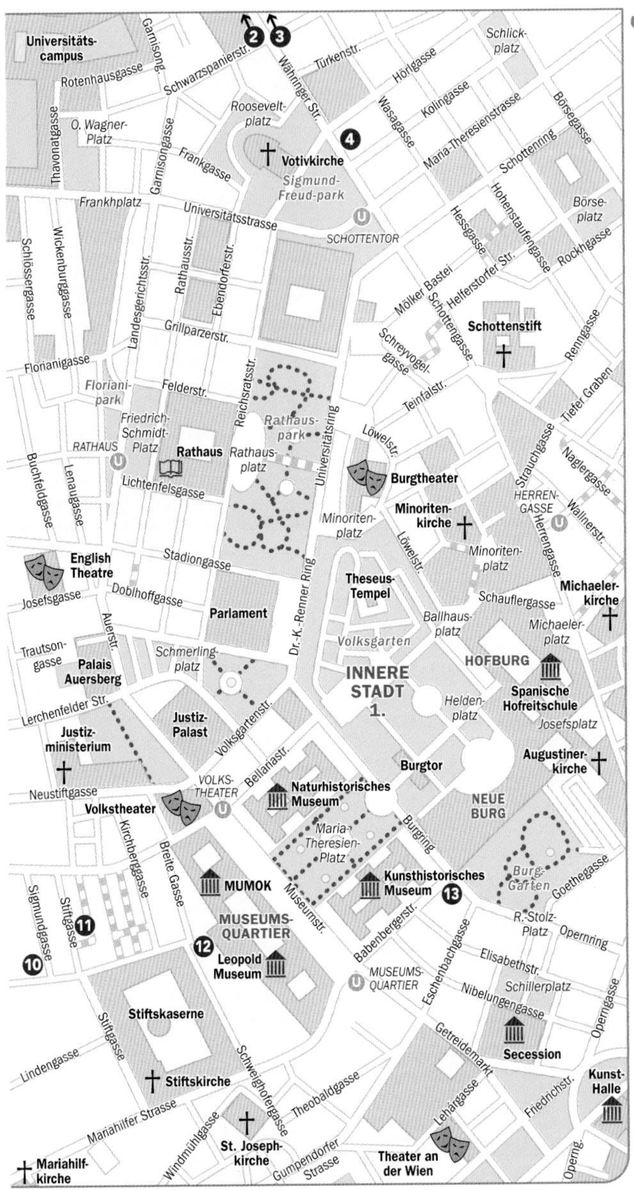
Universitäts-campus
Garnisong.
Schwarzspanierstr.
Währinger Str.
Türkenstr.
Schlick-platz
Hörlgasse
Rotenhausgasse
Roosevelt-platz
Wasagasse
Kolingasse
Maria-Theresienstrasse
Börsegasse
Thavonatgasse
O. Wagner-Platz
Garnisongasse
Frankgasse
Votivkirche
Sigmund-Freud-park
Schottenring
Frankhplatz
Universitätsstrasse
SCHOTTENTOR
Hohenstaufengasse
Hessgasse
Börse-platz
Rockhgasse
Schlössergasse
Wickenburgasse
Landesgerichtsstr.
Rathausstr.
Ebendorferstr.
Mölker Bastei
Helferstorfer Str.
Schottengasse
Schottenstift
Renngasse
Grillparzerstr.
Schreyvogel-gasse
Florianigasse
Reichsratsstr.
Teinfaltstr.
Tiefer Graben
Floriani-park
Felderstr.
Friedrich-Schmidt-Platz
Rathaus-park
Universitätsring
Löwelstr.
Strauchgasse
Naglergasse
RATHAUS
Rathaus
Rathaus-platz
Burgtheater
Buchfeldgasse
Lenaugasse
Lichtenfelsgasse
HERREN-GASSE
Wallnerstr.
Minoriten-kirche
Minoriten-platz
Herrengasse
English Theatre
Stadiongasse
Dr.-K.-Renner Ring
Theseus-Tempel
Michaeler-kirche
Josefsgasse
Doblhoffgasse
Parlament
Schauflergasse
Ballhaus-platz
Michaeler-platz
Auerstr.
Volksgarten
Trautson-gasse
Palais Auersberg
Schmerling-platz
INNERE STADT 1.
HOFBURG
Spanische Hofreitschule
Lerchenfelder Str.
Helden-platz
Justiz-ministerium
Justiz-Palast
Volksgartenstr.
Josefsplatz
Augustiner-kirche
Burgtor
Bellariastr.
VOLKS-THEATER
Naturhistorisches Museum
Neustiftgasse
Volkstheater
NEUE BURG
Maria-Theresien-Platz
Burgring
Kirchberggasse
Breite Gasse
Burg-Garten
Goethegasse
MUMOK
Kunsthistorisches Museum
Museumstr.
Sigmundgasse
Stiftgasse
MUSEUMS-QUARTIER
R.-Stolz-Platz
Opernring
Babenbergerstr.
Eschenbachgasse
Leopold Museum
Elisabethstr.
MUSEUMS-QUARTIER
Schillerplatz
Nibelungengasse
Operngasse
Stiftskaserne
Getreidemarkt
Secession
Lindengasse
Stiftgasse
Schweighofergasse
Stiftskirche
Kunst-Halle
Theobaldgasse
Lehárgasse
Friedrichstr.
Mariahilfer Strasse
Windmühlgasse
St. Joseph-kirche
Gumpendorfer Strasse
Theater an der Wien
Operng.
Mariahilf-kirche

Vienna Dining A to Z

★★ Amerlingbeisl SPITTELBERG *AUSTRIAN* This informal eatery serves simple but varied light bites, including good vegetarian options. Sit outside in the pretty, cobbled courtyard. *Stiftgasse 8. ☎ 01 526 1660. Entrees €7–€12. Breakfast, lunch, and dinner daily. Tram 49 (Stiftgasse). Map p 114.*

★★★ Bitzinger CITY CENTER *AUSTRIAN* The city's most famous sausage stand attracts everyone from opera goers to party animals. All gather in tiny booths for sausages and beer—or champagne. Cash only. *Augustinerstrasse 1. ☎ 01 533 1026. Entrees €3.40–€8. Daily 10am–5am. U-Bahn 1/4 (Karlsplatz). Map p 112.*

★★ The Brickmakers Pub & Kitchen NEUBAU *AMERICAN* This craft beer pub serves up all the meat you can handle with specials like 13-hour brisket or pulled-pork sandwiches. *Zieglergasse 42. ☎ 01 9974414. Entrees €7.90–€24. Mon–Fri 5pm–2am; Sat–Sun 10am–2am. Tram 49 (Zieglergasse). Map p 114.*

★ burg.ring1 CITY CENTER *CAFE* Heaven for breakfast lovers. The menu is huge, and you can create the most important meal of the day just the way you want it. The MuseumsQuartier (MQ) is steps away. *Burgring 1. ☎ 01 581 1393. Entrees €5.60–€11. Mon–Thurs 11am–1am; Fri 11am–2am; Sat 9am–2am; Sun 9am–6pm. U-Bahn 2 (MQ) Map p 114.*

★ kids Café der Provinz JOSEFSTADT *CAFE* This mellow cafe draws students and locals in with its simple menu of salads and savory and sweet pancakes, not to mention homemade lemonade and a great weekend brunch. *Maria-Treu-Gasse 3. ☎ 01 944 2272. €4.80–€7.80. Breakfast, lunch, and dinner daily. U-Bahn 2 (Rathaus). Map p 114.*

Amerlingbeisl is a true local watering hole.

★ Café Drechsler NASCHMARKT *CAFE* This cult cafe by the market with its cool, Conran-designed interior never closes. What's more, it serves sensational brunches, and regularly hosts DJs. *Linke Wienzeile 22/Girardigasse 1. ☎ 01 581 20 44. Entrees €4.90–€15. Open 24 hr. U-Bahn 1/2/4 (Karlsplatz). Map p 111.*

★★ Café Francais VOTIVKIRCHE *CAFE* Close to the University of Vienna, this hip cafe attracts the bobo students for their coffee and breakfast. The lofty, light-flooded space is good for a stop on a sightseeing trip through the city. *Währingerstrasse 6-8. ☎ 01 319 0903. Entrees €5–€13. Mon–Sat 9am–midnight. U-Bahn 2 (Schottentor). Map p 114.*

★★ Café Leopold MQ *CAFE* Hip, arty types frequent the Leopold Museum's cool cafe-bar for tasty brunches, bagels, and wraps during the day, followed by cocktails and funky DJ sounds at night. *Museumsplatz 1. ☎ 01 523 6732. Entrees €3.90–€11. Sun–Wed 10am–2am; Thurs–Sat 10am–4am. U-Bahn 2 (MuseumsQuartier). Map p 112.*

★ kids Café Meirerei Volksgarten HOFBURG *CAFE* Come to this tiny garden pavilion for its sensational alfresco Buck's Fizz breakfasts (the Fizz is much like a mimosa), gooey gateaux, and ice-cream sundaes. *Volksgarten. ☎ 01 533 2105. Entrees €3.80–€13. Breakfast, lunch, and dinner daily (Apr–Oct only). Tram 1/2/D (Dr-Karl-Renner Ring). Map p 112.*

★★★ Café Sacher CITY CENTER *CAFE* The place to try Vienna's famous chocolate cake, *Sachertorte*, made to a secret recipe and served with whipped cream in a posh, traditional tearoom. *Philharmonikerstrasse 4. ☎ 01 51 456-0. Entrees €17–€22. Breakfast, lunch, and dinner daily. Tram 1/2/D (Oper). Map p 112.*

★★★ Café Sperl MQ *CAFE* One of Vienna's best-loved cafes, serving local dishes in a plush, *fin-de-siècle* setting. Newspapers and billiard tables add to the relaxed ambience. *Gumpendorferstrasse 11. ☎ 01 586 4158. Entrees €7.10–€9.80. Mon–Sat 7am–11pm; Sun 11am–8pm (closed Sun July–Aug). U-Bahn 1/2/4 (Karlsplatz). Map p 111.*

★★★ Demel CITY CENTER *CAFE* Famous for its cakes and sweets, this temple of indulgence has also been a haven for tea lovers since 1786. Relax in the original rococo salon. *Kohlmarkt 14. ☎ 01 535 1717 0. Entrees €9.50–€21. Daily 9am–7pm. U-Bahn 1/3 (Stephansplatz). Map p 112.*

★ Disco Volante MARGARETEN *ITALIAN* The oven is shaped like a disco ball in this otherwise minimalist establishment. The focus here is all on the pizza, which is thin, traditional, and very Italian. *Gumpendorferstrasse 98. ☎ 0664 195 2345. Entrees €8.10–€9.20. Mon–Sat noon–midnight; Sun noon–11pm. U-Bahn 4 (Pilgramgasse). Map p 111.*

★★★ Eis Greissler CITY CENTER *ICE CREAM* Vienna's hippest ice cream is made with Austrian organic milk and dispensed from this tiny hole-in-the-wall. They serve classic flavors as well as rarities like goat cheese and poppy seed. Vegan ice cream is also available. Cash only. *Rotenturmstrasse 14. No phone. Entrees €1.30. Daily 11am–11pm. U-Bahn 1/3 (Stephansplatz). Map p 112.*

★★ Fabios FREYUNG *MEDITERRANEAN* See and be seen in this sophisticated, minimalist restaurant where the decor is sleek, the waiters suave, and the modern-Mediterranean cuisine impeccable.

Visit Café Sperl for the classic Viennese coffeehouse experience.

Insalata di pesce at Fabios.

Save room for dessert. *Tuchlauben 4–6. ☎ 01 532 2222. Entrees €29–€35. Lunch and dinner Mon–Sat. U-Bahn 3 (Herrengasse). Map p 112.*

★ **Figar** NEUBAU *CAFE* You'll find the creative hipsters of the 7th district here for breakfast, lunch, dinner, coffee, or just drinks. They're here a lot, but Figar manages to delight on all accounts. *Kirchengasse 18. ☎ 01 890 9947. Entrees €4.50–€14. Mon–Fri 8am–midnight; Sat 9am–2am; Sun 9am–10pm. U-Bahn 3 (Neubaugasse). Map p 114.*

★★★ **Glacis Beisl** MQ *AUSTRIAN* In a hidden corner of the MQ, this eatery is shaded by trees and overgrown vines, under which cordial staffers serve Austrian cuisine in a casual and relaxed setting. Try the delectable Kalbsbutterschnitzel (buttered veal schnitzel). *Breite Gasse 4(MQ). ☎ 01 526 5660. Entrees €9.80–€24. Daily 11am–2am. U-Bahn 2/3 (Volksgarten). Map p 114.*

★★★ **Hawelka** CITY CENTER *CAFE* This scruffy, bohemian, cash-only cafe has long attracted artists and local literati. Join them here at 10pm when hot *Buchteln* (jam doughnuts) are served. Scrumptious with coffee. *Dorotheergasse 6. ☎ 01 512 8230. Snacks €3.50–€4.30. Mon–Sat 8am–2am; Sun 10am–2am. U-Bahn 1/3 (Stephansplatz). Map p 112.*

★★★ **Indian Pavilion** NASCHMARKT *INDIAN* Try the specialty *thali* (mixed curry platter) on the pavement terrace of this tiny market cafe, and wash it down with a Cobra beer, a mango *lassi* (yogurt drink), or Darjeeling tea with cardamom. Cash only. *Naschmarkt 74–75. ☎ 01 587 8561. Entrees €9.50–€13. Mon–Fri 11am–6:30pm; Sat 11am–5pm. U-Bahn 1/2/4 (Karlsplatz). Map p 111.*

★★ **Joseph Brot vom Pheinsten** CITY CENTER *BAKERY* Come for the crispy bread and the rich breakfast menu, stay for the salads, and then dig into the dry-aged cheeseburger. Joseph tries to have it all—and succeeds. Cash only. *Naglergasse 9. ☎ 01 710 2881. Entrees€10–€16. Mon–Fri 7am–7pm; Sat 8am–6pm. Map p 112.*

★★ **Kim** WÄHRING *ASIAN* It has been a long journey for one of Vienna's most talented chefs and now Sohyi Kim has found her way back to her tiny kitchen where she personally cooks the most celebrated Asian dishes in the country. Reservations required in advance; credit cards accepted for groups of six or more only. *Währinger Strasse 46. ☎ 0664 425 8866. Set menu only. Prices vary. Wed–Sat noon–3pm and 6–11pm. Tram 5,37,38,40,41,42 (Spitalgasse). Map p 114.*

★★★ **Kulinarium 7** SPITTELBERG *MODERN AUSTRIAN* This refined wine bar serves sophisticated cuisine to accompany its top-notch international wine selection. Try snails from Vienna's vineyards followed by beef poached in Bordeaux. *Sigmundsgasse/corner Siebensterngasse. ☎ 01 522 3377.*

Set menus only €50–€70. Tues–Sat 5–11:30pm. U-Bahn 2/3 (Volkstheater). Map p 114.

★★★ **Kuishimbo** NASCHMARKT *NOODLE BAR* This tiny hole-in-the-wall serves perhaps the most authentic Japanese food you'll find in Vienna. The delicious udon soup and soba noodles and the courteous Japanese proprietors transport you straight to Tokyo. Cash only. *Linke Wienzeile 40. ☎ 0699 17192355. Entrees €5–€18. Mon–Sat noon–9pm U-Bahn 4 (Kettenbrückengasse). Map p 111.*

★ kids **Kunsthistorisches Museum** MQ *CAFE* Grab a coffee or a light snack between galleries in the KHM's grand cupola hall. Book in advance for the special Sunday Art and Buffet brunch and art tour. *KHM, Maria-Theresien-Platz. ☎ 0644 966 4546. Brunch €39 adults, €23 kids. Tues–Sun 10am–5pm. Tram 1/2/D (Burgring). Map p 112.*

★★ **Labstelle** CITY CENTER *AUSTRIAN* Here the modern dishes are simple, flavorful, and elegant—and that culinary style is reflected in the clean and simple interior. *Lugeck 6. ☎ 01 236 2122. Entrees €16–€27. Mon–Fri 11:30am–2am; Sat 10am–2am. U-Bahn 1/3 (Stephansplatz). Map p 112.*

★★★ **Le Loft** KARMELITER *FRENCH* This minimalist, glassy dining space atop the Sofitel Hotel offers gourmet French cuisine and the best aerial views in town. Book several weeks in advance. *Hotel Sofitel (18th floor), Praterstrasse 1. ☎ 01 906 161-0. Entrees €31–€85; bar menu €9–€25. Breakfast Mon–Fri 6:30–10:30am, Sat–Sun until 11am; lunch daily noon–2:30pm; dinner daily 6pm–midnight. Bar open daily 10am–midnight. U-Bahn 1/4 (Schwedenplatz). Map p 112.*

★★★ **Miznon** CITY CENTER *ISRAELI* Wonderful, chaotic, crowded, and loud. Miznon's self-serve eatery offers mouthwatering Israeli dishes to a lively crowd. Eating there is an experience in itself. Cash only. *Schulerstrasse 4. ☎ 01 512 1053. Entrees €3–€13. Daily*

Experience modern Austrian cuisine at Labstelle.

noon–11pm. U-Bahn 1/3 (Stephansplatz). Map p 112.

★★★ Mochi CITY CENTER *ASIAN* A favorite among locals, this cash-only restaurant is situated on a picturesque little square and serves delectable Japanese fusion dishes. Reservations required for dinner. *Praterstrasse 15. ☎ 01 925 13 80. Entrees €9–€23. Mon–Sat 11:30am–10pm. U-Bahn 1 (Nestroyplatz). Map p 112.*

★★★ modern korean WÄHRING *KOREAN* Opposite Vienna famous Volksoper opera house, diners are surrounded by hip wooden décor and served a perfect fusion of Korean and Austrian cuisines. The attentive staff makes any evening unforgettable. *Lustkandlgasse 4. ☎ 0664 196 7972. Entrees €11–€28. Mon–Fri noon–3pm and 6pm–midnight. U-Bahn 6 (Währinger Strasse). Map p 114.*

★★ Motto am Fluss CITY CENTER *MODERN AUSTRIAN* This sleek restaurant serves affordable gourmet Austrian cuisine in the main boat terminal, overlooking the Danube Canal. On the upper deck, the cafe is popular for alfresco breakfasts, coffees, and light bites. *Schiffstation Wien-City, Schwedenplatz 2. ☎ 01 25 255 10. Entrees €11–€26. Lunch and dinner daily; bar 6pm–4am. U-Bahn 1/4 (Schwedenplatz). Map p 112.*

★★★ Mraz & Sohn BRIGITTENAU *AUSTRIAN* Two Michelin stars says it all. This is a temple of food for all those who appreciate the work and art that go into creating an incredible culinary experience. *Wallensteinstrasse 59. ☎ 01 330 4594. Prix fixe menus only, starting at €65. Mon–Fri 11am–3pm and 7pm–midnight. Tram 5 (Rauscherstrasse). Map p 112.*

★★★ kids Naschmarkt Deli NASCHMARKT *CAFE* Come here for hearty all-day breakfasts, market-fresh salads, and mighty triple-decker sandwiches. It's also a trendy bar by night. Cash only. *Naschmarkt 421–436. ☎ 01 585 0823. Entrees €4.50–€5.50. Breakfast, lunch, and dinner Mon–Sat. U-Bahn 1/2/4 (Karlsplatz). Map p 111.*

★ kids Naturkost St. Josef NEUBAU *VEGETARIAN* Choose from two tasty menus—the dishes change daily—or sample the soups and juices at this simple, quality vegetarian cafe-cum-health food store. *Zollergasse 26. ☎ 01 526 6818. Set menus €7.20–€8.60. Mon–Fri 8am–5pm; Sat 8am–4pm. U-Bahn 3 (Neubaugasse). Map p 114.*

★★★ Nihonbashi CITY CENTER *JAPANESE* Serving top-notch Japanese food, and exquisite sushi in particular, Nihonbashi completes the experience with an authentic atmosphere. You can even dine in a Karaoke room. *Kärntner Strasse 44. ☎ 01 890 7856. Entrees €9.90–€40. Lunch and dinner Mon–Sat. U-Bahn 1/4 (Karlsplatz). Map p 111.*

★★ Ofenloch FREYUNG *VIENNESE* This traditional restaurant serves classic Viennese fare with a modern twist in a series of intimate, romantic dining rooms. The *Zwiebelrostbraten* (steak heaped with crispy onions) is especially tasty. *Kurrentgasse 8. ☎ 01 533 8844. Entrees €11–€19. Lunch and dinner Mon–Sat. U-Bahn 1/3 (Stephansplatz). Map p 112.*

★★ Pizza Quartier KARMELITER *ITALIAN* In one of the city's favorite markets, this is the go-to for authentic Neapolitan pizza. The house favorite is the Calabria (salami), but people also come for the handmade pasta, local produce, and the owner's love of the craft. *Karmelitermarkt 96. ☎ 01 212*

4994. *Entrees €8.50–€24. Mon–Fri 11am–11pm; Sat 8:30am–11pm. U-Bahn 2 (Taborstrasse). Map p 112.*

★★ **Plachutta** CITY CENTER *VIENNESE* One of the city's finest restaurants, where the local specialty *Tafelspitz* (boiled beef) has been elevated to an art form. Choose from 10 cuts of beef. *Wollzeile 38. ☎ 01 512 1577. Entrees €15–€25. Lunch and dinner daily. Tram 1/2. U-Bahn 3 (Stubentor). Map p 112.*

★ **Pure Living Bakery** NEUBAU *BAKERY* The irresistibly friendly staff serves you cake and sweets in a vintage interior while you sip an artisanal cappuccino. Cash only. *Burggasse 68. No phone. Entrees €7–€11. Mon–Thurs 9:30am–5:30pm; Fri–Sun 9:30am–6pm. Tram 46 (Strozzigasse). Map p 114.*

★ **Shanghai Tan** MQ *ASIAN* The black-and-red decor of this large, dark restaurant affords an intimate ambience in which to savor its extensive menu of oriental (primarily Chinese) delicacies. Known for its aromatic noodle dishes, it also serves delicious sushi, dim sum, and satay. *Gumpendorferstrasse 9. ☎ 01 585 4988. Entrees €12–€17. Lunch and dinner Mon–Sat. U-Bahn 1/2/4 (Karlsplatz). Map p 111.*

★★ **Silvio Nickol** CITY CENTER *INTERNATIONAL* Eating in a Palais is an experience in itself. Pair it with a star-studded chef and elegant service and an unforgettable dining experience awaits. *Coburgbastei 4. ☎ 01 518 1813 0. Prix fix menus only, €148–€299. Tues–Sat 6–9:30pm. Tram 2 (Weihburggasse). Map p 112.*

★ **Skopik & Lohn** KARMELITER *AUSTRIAN* The mixture of artsy and traditional decor invites the eye to explore its surroundings. The waiters dressed in white hurry through the isles delivering hearty dishes with a creative twist. *Leopoldsgasse 17. ☎ 01 219 8977. Entrees €12–€27. Mon–Sat 6pm–1am. U-Bahn 2 (Taborstrasse). Map p 112.*

★★★ **Steirereck im Stadtpark** STADTPARK *MODERN AUSTRIAN* Viennese gossip magazines always feature celebrity diners at this upscale riverside restaurant, long ranked Austria's top gourmet temple. The restrooms are among Europe's quirkiest. *Am Stadtpark. ☎ 01 713 3168. Entrees €28–€44. Lunch and dinner Mon–Fri. U-Bahn 4 (Stadtpark). Map p 112.*

★★ **Tel Aviv Beach** KARMELITER *CAFE* On the banks of the Danube canal, this sandy oasis is a local fave for sundowner lounging and after-work relaxation. Summer evenings are perfectly accompanied by violet-flavored spritzers or a delectable hummus plate. *Donaukanal Straße 26. No phone. Entrees €4.50–€12. Apr–Oct (in fair weather) daily noon–midnight. U-Bahn 2 (Schottenring). Map p 112.*

★★ **Tian** CITY CENTER *VEGETARIAN* Innovative meatless cuisine is

Prepare to be wowed at Steirereck.

Wrenkh has a way with vegetables.

the attraction here where seasonal, organic vegetables are combined for delectable creations. For hungry herbivores, there are two Tian Bistros locations in the city at Schrankgasse 4, Spittelberg (☎ 01 5269491) and Kunsthaus Wien, Weißgerberlände 14, Landstrasse (☎ 01 890 9510). *Himmelpfortgasse 23. ☎ 01 890 4665 27. Entrees €9–€42. Mon–Sat noon–midnight. Tram 2 (Weihburggasse). Map p 112.*

★★ **Umarfisch** NASCHMARKT *FISH* It's worth squeezing round the tiny tables at this Mediterranean-style market-cafe, as it serves the freshest fish and shellfish in town. *Naschmarkt 76–79. ☎ 01 587 0456. Entrees €13–€28. Lunch and dinner Mon–Sat. U-Bahn 1/2/4 (Karlsplatz). Map p 111.*

★★ **Wiener** NEUBAU *AUSTRIAN* Come here for savory Viennese dining and join the locals who go there for the classics. Their Schnitzel is famous. *Hermanngasse 27a. ☎ 01 524 5252. Entrees €11–€29. Mon–Sat 5pm–2am; Sun 5pm–midnight. Tram 49 (Siebensterngasse). Map p 114.*

★★ **Wrenkh** CITY CENTER *VEGETARIAN* The city's leading vegetarian restaurant, in a modern yet comfortable setting. *Bauernmarkt 10. ☎ 01 533 1526. Mon–Sat noon–10pm. U-Bahn 1/3 (Stephansplatz). Map p 112.*

7 The Best Nightlife

Nightlife Best Bets

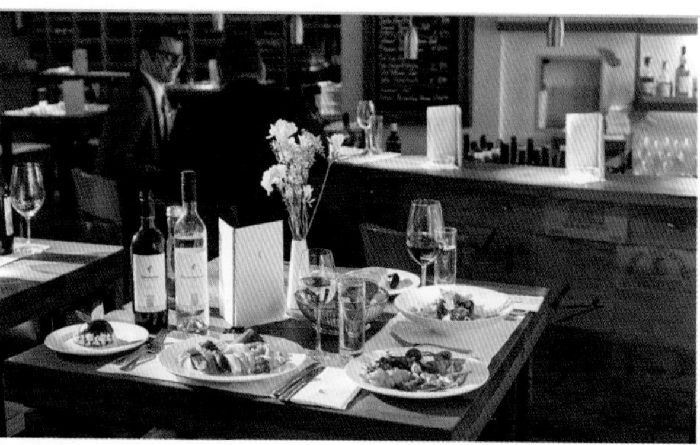

Meinl's beautiful but relaxed wine bar.

Best for Party Animals
★★ passage, *Babenburgerpassage, Burgring 1 (p 131)*

Best Jazz Club
★★ Porgy & Bess, *Riemergasse 11 (p 132)*

Best Dinner Club
★★★ Albertina Passage, *Opernring/Operngasse (p 132)*

Most Creative Cocktails
★★★ Tür7, *Buchfeldgasse 7 (p 130)*

Best Beer
★ 1516 Brewing Company, *Schwarzenbergstrasse 2 (p 130)*

Best Gay Bar
★★ Mango Bar, *Laimgrubengasse 3 (p 132)*

Best Wines
★★ Meinl's Weinbar, *Graben 19 (entrance at Näglergasse 8) (p 129)*

Best Dance Club
★★ Grelle Forelle, *Spittelauer Lände 12 (p 131)*

Best Cocktail Lounge
★★ Roberto American Bar, *Bauernmarkt 11–13 (p 130)*

Best Dressed Crowd
★★ Motto, *Rüdigergasse 1 (p 129)*

Best for Romance
★★★ Ritz-Carlton Rooftop Bar, *Schubertring 5 (p 129)*

Best People-Watching
★★★ Volksgarten, *Burgring 1 (p 132)*

Best for Cutting-Edge Sounds
★★ Auslage, *Lerchenfelder Gürtel 43 (p 130)*

Most Eccentric Bar
★★ R&Bar, *Lindengasse 1 (p 129)*

Best Champagne Bar
★★ Le Cru, *Petersplatz 8 (p 129)*

Best Views
★★★ Le Loft, *Hotel Sofitel, Praterstrasse 1 (p 129)*

Best Jugendstil Bar
★★ Kleinod, *Singerstrasse 7 (p 129)*

Best Beach Party in the City
★★ Strandbar Herrmann, *Hermannpark/Urania (p 130)*

Previous page: An evening stroll along Graben Street.

Neubau & Naschmarkt Nightlife

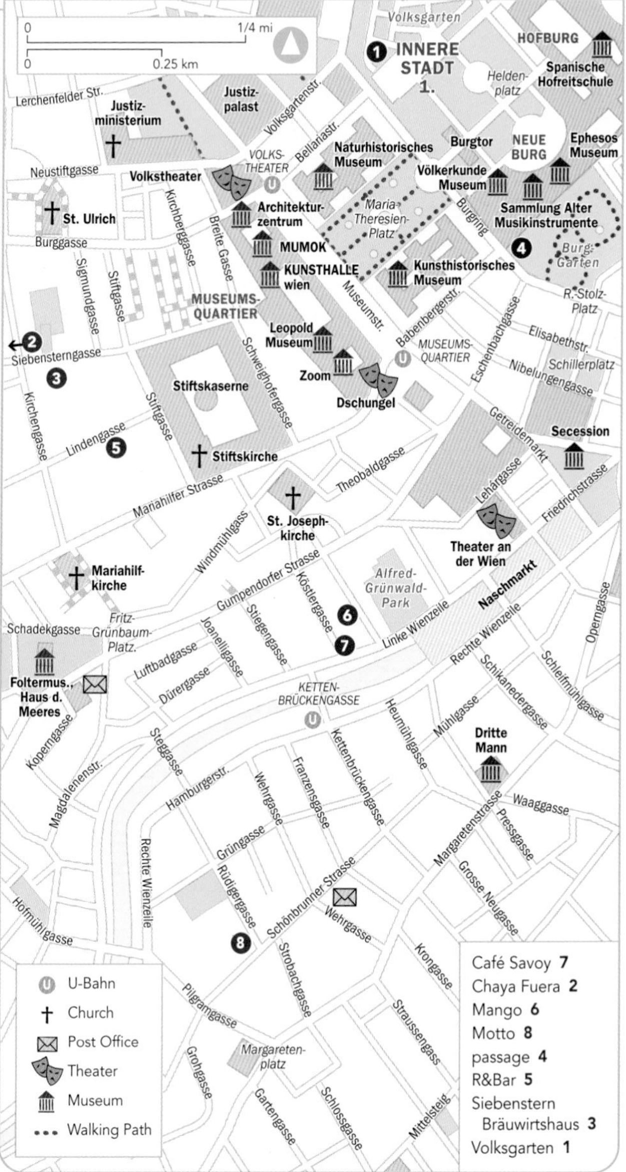

City Center Nightlife

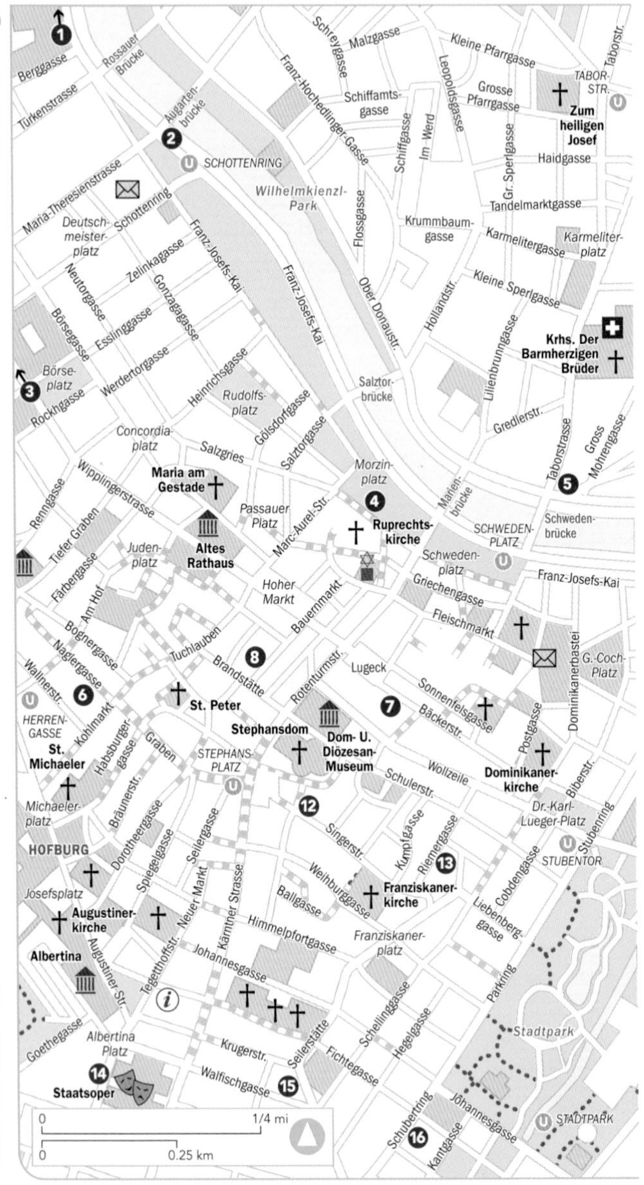

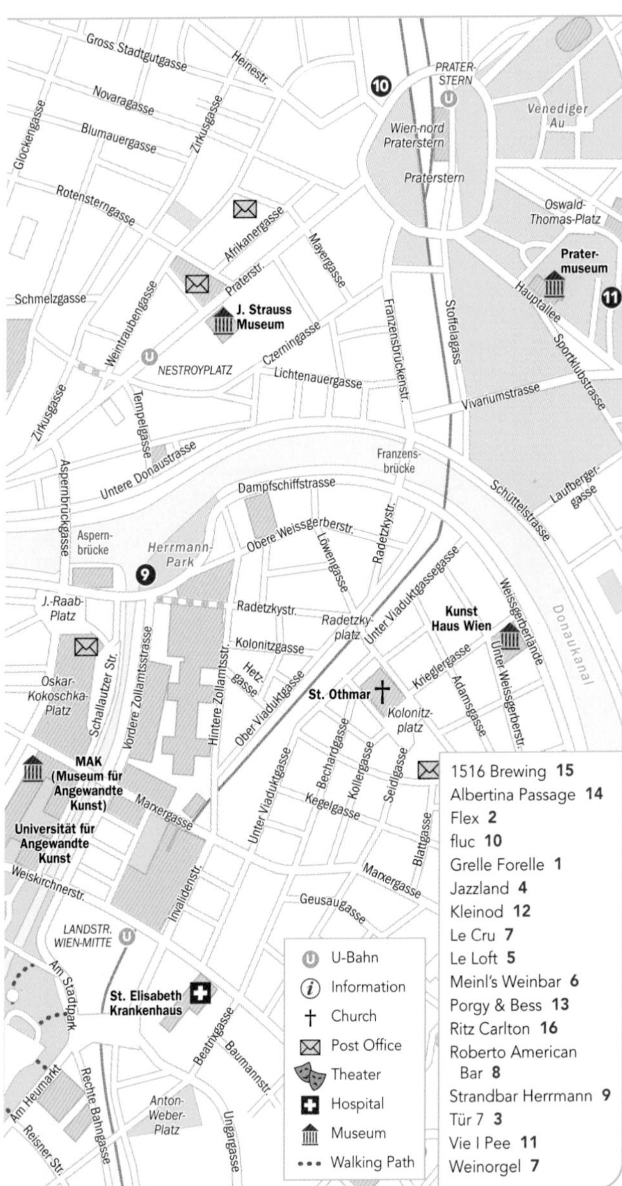
Gross Stadtgutgasse
Heinestr.
Novaragasse
Blumauergasse
Glockengasse
Zirkusgasse
Rotensterngasse
PRATER-STERN
Wien-nord Praterstern
Praterstern
Venediger Au
Oswald-Thomas-Platz
Prater-museum
Hauptallee
Sportklubstrasse
Afrikanergasse
Praterstr.
Mayergasse
Schmelzgasse
Weintraubengasse
J. Strauss Museum
NESTROYPLATZ
Czerningasse
Lichtenauergasse
Franzensbrückenstr.
Stoffelagass
Vivariumstrasse
Tempelgasse
Untere Donaustrasse
Franzens-brücke
Schüttelstrasse
Laufberger-gasse
Aspernbrückgasse
Aspern-brücke
Herrmann-Park
Dampfschiffstrasse
Obere Weissgerberstr.
Löwengasse
Radetzkystr.
Unter Viaduktgassegasse
Weissgerberlände
Donaukanal
J.-Raab-Platz
Radetzky-platz
Kunst Haus Wien
Kolonitzgasse
Unter Weissgerberstr.
Oskar-Kokoschka-Platz
Schallautzer Str.
Vordere Zollamtsstrasse
Hintere Zollamtsstr.
Hetz-gasse
Ober Viaduktgasse
St. Othmar
Krieglergasse
Adamsgasse
Kolonitz-platz
MAK (Museum für Angewandte Kunst)
Marxergasse
Unter Viaduktgasse
Bechardgasse
Kollergasse
Seidlgasse
Kegelgasse
Blattgasse
Universität für Angewandte Kunst
Weiskirchnerstr.
Invalidenstr.
Geusaugasse
LANDSTR. WIEN-MITTE
Am Stadtpark
St. Elisabeth Krankenhaus
Beatrixgasse
Baumannstr.
Am Heumarkt
Rechte Bahngasse
Anton-Weber-Platz
Ungargasse
Reisner Str.
U-Bahn
Information
Church
Post Office
Theater
Hospital
Museum
Walking Path
1516 Brewing 15
Albertina Passage 14
Flex 2
fluc 10
Grelle Forelle 1
Jazzland 4
Kleinod 12
Le Cru 7
Le Loft 5
Meinl's Weinbar 6
Porgy & Bess 13
Ritz Carlton 16
Roberto American Bar 8
Strandbar Herrmann 9
Tür 7 3
Vie I Pee 11
Weinorgel 7

Gürtel Nightlife

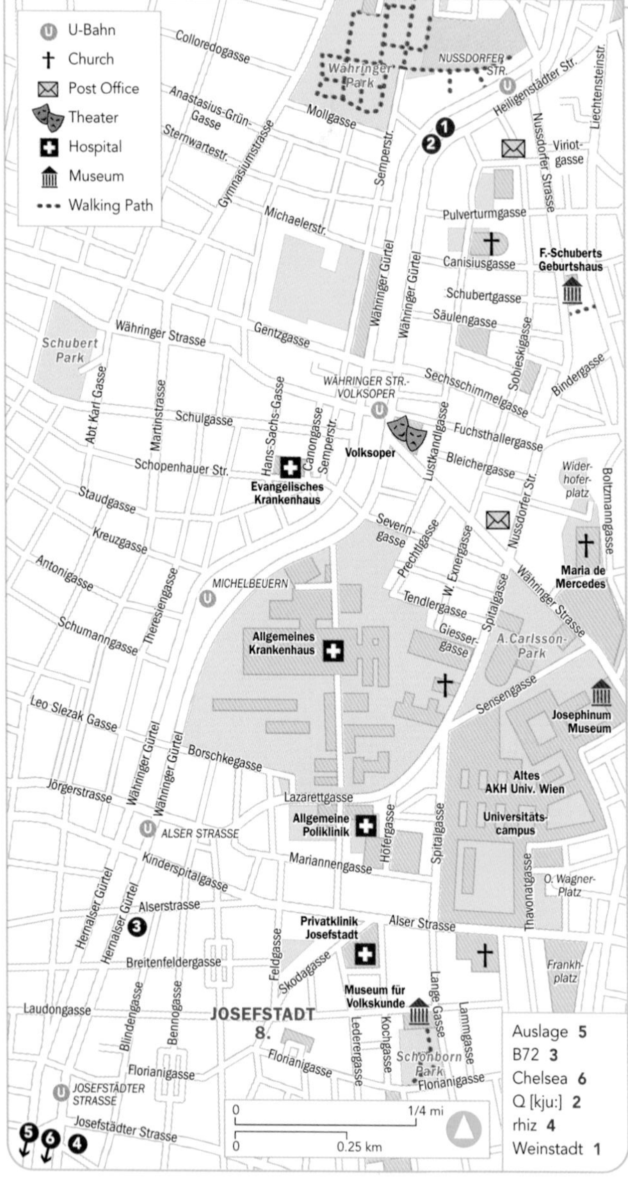
U-Bahn
Church
Post Office
Theater
Hospital
Museum
Walking Path
Colloredogasse
Anastasius-Grün-Gasse
Sternwartestr.
Gymnasiumstrasse
Mollgasse
Währinger Park
NUSSDORFER STR.
Heiligenstädter Str.
Liechtensteinstr.
Semperstr.
Nussdorfer Strasse
Viriot-gasse
Michaelerstr.
Pulverturmgasse
Canisiusgasse
F.-Schuberts Geburtshaus
Währinger Gürtel
Schubertgasse
Säulengasse
Währinger Strasse
Gentzgasse
Schubert Park
Sobieskigasse
Bindergasse
WÄHRINGER STR.-VOLKSOPER
Sechsschimmelgasse
Abt Karl Gasse
Martinstrasse
Hans-Sachs-Gasse
Canongasse
Schulgasse
Fuchsthallergasse
Lustkandlgasse
Volksoper
Bleichergasse
Schopenhauer Str.
Evangelisches Krankenhaus
Wider-hofer-platz
Boltzmanngasse
Staudgasse
Severin-gasse
Kreuzgasse
Prechtlgasse
W. Exnergasse
Nussdorfer Str.
Antonigasse
Theresiengasse
MICHELBEUERN
Maria de Mercedes
Tendlergasse
Spitalgasse
Währinger Strasse
Schumanngasse
Allgemeines Krankenhaus
Giessergasse
A.Carlsson-Park
Sensengasse
Josephinum Museum
Leo Slezak Gasse
Borschkegasse
Altes AKH Univ. Wien
Jörgerstrasse
Lazarettgasse
Allgemeine Poliklinik
Höfergasse
Universitäts-campus
ALSER STRASSE
Kinderspitalgasse
Mariannengasse
Thavonatgasse
O. Wagner-Platz
Hernalser Gürtel
Alserstrasse
Privatklinik Josefstadt
Alser Strasse
Breitenfeldergasse
Feldgasse
Skodagasse
Frankh-platz
Laudongasse
Blindengasse
Bennogasse
JOSEFSTADT 8.
Museum für Volkskunde
Lange Gasse
Lammgasse
Lederergasse
Kochgasse
Schönborn Park
Florianigasse
JOSEFSTÄDTER STRASSE
Josefstädter Strasse
0
1/4 mi
0.25 km

Auslage **5**
B72 **3**
Chelsea **6**
Q [kju:] **2**
rhiz **4**
Weinstadt **1**

Vienna Nightlife A to Z

Bars

★★ Kleinod CITY CENTER This swank cocktail bar with gorgeous Jugendstil details is a great launch pad for an evening out in Vienna. Arrive early to avoid the masses. *Singerstrasse 7. ☎ 01 512 0325. www.kleinod.wien. U-Bahn 1/3 (Stephansplatz). Map p 127.*

★★ Le Cru CITY CENTER The well-informed staff will serve every champagne or sparkling wine that your heart desires. *Petersplatz 8. ☎ 01 533 4791 22. www.lecru.at. U-Bahn 1/3 (Stephansplatz). Map p 127.*

★★★ Le Loft KARMELITER Sip champagne with Vienna's elite in this boxy minimalist bar with wraparound glass and dazzling city vistas on the 18th floor of the Sofitel Hotel. Advance booking for cocktails at sunset is essential at weekends. *Hotel Sofitel (18th floor), Praterstrasse 1. ☎ 01 906 161-0. U-Bahn 1/4 (Schwedenplatz). Map p 127.*

★★ Meinl's Weinbar CITY CENTER Informal yet classy, this beautiful basement wine bar is part of the city's celebrated Meinl delicatessen empire. It serves an impressive range of wines, grappas, champagnes, and brandies by the glass. *Graben 19 (entrance at Näglergasse 8). ☎ 01 532 33 34 6100. U-Bahn 1/3 (Stephansplatz). Map p 127.*

★★ Motto MARGARETEN For over 40 years, this place has been attracting Vienna's cool and suave. Act like a regular and order the beef tartare. After Motto's fourth reinvention, the glamour is still unbroken. *Rüdigergasse 1. ☎ 01 587 0672. www.motto.wien. U-Bahn 4 (Pilgramgasse). Map p 125.*

★★ R&Bar MQ A hub for the creative crowd, this beautiful bar serves eccentric drinks and tiny pizzas with a smile. As soon as you finish one, you'll find yourself ordering another. *Lindengasse 1. ☎ 01 522 44 47. www.dierundbar.com. U-Bahn 3 (Neubaugasse). Map p 125.*

★★★ Ritz-Carlton Rooftop Bar STADTPARK Venture to the top of the city for drink. Day or night, this bar provides the right setting for an unforgettable

Le Loft offers gorgeous city views.

experience with a very attentive staff. *Schubertring 5. ☎ 01 311 88. www.ritzcarlton.com. U-Bahn 4 (Stadtpark). Map p 127.*

★★ Roberto American Bar CITY CENTER Steps from the city center this lively and crowded bar with a plush interior serves great cocktails to the hip and mighty. *Bauernmarkt 11–13. ☎ 01 535 0647. www.robertosbar.com. U-Bahn 1/3 (Stephansplatz). Map p 127.*

★★ Strandbar Herrmann CITY CENTER Soak up the holiday mood at this lively summertime beach bar beside the Danube Canal, with its golden sandy beach, cheerful cocktails, and trendy DJ sounds. *Herrmannpark/Urania. No phone. www.strandbar-herrmann.at. U-Bahn 1/4 (Schwedenplatz). Map p 127.*

★★★ Tür 7 CITY CENTER For some of the best cocktails in town, head to this little bar, hidden on a small street and marked by a golden 7 and a doorbell. Call ahead for a table at this choice establishment. *Buchfeldgasse 7. ☎ 0664 546 3717. www.tür7.at. U-Bahn 2 (Rathaus). Map p 127.*

★ Weinorgel CITY CENTER This tiny brick-clad wine bar is in the vaults of a former Gothic monastery with peanuts and sawdust strewn on the simple wooden floor. *Bäckerstrasse 2. ☎ 01 513 1227. www.weinorgel.at. U-Bahn 1/3 (Stephansplatz). Map p 127.*

Beer Cellars

★ 1516 Brewing Company CITY CENTER For years this pub has been voted the best craft beer pub and brewery in town. In the summer, you can enjoy a cold one outside on the terrace. *Schwarzenbergstrasse 2. ☎ 01 961 1516.*

1516 Brewing Company is a local favorite.

www.1516brewingcompany.com. Tram 2, D, 71 (Schwarzenbergplatz). Map p 127.

★ Siebenstern Bräuwirtshaus NEUBAU A lively brewpub with its own range of eight distinctive beers brewed in situ and served in rustic cellar rooms or under the shade of chestnut trees in the beer garden. Try the Chili Beer. *Siebensterngasse 19. ☎ 01 523 8697. www.7stern.at. Tram 49 (Stiftgasse). Map p 125.*

Dance Clubs

★★★ Auslage GÜRTEL Attracting talented artists with a solid sound system, this club is a prime location to party all night long to pumping music. *Lerchenfelder Gürtel 43. U-Bahn 6 (Lerchenfelderstrasse). Map p 128.*

★ Flex ALSERGRUND The best dance club in town, famous for its awesome sound system, with top-notch DJs and a huge variety of cutting-edge beats, including techno, Indie, and underground rock. Go on Tuesday nights for Viennese electronica at its best.

Gürtel Party Tour

The Gürtel ring-road is currently the nerve center of Vienna's nightlife. Beneath the Jugendstil arches of the city railway designed by Otto Wagner lies a mixed bag of dance clubs, pubs, and bars. It's the in-place to party all night long to the sound of trains rumbling overhead. START: **Josefstädter Strasse U-Bahn station.**

★★ **rhiz** One of the cradles of Vienna's renowned electronica scene, this laid-back Internet cafe-bar remains a popular platform for new projects and experiments in electronic music. *Stadtbahnbögen 37–38, Lerchenfelder Gürtel.* ☎ *01 409 2505. www.rhiz.org. Map p 128.*

★ **B72** Situated under Arch 72 of the Gürtel, this old-timer's specialty is alternative live music and electronic sounds. Dark, smoky, and split-level, it draws a lively young crowd. *Stadtbahnbögen 72–73, Hernalser Gürtel.* ☎ *01 409 2128. www.b72.at. Map p 128.*

★★★ **Q [kju:]** There's always a great party mood at Q, where the clientele are young and carefree, the cocktails potent, the barmen flashy, and the dance music loud. It's easy to find, occupying three arches bathed in pink, red, and green fluorescent light. Relaxed door policy. *Stadtbahnbögen 142–144, Währinger Gürtel.* ☎ *01 804 5055. www.kju-bar.at. Map p 128.*

★★ **Weinstadt** This soothing wine bar, simply decorated with bare brick vaults, is the perfect place to relax with friends. It offers an excellent choice of local and international wines, including chalkboard specials, to wash down platters of cold cuts, cheeses, and olives. *Stadtbahnbögen 154, Währinger Gürtel.* ☎ *0664 734 11 786. www.weinstadt.cc. Map p 128.*

★★★ **Chelsea** A grungy live-music venue for the young or young-at-heart. Here, the lack of a dress code, the cheap beer, and the relaxed atmosphere guarantee a laid-back evening. *Stadtbahnbögen 29–30, Lerchenfelder Gürtel.* ☎ *01 407 9309. www.chelsea.co.at. Map p 128.*

Donaukanal (by the Augartenbrücke). ☎ *01 533 7525. www.flex.at.U-Bahn 2/4 (Schottenring). Map p 127.*

★★ **Grelle Forelle** SPITTELAU A varied, eclectic sound selection from techno to hip-hop. A bit off the beaten path, this club is always worth a visit. *Spittelauer Lände 12 (on the waterfront). www.grelleforelle.com U-Bahn 4/6 (Spittelau). Map p 127.*

★★ **passage** RINGSTRASSE This futuristic club in a former subway has minimalist decor and an ultra-cool lighting system. Backdrops morph to suit varying sounds (house, disco, hip-hop, funk, and so on) on different nights. *Babenburgerpassage, Burgring 1.* ☎ *01 961 8800. www.sunshine.at. Tram 1/2/D (Burgring). Map p 125.*

★ **Vie I Pee** PRATER This classic hip-hop and soul club—just steps from the Prater's rollercoasters—serves deep sounds for tonight's it crowd. *Waldsteingartenstrasse 135. U-Bahn 2 (Messe-Prater). Map p 127.*

★★★ **Volksgarten** RINGSTRASSE Vienna's beautiful people love this hot and happening complex. It's all here—house, soul, techno, funk, salsa . . . plus an idyllic garden and an electronic roof that opens for moonlit dancing in summer. *Burgring 1. ☎ 01 532 4241. www.volksgarten.at. Fri–Sat from 11pm. Tram 1/2/D (Burgring). Map p 125.*

Gay & Lesbian

★★ **Café Savoy** NASCHMARKT This long-established gay bar offers a traditional cafe atmosphere, with plush furnishings, giant mirrors, and stucco decor. *Linke Wienzeile 36. ☎ 699 181 26391. www.savoy.at. U-Bahn 4 (Kettenbrückengasse). Map p 125.*

★★ **Mango Bar** NASCHMARKT Every night a young, mostly male crowd dances to the hits at this mirror-lined bar. Kick-start or end your party here. *Laimgrubengasse 3. ☎ 01 920 4714. www.why-not.at. U-Bahn 4 (Kettenbrückengasse). Map p 125.*

Live Music

★★★ **Albertina Passage** RINGSTRASSE This dinner club next to the opera was built into an old underpass. It serves food and drink to Vienna's haute monde. Dress to impress. *Opernring/Operngasse. ☎ 01 512 0813. www.albertinapassage.at. U-Bahn 1/4 (Karlsplatz). Map p 127.*

★ **Chaya Fuera** NEUBAU Great cocktails, minimal design, and an eclectic assortment of live music acts that will have you dancing until the wee hours. *Kandlgasse 19–21. ☎ 01 544 0036 250. www.chayafuera.com. U-Bahn 6 (Burggasse). Map p 125.*

★ **fluc** PRATER This rugged bar is one of Vienna's best places to hear live, experimental, electronic, and Indie acts. Fluc Wanne (in the basement) stages electro and disco parties and a range of DJ sounds. *Praterstern 5. ☎ 01 218 2824. www.fluc.at. U-Bahn 1/2 (Praterstern). Map p 127.*

★★ **Jazzland** CITY CENTER For over 30 years, this brick-built club in a cellar under Ruprechtskirche (St. Rupert's Church) has showcased the best of Austrian and international jazz—blues, Dixie, and swing to modern jazz. *Franz-Josefs-Kai 29. ☎ 01 533 2575. www.jazzland.at. Mon–Sat. U-Bahn 1/4 (Schwedenplatz). Map p 127.*

★★ **Porgy & Bess** STADTPARK This relaxed, modern jazz joint in a former porn cinema is hugely popular thanks to its world-class eclectic program of homegrown, international modern, and non-traditional jazz acts. *Riemergasse 11. ☎ 01 512 8811. www.porgy.at. U-Bahn 3 (Stubentor). Map p 127.*

8 The Best Arts & Entertainment

Arts & Entertainment Best Bets

You'll find the best acoustics at Musikverein.

Best **Acoustics**

★★★ Musikverein, *Karlsplatz/ Bösendorferstrasse 12 (p 137)*

Best **Jazz Joint**

★★★ Porgy & Bess, *Riemergasse 11 (p 139)*

Best **Show for Kids**

★★ Lilarum Puppet Theater, *Göllnergasse 8 (p 140)*

Best **"Jungle" in Town**

★★ Dschungel Wien, *Museumsplatz 1 (p 140)*

Best **Modern Dance**

★★★ Tanzquartier Wien, *Museums Quartier (p 138)*

The **Hottest Ticket in Town**

★★★ Staatsoper, *Opernring 2 (p 139)*

Best **Ecclesiastical Sounds**

★★ Augustinerkirche, *Augustinerstrasse 3 (p 137)*

Best **Retro Cinema**

★★★ Burgkino, *Opernring 19 (p 138)*

Best **Public Viewing**

Film Festival Rathausplatz, *Rathausplatz (p 138)*

Best **Chance of Getting Standing-Room Tickets**

★★ Volksoper, *Währingerstrasse 78 (p 139)*

Best **Ballet**

★★★ Das Wiener Staatsballett, *Staatsoper, Opernring 2 (p 138)*

Previous page: Mozart souvenirs.

City Center A&E

Akademietheater 11
Arena Wien 14
Augustinerkirche 3
Bösendorfer Hall at the Mozarthaus 7
Burgkino 4
Das Wiener Staatsballett 5
Kammeroper 8
Konzerthaus 10
Lilarum Puppet Theater 13
Musikfilmfestival 1
Musikverein 9
Porgy & Bess 12
Staatsoper 6
Wiener Sängerknaben 2

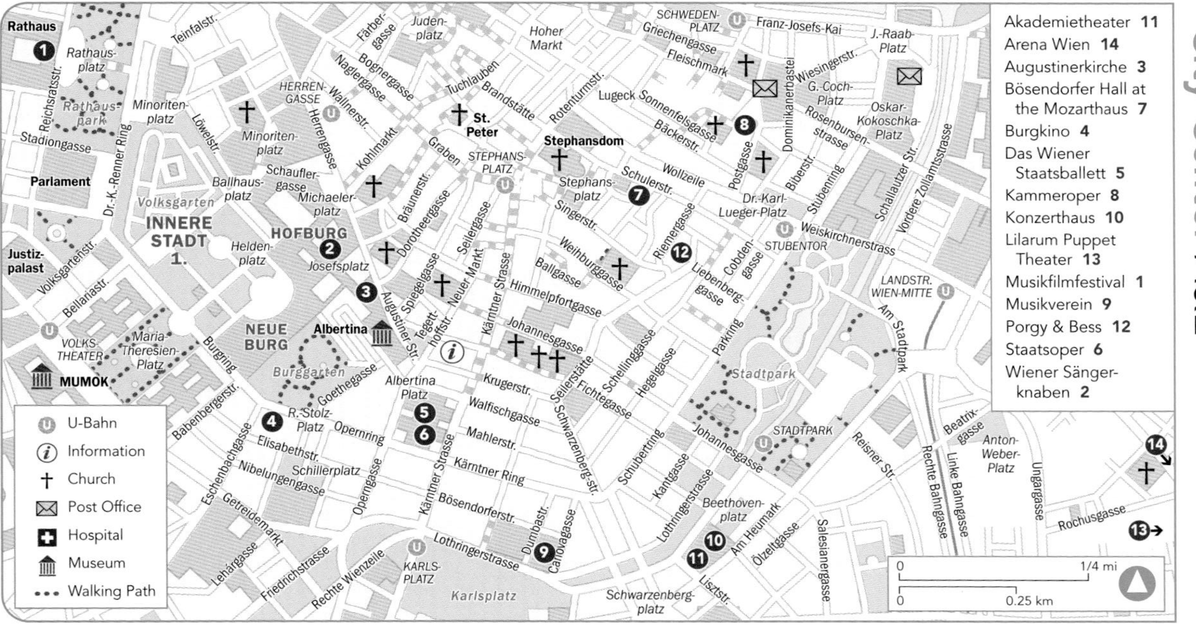

MQ A&E

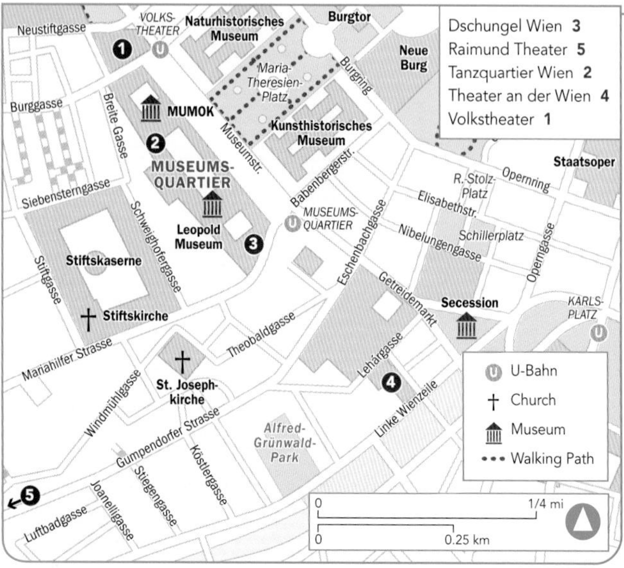

Dschungel Wien 3
Raimund Theater 5
Tanzquartier Wien 2
Theater an der Wien 4
Volkstheater 1

U-Bahn
Church
Museum
Walking Path

City Center West A&E

U-Bahn

Burgtheater 5
Schauspielhaus 2
Theater in der Josefstadt 3
Vienna's English Theatre 4
Volksoper 1

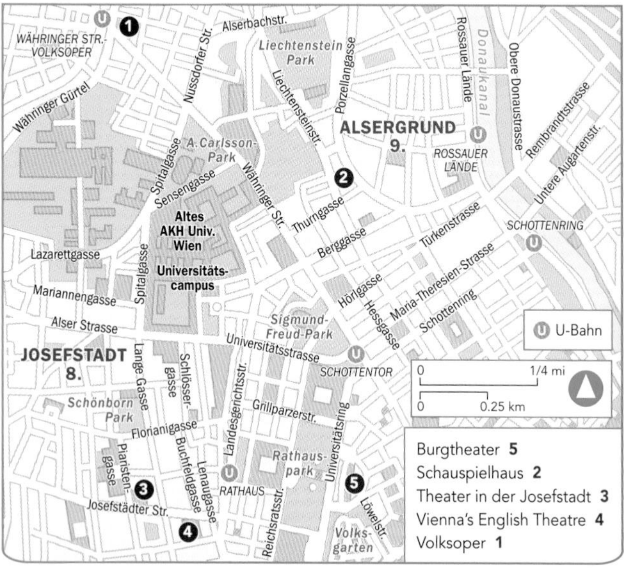

Arts & Entertainment A to Z

Classical Music

★★ Augustinerkirche HOFBURG The Gothic Augustinian church boasts fine acoustics, and sacred works by Haydn, Mozart, and Schubert are frequently performed here during Sunday Mass (11am). *Augustinerstrasse 3 (entrance on Josefsplatz). ☎ 01 533 70990. www.hochamt.at. Free admission. U-Bahn 3 (Herrengasse). Map p 135.*

★ Bösendorfer Hall at the Mozarthaus CITY CENTER Listen to Mozart, Haydn, Schubert, and Beethoven chamber music in this intimate space. Check the website for concert info. *Domgasse 5. ☎ 01 504 6651-311. www.mozarthausvienna.at. Tickets €20–€25. U-Bahn 1/3 (Stephansplatz). Map p 135.*

★★ Konzerthaus STADTPARK A major venue for classical symphony and chamber music, performed by the resident Vienna Symphony Orchestra and other renowned ensembles. *Lothringerstrasse 20. ☎ 01 242 002. konzerthaus.at. Ticket prices vary. U-Bahn 4 (Stadtpark). Map p 135.*

★★★ Musikverein CITY CENTER It is hailed as one of the concert halls with the best acoustics in the world. It's also the site for the city's celebrated New Year's Day concert, performed by the Vienna Philharmonic Orchestra, one of the world's finest. *Karlsplatz/Bösendorferstrasse 12. ☎ 01 505 8190. www.musikverein.at. Tickets €6 (standing room) to €79. U-Bahn 1/2/4 (Karlsplatz). Map p 135.*

★★★ Wiener Sängerknaben HOFBURG Founded over 500 years ago, the Vienna Boys' Choir is

How to Get Tickets

Get details of what's on when from tourist offices, or in the city magazine *Metropole* (www.metropole.at), published monthly and available online and from a *tabak* (newsagent) or a sidewalk kiosk. Tickets can be bought in advance directly from the individual venues or online at ticketing agencies such as Austria Ticket Online (www.austriaticket.at) or Club Ticket (www.clubticket.at).

The Wien-Ticket Pavilion ticket booth beside the opera house (Karajanplatz; ☎ 01 588 85; Mon–Sat 10am–7pm) sells tickets for all venues. The Bundestheaterkassen (State ticket office) sells tickets for the Akademietheater, Burgtheater, Staatsoper, and Volksoper (Operngasse 2; ☎ 01 514 447 880; www.bundestheater.at; Mon–Fri 8am–6pm, Sat–Sun 9am–noon; Tram 1/2/D [Oper]).

Book as early as you can: Ticket sales at many venues, including the Staatsoper, Volksoper, and Musikverein, begin months ahead of the performance. Some venues offer limited numbers of last-minute standing-only tickets. The Staatsoper, for instance, releases 567 standing-room tickets 80 minutes before the performance starts—a bargain if you're patient enough to stand in line.

For classical concerts head to Konzerthaus.

perhaps the most famous of its kind in the world. Hear them sing Mass at the Hofburg's ancient Burgkapelle on Sundays (mid-Sept to June) at 9:15am. *Schweizerhof.* ☎ *01 553 9927. www.hofburgkapelle.at, www.wsk.at. Tickets €10–€36. U-Bahn 3 (Herrengasse). Map p 135.*

Cinema

★★★ Burgkino RINGSTRASSE This tiny, old-fashioned cinema shows only English-language movies, and regular late-night screenings of *The Third Man* (set in post-World-War-II Vienna) in its original English language version. *Opernring 19.* ☎ *01 587 8406. www.burgkino.at. Tickets €7–€8.50. Tram 1/2/D (Oper). Map p 135.*

★★ Film Festival Rathausplatz RINGSTRASSE Vienna has 15 different venues for open-air cinema during the summer festival season. The Film Festival on Rathausplatz is a great choice. It takes place from mid-July to early September. There are international food stands and bars lining the square and when darkness falls, free screenings of opera and concerts are shown against a dramatic illuminated backdrop of the City Hall. *Rathausplatz. http://filmfestival-rathausplatz.at. Tram 2 (Rathaus).*

Dance

★★★ Das Wiener Staatsballett CITY CENTER World-class ballet productions, plus a glittering list of guest artists. *Staatsoper, Opernring 2.* ☎ *01 514 440. Tickets €3–€4 (standing only), €12–€186. U-Bahn 1/2/4 (Karlsplatz), Tram 1/2/D (Oper). Map p 135.*

★★★ Tanzquartier Wien MQ Vienna's leading dance center hosts an ambitious program of local and international troupes, with the main emphasis on experimental dance. It also hosts the international dance festival Impulstanz in July and August. *Halle E+G, Studios, MQ, Museumsplatz 1.* ☎ *01 581 3591. www.tqw.at. U-Bahn 2 (MQ). Map p 136.*

Live Music

★★★ Arena Wien LANDSTRASSE A former squatting ground in the far reaches of the 3rd district, this alternative venue has cult status. With the capacity for 3,000 concertgoers, Arena features world-famous rock acts as well as music festivals and leading Austrian and European rock artists. *Baumgasse 80.* ☎ *01 798 8595. www.arena.co.at. U-Bahn 3 (Erdberg). Map p 135.*

★★★ **Porgy & Bess** CITY CENTER This downtown venue boasts the hottest jazz acts from all over the world as well as a small but choice selection of rock and pop artists. *Staatsoper, Riemergasse 11.* ☎ *01 503 70 09. Tickets €3–€4 (standing only), €18–€32. U-Bahn 3 (Stubentor). Map p 135.*

Opera & Musicals

★★ **Kammeroper** CITY CENTER This small opera house puts on a varied repertoire of everything from classic operetta and *opera buffa* (comic opera) to rock opera and more quirky contemporary musical theater. *Fleischmarkt 24.* ☎ *01 512 0100-77. www.wienerkammeroper.at. Tickets €10–€51. U-Bahn 1/4 (Schwedenplatz). Map p 135.*

★★ **Raimund Theater** MARIAHILF This theater has made its name as the definitive venue for musicals and musical comedy, premiering the German-language versions of blockbuster hits such as *Cats* and *Phantom of the Opera*. *Wallgasse 18–20.* ☎ *01 588 85. www.musicalvienna.at. Tickets €5 (standing only), €20–€125. U-Bahn 6 (Gumpendorfer Strasse). Map p 136.*

★★★ **Staatsoper** CITY CENTER One of Europe's finest opera houses, with daily performances from September to June, and children's opera in summer. *Opernring 2.* ☎ *01 514 447 880 (tickets). www.wiener-staatsoper.at. Tickets €3–€4 (standing only), €8–€250. Tram 1/2/D (Oper). Map p 135.*

★★ **Theater an der Wien** NASCHMARKT Founded in 1801 as an opera house, this plush theater premiered Mozart's *Die Zauberflöte*, Beethoven's *Fidelio*, and Johann Strauss's *Die Fledermaus*. Today, it's Vienna's second opera house and its program changes monthly. *Linke Wienzeile 6.* ☎ *01 58885. www.theater-wien.at. Tickets €12–€160. U-Bahn 1/2/4 (Karlsplatz). Map p 136.*

★★ **Volksoper** ALSERGRUND Affordable and fun, the "People's Opera" is the city's leading operetta house. It also stages light opera, classical musicals, and ballet. *Währingerstrasse 78.* ☎ *01 514 44-3318. www.volksoper.at. Tickets €3–€4 (standing only), €6–€89. U-Bahn 6 (Volksoper). Map p 136.*

Theater

★ **Akademietheater** STADTPARK This excellent repertory theater (a second venue for the Burgtheater) offers productions

Vienna Boys' Choir

The Vienna Boys' Choir (Wiener Sängerknaben, www.wsk.at) was founded in 1498 as part of the imperial choir. Originally, it comprised just 12 boys. Over the centuries it grew in size, and counted musical luminaries such as Haydn and Schubert among its members. Nowadays Vienna's leading choir is a highly commercialized and rather overhyped organization. Four separate choirs, each consisting of 24 angelic choirboys, continuously tour the world, no longer dressed in imperial costumes, but in twee blue sailor suits. In Vienna, they sing Sunday Mass in the Burgkapelle and give occasional concerts in the Musikverein.

Book your tickets in advance for a night at the opera.

ranging from classic to contemporary drama. *Lisztstrasse 1. ☎ 01 514 44-4140. www.akademietheater.at. Tickets €2.50 (standing only), €3.50–€59. U-Bahn 4 (Stadtpark). Map p 135.*

★★★ Burgtheater RINGSTRASSE Actors dream of standing on this stage, what many deem the best theater in the German-speaking world. The resplendent foyer has stairway frescoes painted by Klimt. *Dr-Karl-Lueger-Ring 2. ☎ 01 514 44-4140. www.burgtheater.at. Tickets €2.50 (standing only), €3.50–€59. Tram 1/2/D (Burgtheater). Map p 136.*

★★ kids Dschungel Wien MQ Language is no barrier for kids at the lively "Jungle" family arts center with theater, dance, puppet shows, video, and music workshops for kids aged 2 and over. *Museumsplatz 1. ☎ 01 522 0720-20. www.dschungelwien.at. Tickets €9. U-Bahn 2 (MQ). Map p 136.*

★★ kids Lilarum Puppet Theater LANDSTRASSE Lilarum's charming hand-and-rod puppets make for enchanting theater for kids ages 3 to 10. The stories transcend language barriers. *Göllnergasse 8. ☎ 01 710 2666. www.lilarum.at. Tickets €8.50. U-Bahn 3 (Kardinal-Nagl-Platz). Map p 135.*

★★★ Schauspielhaus ALSERGRUND Of Vienna's 50-plus theaters, the Schauspielhaus is at the forefront of contemporary productions—often of a thought-provoking, controversial, or alternative nature. *Porzellangasse 19. ☎ 01 317 0101. www.schauspielhaus.at. Tickets €20 adults; €10 students; €15 concessions. Tram D (Bauernfeldplatz). Map p 136.*

★ Theater in der Josefstadt JOSEFSTADT One of Vienna's oldest, best-loved, and most ornate theaters, founded in 1788, and known for its lightweight plays, comedies, and farces. *Josefstädterstrasse 26. ☎ 01 42700-300. www.josefstadt.org. Tickets €4 (standing only), €7–€74. Bus 13A (Theater in der Josefstadt). Map p 136.*

★★ Vienna's English Theatre JOSEFSTADT Continental Europe's oldest English-language theater was founded in 1963 and offers year-round performances of English and American classics, comedies, and contemporary works. *Josefgasse 12. ☎ 01 402 12600. www.englishtheatre.at. Tickets €24–€47. U-Bahn 2 (Rathaus). Map p 136.*

★ Volkstheater MQ With an auditorium holding nearly a thousand people, this is one of the city's largest theaters. It puts on an exceptionally broad repertoire, embracing classic and modern plays and operetta. *Neustiftgasse 1. ☎ 01 52 111-400. www.volkstheater.at. Tickets €5–€48. U-Bahn 2/3 (Volkstheater). Map p 136.* ●

9 The Best Lodging

Lodging Best Bets

The Sacher is Vienna's most historic hotel.

Best **Urban Luxury**
★★★ Sofitel Vienna Stephansdom, *Praterstrasse 1 (p 154)*

Best **"Beach" Hotel**
★★ Strand Hotel Alte Donau, *Wagramerstrasse 51 (p 154)*

Best **Boutique Hotel**
★★★ Altstadt, *Kirchengasse 41 (p 148)*

Best for a **Romantic Getaway**
★★★ Hollmann Beletage, *Köllnerhofgasse 6 (p 150)*

Best **Spa Hotel**
★★ The Ring, *Kärtner Ring 8 (p 153)*

Best **See-and-be-Seen Hotel**
★★★ Park Hyatt, *Am Hof 2 (p 152)*

Best for **Families**
★★ 25hours Hotel, *Lerchenfelderstrasse 1–3 (p 148)*

Most **Historic Hotel (also Best for Chocolate Cake)**
★★★ Sacher, *Philharmonikerstrasse 4 (p 153)*

Biggest **Splurge**
★★★ Palais Coburg Residenz, *Coburgbastei 4 (p 152)*

Best for **Design Buffs**
★★★ Hotel Daniel, *Landstrasser Gürtel 5 (p 151)*

Most **Eccentric Decor**
★★ Kuchlmasterei, *Obere Weissgerberstrasse 6 (p 152)*

Most **Centrally Located**
★★★ Do & Co, *Stephansplatz 12 (p 149)*

Most **Socially Aware Hotel**
★★ Magdas Hotel, *Laufbergergasse 12 (p 152)*

Most **Spectacular Cityscapes**
★★★ Ritz-Carlton, *Schubertring 5–7 (p 153)*

Best for a **Homey Feel**
★★ Schreiners Essen & Wohnen, *Westbahnstrasse 42 (p 154)*

Most **Royal Welcome**
★★★ Imperial, *Kärtner Ring 16 (p 151)*

Previous page: Do & Co's delightful Onyx Bar.

City Center South Lodging

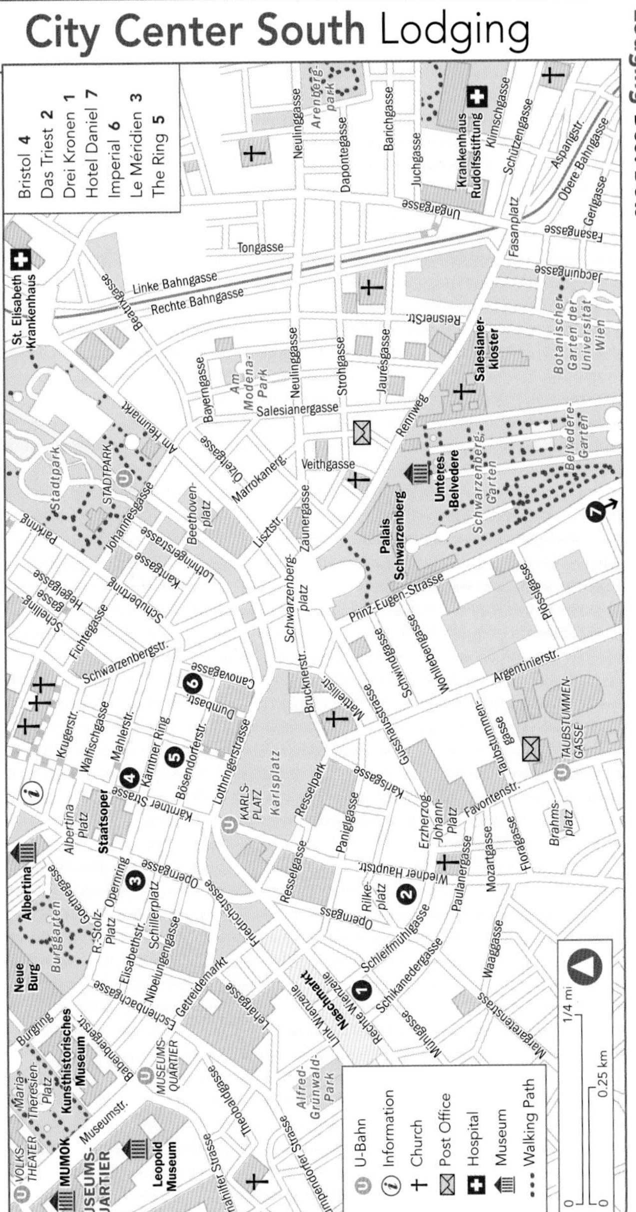

City Center Lodging

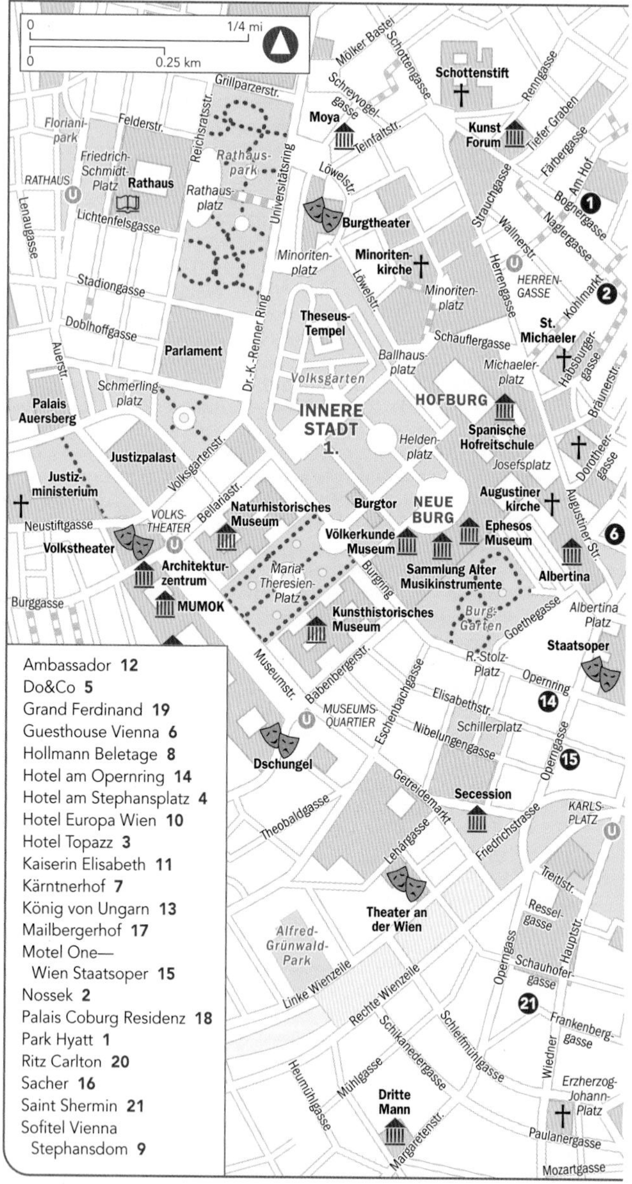

Ambassador **12**
Do&Co **5**
Grand Ferdinand **19**
Guesthouse Vienna **6**
Hollmann Beletage **8**
Hotel am Opernring **14**
Hotel am Stephansplatz **4**
Hotel Europa Wien **10**
Hotel Topazz **3**
Kaiserin Elisabeth **11**
Kärntnerhof **7**
König von Ungarn **13**
Mailbergerhof **17**
Motel One—Wien Staatsoper **15**
Nossek **2**
Palais Coburg Residenz **18**
Park Hyatt **1**
Ritz Carlton **20**
Sacher **16**
Saint Shermin **21**
Sofitel Vienna Stephansdom **9**

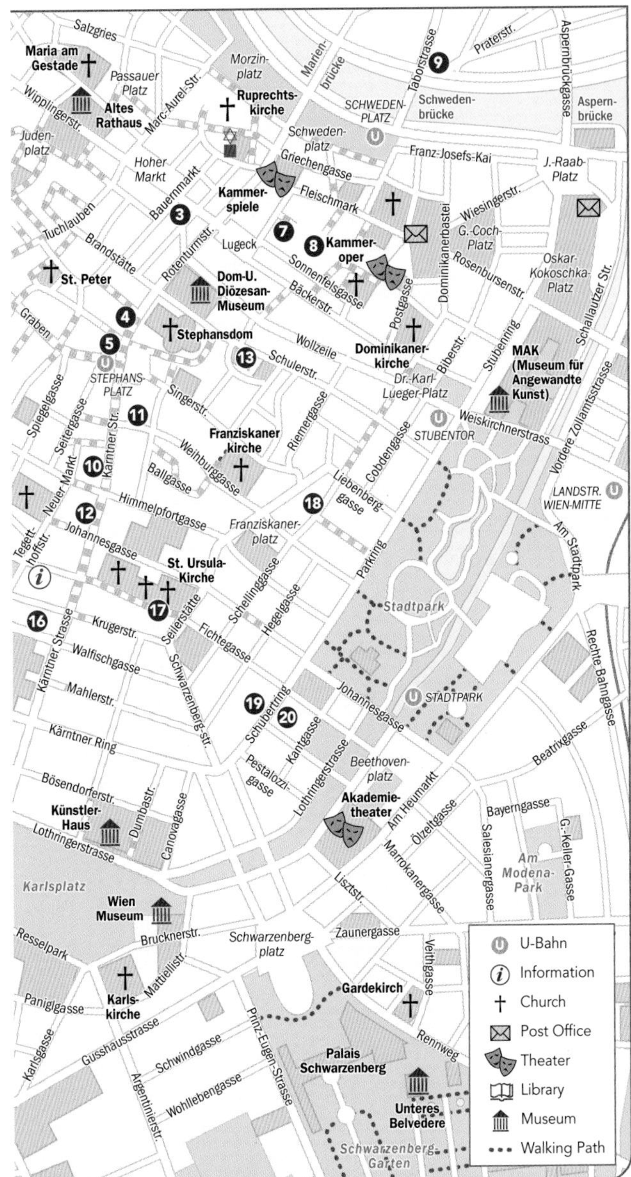
Salzgries
Maria am Gestade
Passauer Platz
Morzin-platz
Marien-brücke
Taborstrasse
Praterstr.
Asperbrückgasse
Wipplingerstr.
Altes Rathaus
Marc-Aurel-Str.
Ruprechts-kirche
SCHWEDEN-PLATZ
Schweden-brücke
Aspern-brücke
Juden-platz
Hoher Markt
Schweden-platz
Griechengasse
Franz-Josefs-Kai
J.-Raab-Platz
Bauernmarkt
Kammer-spiele
Fleischmarkt
Tuchlauben
Wiesingerstr.
G.-Coch-Platz
Brandstätte
Rotenturmstr.
Lugeck
Kammer-oper
Dominikanerbastei
Rosenbursenstr.
Oskar-Kokoschka-Platz
St. Peter
Dom-U. Diözesan-Museum
Sonnenfelsgasse
Bäckerstr.
Postgasse
Schallautzer Str.
Graben
Stephansdom
Wollzeile
Dominikaner-kirche
Biberstr.
Stubenring
MAK (Museum für Angewandte Kunst)
Schulerstr.
STEPHANS-PLATZ
Dr.-Karl-Lueger-Platz
Spiegelgasse
Seitergasse
Singerstr.
Riemergasse
Weiskirchnerstrass
STUBENTOR
Vordere Zollamtsstrasse
Kärntner Str.
Franziskaner kirche
Cobdengasse
Neuer Markt
Weihburggasse
Ballgasse
Liebenberg-gasse
LANDSTR. WIEN-MITTE
Himmelpfortgasse
Franziskaner-platz
Tegett-hoffstr.
Johannesgasse
Parkring
Am Stadtpark
St. Ursula-Kirche
Schellinggasse
Hegelgasse
Stadtpark
Seilerstätte
Krugerstr.
Fichtegasse
Rechte Bahngasse
Kärntner Strasse
Walfischgasse
Schwarzenberg-str.
Mahlerstr.
Schubertring
STADTPARK
Kantgasse
Kärntner Ring
Lothringerstrasse
Beethoven-platz
Beatrixgasse
Pestalozzi-gasse
Bösendorferstr.
Am Heumarkt
Akademie-theater
Künstler-Haus
Dumbastr.
Canovagasse
Ölzeltgasse
Bayerngasse
Salesianergasse
G.-Keller-Gasse
Am Modena-Park
Marrokanergasse
Lisztstr.
Karlsplatz
Wien Museum
Bruckner str.
Schwarzenberg-platz
Zaunergasse
Veithgasse
Resselpark
Mattiellistr.
Gardekirch
Karls-kirche
Paniglgasse
Gusshausstrasse
Rennweg
Karlsgasse
Schwindgasse
Prinz-Eugen-Strasse
Palais Schwarzenberg
Argentinierstr.
Wohllebengasse
Unteres Belvedere
Schwarzenberg-Garten
U-Bahn
Information
Church
Post Office
Theater
Library
Museum
Walking Path

City Center West Lodging

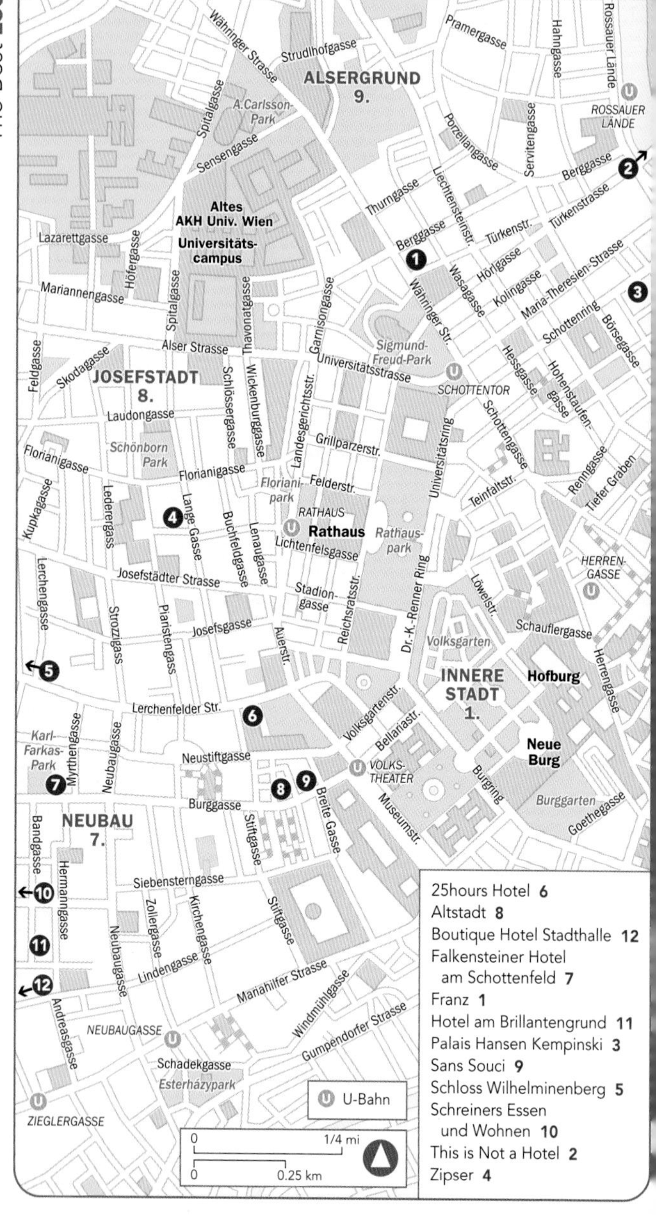

Danube Lodging

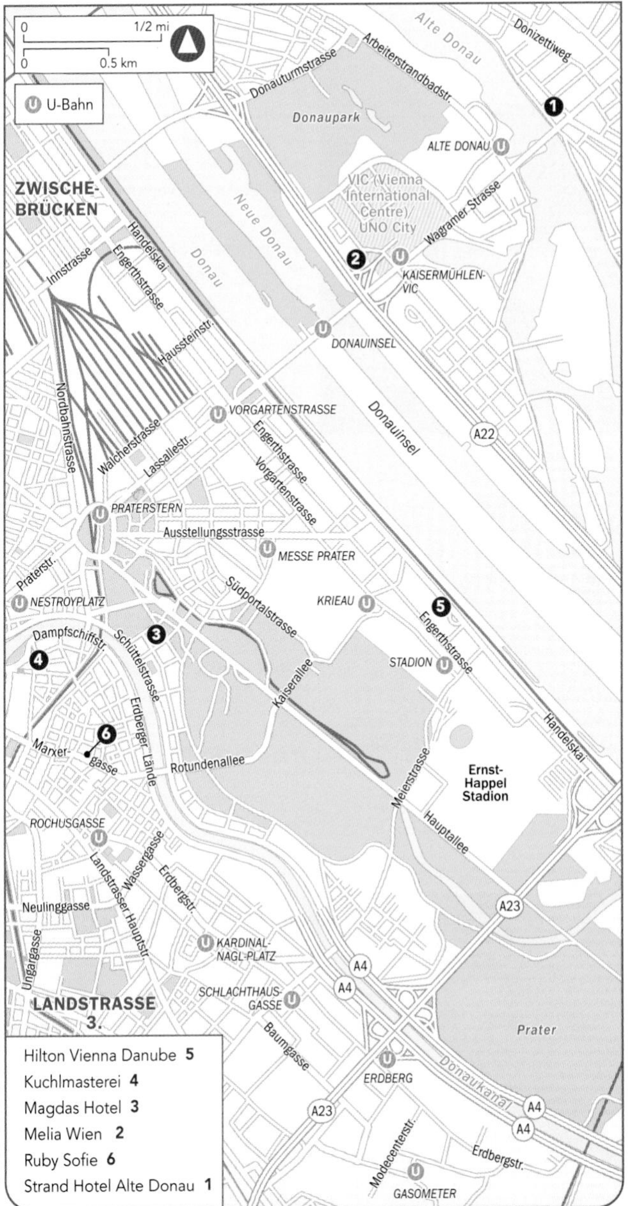

Hilton Vienna Danube 5
Kuchlmasterei 4
Magdas Hotel 3
Melia Wien 2
Ruby Sofie 6
Strand Hotel Alte Donau 1

Vienna Lodging A to Z

The stylish Altstadt.

★★ 25hours Hotel MQ Former student housing turned into a circus-themed hotel, or as the neon sign outside states: "We are all mad here." A charming staff and the hotel's obvious love for design details make this a favorite among young travelers and families. *Lerchenfelderstrasse 1–3. ☎ 01 521 510. www.25hours-hotels.com. 219 units. Doubles €110–€220. U-Bahn 2/3 (Volksgarten). Map p 146.*

★★★ Altstadt SPITTELBERG Exotic and decadent yet homey, this boutique hotel in a converted patrician house oozes style, with lavish wallpapers, velvets, and free-standing bathtubs. *Kirchengasse 41. ☎ 01 522 6666. www.altstadt.at. 42 units. Doubles €139–€169 w/breakfast. U-Bahn 2/3 (Volkstheater). Map p 146.*

★ Ambassador CITY CENTER Add your name to the visitors' book alongside such luminaries as composer Franz Lehár, actress Marlene Dietrich, and writer Mark Twain at this upscale hotel. *Kärtnerstrasse 22/Neuer Markt 5. ☎ 01 961 610. www.ambassador.at. 86 units. Doubles €322–€584. U-Bahn 1/3 (Stephansplatz). Map p 144.*

★ Boutique Hotel Stadthalle STADTHALLE This friendly family-run hotel offers clean, simple rooms and fresh, organic breakfast. The green facade is an eye-catcher in summer. *Hackengasse 20. ☎ 01 982 4272. www.hotelstadthalle.at. 79 units. Doubles €127–€167 w/breakfast. U-Bahn 6 (Burggasse/Stadthalle). Map p 146.*

★★ kids Bristol RINGSTRASSE The exuberant marble lobby of this landmark hotel belies the tasteful *fin-de-siècle* charm of its rooms.

Converted from a 17th-century stable the Das Triest now features a modern aesthetic.

A stylish suite at the well-located Do & Co.

For the ultimate indulgence, get the Prince of Wales suite. *Kärntner Ring 1. ☎ 01 515 160. www.luxurycollection.com/bristol. 140 units. Doubles €279–€529. Tram 1/2/D (Oper). Map p 143.*

★★★ **Das Triest** MARIAHILF Formerly used as a stable on the Vienna–Trieste stagecoach route in the 17th century, this boutique hotel now has chic modern interiors designed by Sir Terence Conran, and attracts an arty clientele. *Wiedner Hauptstrasse 12. ☎ 01 589 180. www.dastriest.at. 72 units. Doubles €220–€292 w/breakfast. Tram 62/65 (Paulanergasse). Map p 143.*

★★★ **Do & Co** CITY CENTER Sophisticated suede walls, teak floors, and deep sofas are the hallmarks of this glossy, bulbous hotel and rooftop restaurant in the iconic Haas Haus, with unparalleled views over Stephansplatz and the cathedral. *Stephansplatz 12. ☎ 01 24188. www.doco.com. 43 units. Doubles €225–€410. U-Bahn 1/3 (Stephansplatz). Map p 144.*

★★ **Drei Kronen** NASCHMARKT The "Three Crowns" (of Austria, Hungary, and Bohemia) are carved on the facade of this simple but comfortable hotel. Ask for a room overlooking the Naschmarkt. *Schliefmühlgasse 25. ☎ 01 587 3289. www.hotel3kronen.at. 41 units. Doubles €65–€149 w/breakfast. U-Bahn 1/2/4 (Karlsplatz). Map p 143.*

★★ **Falkensteiner Hotel am Schottenfeld** NEUBAU Dramatic colored-lighting effects distinguish this trendy, modern hotel. It attracts a young and savvy clientele. *Schottenfeldgasse 74. ☎ 01 526 5181. www.schottenfeld.falkensteiner.com. 144 units. Doubles €105–€230. Tram 48 (Zieglergasse/Burggasse). Map p 146.*

★★ **Franz** SCHOTTENRING Furnished in old-Viennese baroque style, this comfortable guesthouse is a popular budget choice. Its interconnected rooms are good for families. *Währingerstrasse 12. ☎ 01 310 4040-0. www.hotelpensionfranz.at. 24 units. Doubles €79–€95 w/breakfast. U-Bahn 2 (Schottentor). Map p 146.*

★★★ **Grand Ferdinand** CITY CENTER Picturesque views of the city, plus an open-air pool, impeccable design, and affordable rates make this hotel a perfect choice. It's also the only five-star hotel that offers a designer dorm for just €30 per person a night. *Schubertring 10–12. ☎ 01 91 880. www.grandferdinand.com. 188 units. Doubles*

€200–€440. U-Bahn 4 (Stadtpark). Map p 144.

★★ The Guesthouse Vienna CITY CENTER Designed by Sir Terence Conran, this boutique hotel is perfectly situated next to the Opera and the Albertina in the center of Vienna, but it still manages to feel cozy and honest. Don't miss the delectable breakfast. *Führichgasse 10. ☎ 01 512 1320. www.theguesthouse.at. 39 units. Doubles €240–€610. U-Bahn 1/3 (Stephansplatz). Map p 144.*

★★ Hilton Vienna Danube DANUBE One of three Hiltons in the city, this hotel claims some of the most spacious guestrooms in Vienna. Ask for a room with a Danube view. *Handelskai 269. ☎ 01 72777. www.hilton.at/wiendanube. 367 units. Doubles €75–€399. U-Bahn 2 (Ernst Happel Stadion). Map p 147.*

★★★ Hollmann Beletage CITY CENTER Spacious rooms, designer furniture, and plenty of home comforts make this hotel an inner-city sanctuary. *Köllnerhofgasse 6. ☎ 01 961 1960. www.hollman-beletage.at. 16 units. Doubles €140–€250 w/breakfast. U-Bahn 1/4 (Schwedenplatz). Map p 144.*

★ Hotel am Brillantengrund NEUBAU This place revolves around its courtyard. While there are indoor dining rooms, in summer the courtyard cafe cum restaurant fills with neighborhood hipsters and young families who come for Filipino-Austrian fusion dishes served beneath cheap beach umbrellas. The rooms are almost aggressively simple and clean with retro furniture. *Bandgasse 4. ☎ 01 523 3662. www.brillantengrund.com. 34 units. Doubles €69–€129. Tram 5/49 (Westbahnstrasse). Map p 146.*

★★ Hotel am Opernring CITY CENTER Located opposite the celebrated State Opera at the heart of the city, this hotel has stylish contemporary rooms and serves a delicious champagne breakfast buffet. *Opernring 11. ☎ 01 587 55 18. www.opernring.at. 47 units. Doubles €149–€325 w/breakfast. Tram 1/2/D (Oper). Map p 144.*

★★ kids Hotel am Stephansplatz CITY CENTER The central location of this hotel (next to the cathedral) is unbeatable. It operates along eco-friendly lines (sustainable wood, organic meals, and recycling) and the organic breakfasts are delicious. *Stephansplatz 9.*

The welcoming lounge at Hollmann Beletage.

Hotel Daniel is stylish and cool.

☎ 01 534 05-0. www.hotelamstephansplatz.at. 56 units. Doubles €180–€280 w/breakfast. U-Bahn 1/3 (Stephansplatz). Map p 144.

★★★ **Hotel Daniel** HAUPTBAHNHOF This place provides smart luxury for a decent price. There are plenty of perks, including a stylish lounge, hip interior design, homemade cakes, and a generous breakfast buffet. This is also the only hotel with a Dali-esque sailboat dripping from its rooftop. *Landstrasser Gürtel 5. ☎ 01 901 310. www.hoteldaniel.com. Double €95–€112. Tram 18/D/O (Quartier Belvedere). Map p 143.*

★★ **Hotel Europa Wien** CITY CENTER Ideally located on a pedestrian street in the city center, this business-class hotel combines modern furnishings with Austrian charm. *Kärtnerstrasse 18. ☎ 01 51594. www.austria-trend.at/hotel-europa-wien. 160 units. Doubles €450–€650 w/breakfast. U-Bahn 1/3 (Stephansplatz). Map p 144.*

★★ **Hotel Topazz** CITY CENTER From the outside it looks like a submarine married a spaceship but inside you'll find 1920s-inspired elegance. Rooms are like cozy, boutique cocoons—with portholes for watching the city below. *Lichtensteg 3. ☎ 01 532 2250. www.hoteltopazz.com. 32 units. Doubles €198–€248. U-Bahn 1/3 (Stephansplatz). Map p 144.*

★★★ **kids** **Imperial** RINGSTRASSE This sumptuous hotel conjures up the glory days of the Habsburg empire with its palatial rooms. It's the pick of the bunch for visiting heads of state. *Kärtner Ring 16. ☎ 01 501 10-0. www.luxurycollection.com/imperial. 138 units. Doubles €359–€789. Tram 1/2/71/D (Schwarzenbergplatz). Map p 143.*

★★ **Kaiserin Elisabeth** CITY CENTER Formerly frequented by Mozart, Wagner, and Liszt, this hotel offers traditional Viennese elegance with grand (if slightly over-the-top) furnishings. *Weihburggasse 3. ☎ 01 515 26. www.kaiserinelisabeth.at. 63 units. Doubles €216–€245 w/breakfast. U-Bahn 1/3 (Stephansplatz). Map p 144.*

★★ **Kärtnerhof** CITY CENTER Hidden down a tiny lane, this quiet, friendly hotel has traditional furnishings and a roof terrace. It's a popular choice with budget-conscious visitors. *Grasshofgasse 4. ☎ 01 512 1923. www.kartnerhof.com. 44 units. Doubles €110–€179 w/breakfast. U-Bahn 1/4 (Schwedenplatz). Map p 144.*

★★★ **König von Ungarn** CITY CENTER Step inside and take a trip back in time to the days when this grand hotel served as a guesthouse for cathedral dignitaries, and Mozart lived next door. *Schulerstrasse 10. ☎ 01 515 84-0. www.kvu.at. 44 units. Doubles €215 w/breakfast. U-Bahn 1/3 (Stephansplatz). Map p 144.*

★★ **Kuchlmasterei** PRATER Small, stylish, and a little different, Kuchlmasterei began life as a restaurant before adding several opulent suites. Treat yourself to the special bath menu. *Obere Weissgerberstrasse 6. ☎ 01 712 9000. www.kuchlmasterei.at. 7 units. Suite €247. Tram N/O (Hintere Zollamtsstrasse). Map p 147.*

★★★ **Le Méridien** RINGSTRASSE Relax in the sophisticated spa, then join the smart set for cocktails in the glamorous Shambala Bar. Bedrooms are sleekly minimalist. *Opernring 13–15. ☎ 01 588 900. www.lemeridienvienna.com. 294 units. Doubles €180–€465. Tram 1/2/D (Oper). Map p 143.*

★★ **Magdas Hotel** PRATER This laid-back hotel close to the green Prater is unique in several ways. The former nursing home was renovated with a fresh, clean design aesthetic and the Magdas is Vienna's first hotel to employ refugees alongside its hotel professionals. Rooftop doubles offer great views of the Ferris wheel and the Prater. *Laufbergergasse 12. ☎ 01 720 0288. www.magdas-hotel.at. 80 units. Doubles €80–€141. U-Bahn 2 (Praterstern) 10min walk. Map p 147.*

★★ **Mailbergerhof** CITY CENTER A gorgeous hotel in a small baroque palace with stables and a chapel, near the cathedral and the opera house. *Annagasse 7. ☎ 01 512 0641. www.mailbergerhof.at. 40 units. Doubles €110–€190 w/breakfast. U-Bahn 1/3 (Stephansplatz). Map p 144.*

★ **Melia Wien** DANUBE Close to the UN and the Vienna International Centre, the hotel is situated in Austria's highest skyscraper where you have arguably the best view of the city. Its modern interior design and fast connection to the city center add more reasons to stay. *Donau-City-Strasse 7. ☎ 01 901 04. www.melia.com. 253 units. Doubles €166–€796 and way up. U-Bahn 1 (VIC). Map p 147.*

★ **Motel One—Staatsoper** CITY CENTER Despite being part of a chain, this particular property is unique because of its incredible, central location, the outstanding decor in its public areas (what you'd expect from a five-star establishment), and the friendly staff. It cannot be beat at this price. *Elisabethstrasse 5. ☎ 01 585 0505. www.motel-one.com. 400 units. Doubles €140–€150. U-Bahn 1/4 (Karlsplatz). Map p 144.*

★★ kids **Nossek** CITY CENTER Sample true Viennese hospitality in an excellent central location at this friendly little guesthouse, furnished in baroque style. No credit cards. *Graben 17. ☎ 01 533 7041. www.pension-nossek.at. 31 units. Doubles €115–€150 w/breakfast. U-Bahn 1/3 (Stephansplatz). Map p 144.*

★★★ **Palais Coburg Residenz** CITY CENTER The ultimate in traditional luxury, this regal palace has a top-notch gourmet restaurant, a vast wine cellar, and a rooftop pool. *Coburgbastei 4. ☎ 01 518 18-0. www.palais-coburg.com. 35 units. Doubles €670–€2,700. U-Bahn 3 (Stubentor). Map p 144.*

★★★ **Palais Hansen Kempinski** CITY CENTER Inside a palace built for the 1873 World Exhibition you'll find a brilliantly designed hotel with an iPad for room controls, two exquisite restaurants, a spa with pool, and impeccable service. *Schottenring 24. ☎ 01 236 1000. www.kempinski.com. 152 units. Doubles €280–€1,185 and up. U-Bahn 2/4 (Schottenring). Map p 146.*

★★★ **Park Hyatt** CITY CENTER Opened in 2014 in a 19th-century former bank building, this palace

The upscale Palais Hansen Kempinski is renowned for its service.

drips with opulent Viennese decor. This is where the city's who's who grab a drink and where their guests find a comfy bed and a luxurious spa and pool for relaxing. *Am Hof 2. ☎ 01 227 401 234. www.vienna.park.hyatt.com. 143 units. Doubles €475–€975 and up. U-Bahn 3 (Herrengasse). Map p 144.*

★★ **The Ring** RINGSTRASSE Tradition meets modernity at this five-star hotel near the opera house. Behind an impressive 19th-century facade the stylish but comfortable rooms, snazzy suites, and fitness spa ooze casual luxury. *Kärtner Ring 8. ☎ 01 221 22-0. www.theringhotel.at. 68 units. Doubles €199–€470. Tram 1/2/D (Oper). Map p 143.*

★★★ **Ritz-Carlton** CITY CENTER A testimony to opulence, the Ritz has a stunning rooftop bar, a Guerlain Spa, and a restaurant famous for its steak. Marble bathrooms, chocolate treatments, and underwater music—this place doesn't leave the wow factor to chance. *Schubertring 5–7. ☎ 01 311 88. www.ritzcarlton.com. 202 units. Doubles €380–€1,835 and up. U-Bahn 4 (Stadtpark). Map p 144.*

★ **Ruby Sofie Hotel** LANDSTRASSER Built on the ruins of the legendary Sofiensäle, this urban hipster delivers playful design, a stylish hotel bar, and free bike rental. *Marxergasse 17. ☎ 01 361 9660 60. www.ruby-hotels.com. 77 units. Doubles €139–€204. U-Bahn 3 (Wien-Mitte). Map p 147.*

★★★ **Sacher** RINGSTRASSE Vienna's most famous hotel, founded in 1876, Sacher retains its palatial 19th-century style, reveling in opulent, romantic rooms. Its famous *Sachertorte* is on the must-eat list of every tourist. *Philharmonikerstrasse 4. ☎ 01 514 560. www.sacher.com. 152 units. Doubles €310–€828. Tram 1/2/D (Oper). Map p 144.*

★★★ **Saint Shermin** CITY CENTER A lovely little B&B located on the first floor of an old Viennese house with a dedication to champagne. Staying here feels like visiting friends. *Rilke-Platz 7. ☎ 01 586 6183 0. www.shermin.at. 11 units. Doubles €193–€285. -Bahn 1/4 (Karlsplatz). Map p 144.*

★★ **Sans Souci** MQ An exclusive luxury hotel next to the MuseumsQuartier, this place offers a refreshing approach to design with original art, a rooftop terrace, and an indoor pool and spa. *Burggasse 2. ☎ 01 522 2520. www.sanssouci-wien.com. 63 units. Doubles €296–€990. U-Bahn 2/3 (Volksgarten). Map p 146.*

★★★ Schloss Wilhelminenberg OTTAKRING This former castle surrounded by parkland on the western outskirts is now a contemporary-style hotel with sensational city vistas. *Savoyenstrasse 2. ☎ 01 485 03. www.austria-trend.at/wiw. 87 units. Doubles €155–€260. U-Bahn 3 (Ottakring) then Bus 46B/146B (Schloss Wilhelminenberg). Map p 146.*

★★ Schreiners Essen & Wohnen NEUBAU In the artsy 7th district, you can enjoy a homemade breakfast, a beautiful patio, and spacious rooms in this tiny family-run hotel with an in-house restaurant. *Westbahnstrasse 42. ☎ 0676 475 4060. www.schreiners.cc. 6 units. Doubles €177–€208. Tram 5/49 (Westbahnstrasse). Map p 146.*

★★★ Sofitel Vienna Stephansdom KARMELITER A sleek, chic hotel, designed by French architect Jean Nouvel in a minimalist palette of blacks, grays, and whites. With an exotic spa and an acclaimed rooftop eatery (p 119), this is where Vienna's beautiful people hang out. *Praterstrasse 1. ☎ 01 906 16 3100. www.sofitel.com. 182 units. Doubles €285–€555. U-Bahn 1/4 (Schwedenplatz). Map p 144.*

★★ kids Strand Hotel Alte Donau DANUBE A city "beach" hotel, with cheerful rooms, alfresco breakfasts in summer, bikes for hire, and its very own beach complete with rowing boats. *Wagramerstrasse 51. ☎ 01 204 4040. www.strandhotel-alte-donau.at. 29 units. Doubles €100–€150 w/breakfast. U-Bahn 1 (Alte Donau). Map p 147.*

★★ This is Not a Hotel AUGARTEN A bit off the beaten track, this tiny family-run property gives you the personal touches a big chain can't. Your hosts are happy to offer tips for your time in the city and a family breakfast each morning makes it home away from home. *Obere Donaustrasse 9. ☎ 01 348 300. www.thisisnotahotel.at. 3 units; 2-night minimum stay. Doubles €121–€150. U-Bahn 4 (Rossauer Lände). Map p 146.*

★ Zipser JOSEFSTADT Don't be put off by the plain facade of this contemporary hotel. It's a friendly place with attractive, generously sized bedrooms—some have tranquil, tree-shaded balconies. *Lange Gasse 49. ☎ 01 404 54-0. www.zipser.at. 55 units. Doubles €99–€205 w/breakfast. U-Bahn 2 (Rathaus). Map p 146.* ●

The Strand Hotel Alte Donau has its own beach.

The Savvy Traveler

Before You Go

Government Tourist Offices

In the U.S.: 120 West 45th St., 9th floor, New York, NY 10036 (☎ 1 212 944 6880); 6520 Platt Avenue, # 561 West Hills, California, CA 91307-3218 (☎ 1 818 999 4030). **In Canada:** 2 Bloor Street West, # 400 Toronto, ON, M4W 3E2 (☎ 1 416 967 4867). **In the U.K. & Ireland:** 9–11 Richmond Buildings, London, W1D 3HF (☎ 020 7440 3830 or 0845 101 1818). **In Australia:** 1st floor, 36 Carrington Street, Sydney NSW 2000 (☎ 02 9299 3621). Wherever you live, the best place for information is the official website of Vienna Tourism at www.vienna.info.

The Best Times to Go

The best time to visit is from May to October. May, when the lilac and chestnut trees are in bloom, marks the start of *Heuriger* season (wine taverns connected to vineyards). June to August, when the days are long and hot, is ideal for lazy afternoons in Vienna's extensive parks; for swimming and sunbathing at the city's beaches; and for river trips and watersports on the Danube. However, Vienna can get very crowded at the height of summer, especially during school vacations. September marks the start of the theater season as all the major venues launch their new programs and, in October, the city's new wines vineyards are toasted in the city bars and country *Heurigen*. Another popular time is Christmas, when snow has often fallen, festive decorations and lights illuminate the city, and the streets are filled with stalls selling roasted chestnuts, hot punch, and *Glühwein* (mulled wine). Many visitors come to shop at the Christmas markets or to enjoy the city's celebrated New Year's Eve festivities. Whenever you choose to visit, there's always a superb choice of theater and music, and over 80 museums to provide entertainment for all the family, whatever the weather.

Climate

Vienna's mild climate means that you can enjoy visiting the city year-round. As a general rule, Vienna has cold winters, hot summers, and temperatures are mild during spring and fall. May marks the start of balmy days, and alfresco dining (until Sept). No matter what the season, temperatures can change quickly, so think layers. It is hottest between June and August with temperatures ranging from 68° to 75°F (20–23°C). This is also the wettest time of year, but the rain helps to keep the city cool and pleasant. September is one of the best months for sightseeing, with crisp, sunny days, comfortable temperatures, and fewer visitors than during the height of summer. October, too, can be mild and pleasant, when the leaves in the city parks and vineyards start to change color. The notorious *Föhn* wind can blow at any time of year. This warm, dry Alpine wind often brings crystal-clear days (beautiful light for photographs), but it is also blamed for headaches and bad moods. November heralds the first chills of winter. January and February are the coldest months when snow is frequent, although it rarely settles for long in the city center. It can be surprisingly cold during this time, so pack warm clothes.

Previous page: Vienna underground.

VIENNA'S AVERAGE DAILY TEMPERATURE & MONTHLY RAINFALL

	JAN	FEB	MAR	APR	MAY	JUNE
Temp. (°F)	37	35	45	55	59	68
Temp. (°C)	3	2	7	13	15	20
Rainfall (mm)	38	41	40	50	60	72
	JULY	**AUG**	**SEPT**	**OCT**	**NOV**	**DEC**
Temp. (°F)	75	73	62	53	42	35
Temp. (°C)	24	23	17	12	6	2
Rainfall (mm)	60	62	42	40	50	42

Festivals & Special Events

For further information on what's on, check out the "Events" section of www.vienna.info and the website www.whatsonwhen.com.

SPRING The **Spring Marathon** takes place in April and participants make their way from the Schönbrunn Palace to the Rathaus. The **Wiener Festwochen** (Vienna Festival Weeks) follows in May. This is Vienna's main arts festival of opera, theater, and performing arts (from mid-May to mid-June). Spring also marks the start of the **Schönbrunn Palace concert season** (Mar–Oct), the **Prater funfair** (Apr–Oct), and performances of the **Spanish Riding School** (until June).

SUMMER Highlights of this glorious season of balls and open-air entertainment include the **Fête Imperial** summer ball at the Spanish Riding School in July; the **Mozart Opera** series, performed nightly in the Schönbrunn Park until mid-August; and the **Donauinselfest** (last weekend in June), a 3-day pop festival on Danube Island. The free **Musikfilm Festival** at the Rathaus (mid-July to mid-Sept) is one of several open-air cinema venues throughout the city. The **VieVinum** wine festival takes place in the Hofburg (in June), and Vienna's gay community celebrates late June with the flamboyant **Regenbogen Parade** (Rainbow Parade). And there's the **Jazz Fest** (first 2 weeks in July) at the State Opera House and Volkstheater. From mid-July to mid-August, dancers take over the city for the **Impulstanz** Festival.

FALL Fall is the cultural start of the year, when the major theaters and opera houses reopen for the season and launch their new programs. The **Spanish Riding School** begins performances again (Sept–June), and the **Vienna Boys' Choir** sings Mass once more on Sundays (mid-Sept to June) after their summer break. On the **Lange Nacht der Museen** (first Sat in Oct), all the museums in the city open from 6pm to 1am, and one ticket allows entry to all of them. At the end of the month, the **National Holiday** (26th Oct) celebrates the withdrawal of Allied troops in 1955, following the passing of the Neutrality Act. October also sees the start of **Wien Modern** (Oct–end Nov), a modern music festival at the Konzerthaus, and the **Viennale,** Austria's leading film festival. In November, the **Schubertiade** concert series takes place at the Musikverein, and **Christkindlmärkte,** the city's much-loved Christmas markets open (mid-Nov to end Dec).

WINTER **Christmas markets** are in full swing right across the city for the month of December, at Freyung, Karlsplatz, Spittelberg, Schönbrunn, and Heiligenkreuzerhof. On ember 6, St. Nicholas and his ked companion Krampus make their annual appearance in various **St. Nicholas festivities and parades.** Christmas is marked by **Midnight Mass** (arrive early to get a seat in the Stephansdom). **Christmas Day** and **Stefanitag** (Boxing Day) are public holidays. **New Year's Eve** is traditionally celebrated with a performance of **Die Fledermaus** at the Opera House and Volksoper (shown on large screens in Stephansplatz); **Beethoven's 9th Symphony** is performed at the Konzerthaus; and the glittering **Kaiserball** takes place at the Hofburg. The nation's largest **Silvester** (New Year's Eve) party takes place in the city center, with street entertainment, revelry, and dazzling fireworks. The famous **New Year's Day concert** is performed by the Vienna Philharmonic at the Musikverein (requests for tickets for the following year's concert must arrive in writing at the Musikverein on Jan 2, no sooner, no later). Then there's ice-skating for everyone (mid-Jan to Feb) in front of the city hall at **Vienna Ice Dream,** followed by the **Fasching** carnival season (Jan 6 until Ash Wed). Fasching festivities include the **Opera Ball** (last Thurs before Shrove Tues), one of the grandest society events of the year, climaxing at the lavish **Heringschmaus** (Ash Wed) buffet. The **Haydn Tage** concert series (mid-Feb to first week Mar) takes place at the Konzerthaus.

Useful Websites

- **www.vienna.info** The official website for the Vienna Tourist Board contains lots of useful information on where to stay (including a hotel booking facility), what to do (museums, galleries, sights), where to go (restaurants, theaters, nightlife), and much more.
- **www.wien.at** The city's municipal online information service, run by local government, contains maps and all sorts of useful information, with sections on business, culture, health, leisure, history, and politics.
- **www.austria.info** The Austrian National Tourist Board's website contains everything you need to know for vacationing in Austria, plus it has a facility for booking accommodation.
- **www.metropole.at** Vienna's only English-language magazine is available in print and online.
- **www.niederoesterreich.at** Information on Niederösterreich (Lower Austria), the region surrounding Vienna.
- **www.viennaairport.com** Useful for flight planning, with details of airport services and transport to and from the city center.
- **www.oebb.at** Timetables, fares, and online booking for the national rail system, the Österreichische Bundesbahnen (ÖBB).
- **www.wienerlinien.at** Schedules and routes for the city's public transport network, including bus, tram, U-Bahn and night-bus systems, plus details of all the various ticket types on offer.
- **www.ddsg-blue-danube.at** Details of sightseeing cruises and special day trips on the waterways of the Danube.
- **www. viennawuerstelstand.com** A fun, English-language website devoted to the city's leisure activities, nightlife, and cuisine.

Cellphones (Mobiles)

If you're staying longer, it may make sense to buy a cheap pay-as-you-go cellphone at any phone store in Austria for about €40 to €75, which usually includes some prepaid calling time. The major networks—A1, Drei, and T-Mobile—all sell SIM cards. You can top this up using phone cards purchased from supermarkets and **Trafik** (tobacconists/newsstands) for €20 or €40. Local cellphone numbers start with 0650, 0660, 0664, 0676, and 0699, 0680.

Car Rentals

Don't bother! Like New York City or Paris, driving in Vienna is not worth the hassle and parking is expensive. You're much better off sticking to the city's highly efficient public transport system. Vienna is surprisingly compact and many of the main sights are all within easy walking distance. If you'll be travelling outside the city, or simply want to rent a vehicle, it is usually cheaper to reserve a car before leaving home. Be ready for pickup at the airport. Try **Avis** (☎ 01 7007 32700; www.avis.at); **Budget** (☎ 01 7007 32711; www.budget.at); **Europcar** (☎ 0866 16 10; www.europcar.at); **Hertz** (☎ 01 7007 32661; www.hertz.at); or **Sixt** (☎ 01 7007 36517; www.sixt.at).

Getting **There**

By Plane

Most visitors fly into **Vienna International Airport** (☎ 01 7007-0; www.viennaairport.com) at Schwechat, 20km (12 miles) southeast of the city center, although some European charter flights make use of the cheaper **Airport Letisko Bratislava** (☎ +421 2 4857 3353; www.airportbratislava.sk), just 60km (37 miles) east of Vienna.

At Vienna International Airport, the Vienna Tourist Service desk at Baggage Reclaim (☎ 01 7007 32875; daily 6am–11pm) can provide general maps and pamphlets and help you find a hotel room if you haven't reserved ahead. To reach the city center, follow signs to the **S-Bahn suburban train station** (☎ 05 1717; www.oebb.at; 4:34am–11:49pm) for cheap, easy connections. Trains run every 30 minutes. It takes 25 minutes on the S7 to reach Wien Mitte central station and costs €4.40. **The City Airport Train** (CAT; ☎ 01 252 50; www.cityairporttrain.com; 6:05am–11:25pm; €11 adults, kids under 14 ride for free) takes 16 minutes, but it is the more expensive option. **Airport buses** (☎ 01 711-01; 1:20am–12:20am; €8) shuttle every 30 minutes to Erdberg, the Vienna International Center (UN), West Train Station and Schwedenplatz in the city center, where there are U-Bahn connections. Journey time is usually about 20 minutes, depending on traffic. Expect to pay around €35 for a taxi ride to the city center. When traveling to and from the airport, be sure to request airport rates in advance.

On arrival at Airport Letisko Bratislava, a shuttle bus operates 19 times a day to Vienna's Südtiroler Platz. It takes roughly 90 minutes and costs €7.70. Alternatively, catch bus no. 61 (every 10–20 min; 5am–11pm) to the main station, then take a direct train to Vienna's Südbahnhof (almost hourly, 6:50am–11:50pm). From April to October you can arrive by **hydrofoil** along the Danube from Bratislava in 75 minutes (☎ 01 588 80; www.ddsg-blue-danube.at; five sailings daily, from €19). A taxi ride from Bratislava airport to Vienna city center takes around 45 minutes, and costs approximately €200 to €300.

By Car

Austria has an excellent network of motorways but you need an *Autobahnvignette* (toll-sticker) in order to drive on them. These are available at gas stations, tobacconists, and border-crossing points, and must be attached to the inside of your windshield. A 10-day vignette costs €7.90. The main access route from the north is on the A22 Danube motorway (*Donauuferautobahn*); from the west on the A1 western motorway (*Westautobahn*); the A2 and A23 southern motorways (*Südautobahn*); and the A4 eastern motorway (*Ostautobahn*)—the route from Schwechat International Airport. The motorways converge on the *Gürtel* (outer ringroad). From here, follow signs to *Zentrum* (city center).

By Train

Vienna has several mainline railway stations, three of which have international connections. As a general rule, trains from the west (and some from Budapest) arrive at the Westbahnhof; trains from the south and east at the Hauptbahnhof and Wien Meidling; and trains from the north at Franz-Josefs-Bahnhof. Facilities at each include a travel agency, snack bars, newsagents, and shops. If you're arriving by Eurocity train, book in advance (you have to pay a supplement if you book within 72 hours of departure). Reserve a bed if you're traveling overnight. Many of the night trains have no buffet service, so bring some drinks and snacks with you.

By Bus

International coach connections can be long and uncomfortable so I don't recommend them. There is no central bus station, so your arrival destination will vary, depending which company you're traveling with. Wien Mitte coach station handles most of the international coach services as well as domestic routes from eastern Austria. Domestic coach routes from southern and southwestern Austria terminate at the Südbahnhof coach station. **Eurolines** (☎ 01 798 2900; www.eurolines.at) offer coach services throughout Europe, arriving at the bus station at the U3 U-Bahn station of Erdberg, and occasionally at Südbahnhof.

Getting **Around**

On Foot

Vienna is easy to explore on foot. Most of the major attractions lie within the Ringstrasse, and the Tourist Office has an excellent free map to help you. Don't worry if you get lost—the graceful tower of the Stephansdom is never far from sight and always useful for orientation.

Public Transport Ticket System

Vienna's comprehensive public transport system is clean, fast, and very efficient. It comprises the U-Bahn (underground trains), S-Bahn (regional trains), trams, and buses, and it's easy to use. Flat-fare tickets are valid for all modes of transport, and can be purchased at tobacconists and in U-Bahn stations from automatic machines (with instructions in English). Before boarding a train, you must put your ticket in the blue validating machine (*Entwerter*) found at the entrances to the U-Bahn stations. On buses and trams, you must immediately stamp your ticket inside the vehicle upon boarding. While Vienna's public transit runs on an honor system traveling without a valid ticket can result in a heavy fine. Tickets and passes include an *Einzelfahrschein* (single ticket, €2.20); a *Streifenkarte* (Strip Card, €8.80, for four journeys); a *24-Stunden Wien-Karte* (24 hours unlimited travel, €7.60); a *72-Stunden Wien-Karte* (72 hours unlimited travel, €16.50); an *8-Tage-Karte* (valid for 8 days—not necessarily consecutive ones— €38.40) and a *Wochenkarte* (a weekly card, but only valid until Sun, regardless of what day you purchase it, €16.20). The Vienna Card (€21.90) also provides 72 hours of unlimited travel plus other discounts (see Passes, p 165). Kids under 6 travel free; kids under 15 travel free on Sundays and during school holidays.

By U-Bahn

The U-Bahn (underground train) is the fastest way to get around town, although admittedly it's not as scenic as the trams. There are five color-coded routes (U1—red, U2—purple, U3—orange, U4—green, U6—brown). Transport maps are posted in all stations; free maps are available from **Wiener Linien** (☎ 01 790 9100; www.wienerlinien.at), online and at every station. Electronic boards on station platforms indicate the destination of the next train and the waiting time until its arrival. The U-Bahn runs daily from about 5am until just after midnight, with trains running at approximately 5-minute intervals (more frequent at rush hour); after 8:30pm, the trains slow to every 7 to 8 minutes. On weekends they run 24 hours a day.

By Tram or Bus

Trams operate at the perfect speed for taking in the sights. Those that run along the Ringstrasse offer great sightseeing opportunities, or just board the Ring Tram (see p 58) to admire the fine architecture of the city center. As with buses, trams are identified by numbers and/or letters. Bus routes 1A, 2A, and 3A are city-center mini-hoppers. Most routes operate from 5am until midnight, when a useful network of night buses (marked with a blue "N") operates until 5am. Details of individual routes can be found at www.wienerlinien.at.

By Taxi

There are taxi ranks at many busy junctions and outside most large hotels. You can hail a taxi in the street if its yellow sign is lit, or book one by phone (☎ 01 60 160; ☎ 01 40 100; ☎ 01 31 300). Taxis charge around €2 pickup fee when ordered by phone. The private-driver app Uber is also available in Vienna.

By Car

Vienna's maze of narrow one-way streets, its expensive, restricted parking, and ubiquitous trams (which always take priority over other traffic) make driving in the city center decidedly stressful and best avoided.

Fast **Facts**

APARTMENT RENTALS For long-term accommodation (including short-term lets) look at *airbnb.com* or *interhome.at*. Chapter 9 ("The Best Hotels") contains details of a couple of apartment-hotels.

ATMS The easiest way to get euros is via bank or credit card at an ATMs (called *Bankomat*), which are dotted about the city. Be warned, however, you may be charged a fee for withdrawing money from your home bank account, and credit-card companies charge interest.

BABYSITTING Many mid- to upper-range hotels can arrange babysitting services. Otherwise, contact **WienXtra-Kinderinfo** (☎ 01 4000 84 400; www.kinderinfowien.at) for details of reputable babysitting agencies.

BANKING HOURS Most banks are open Monday through Friday from 9am to 3pm (Thurs until 4:30pm).

BIKE RENTALS Vienna has over 300km (186 miles) of marked cycle paths and plenty of bike-hire outlets (open Mar–Oct), including **Pedal Power,** Ausstellungsstrasse 3 (☎ 01 729 7234; www.pedalpower.at); **Bicycle Rental Hochschaubahn,** Prater 113, near the rollercoaster (☎ 01 729 5858, www.radverleih-hochschaubahn.com). Prices start at around €5 for an hour, €15 for a half-day, and €24 for a full day. Vienna's bike-hire system, called Citybike (www.citybikewien.at), has over 120 pickup points around town—look out for the distinctive circular red "Citybike" sign. All you need is a credit card (Mastercard or Visa), or a debit card with a chip to release a bicycle at one of the bike stations. You can only hire one Citybike per card. The first hour is free of charge (following a one-time registration charge of €1), then rates increase from €1 for 2 hours to €4 for 4 hours. You can return the Citybike to any bike station. The fee debited will depend on the time you return the bicycle to an empty bike box. If you don't have a credit card, you can buy a Tourist Card (€2 per day plus a small deposit) from Royal Tours, Herrengasse 1–3 (daily 8–11:30am and 1–6pm) or Pedal Power, Ausstellungsstrasse 3 (daily 9am–5pm) and then pay the accrued fees when you return the card.

BUSINESS HOURS Most stores open Monday through Friday 9am to 6pm and Saturday from 9am to 5pm. Some larger stores open late on Thursdays until 9pm. Supermarkets open Monday through Friday 8am to 6 or 7pm; Saturday from 8am to 5pm. General office hours are Monday through Friday 8am to 3:30pm (or sometimes 4pm or 5pm).

CLIMATE See "The Best Times to Go" and "Climate," p 156.

CONCERTS See "How to Get Tickets," p 137.

CONSULATES & EMBASSIES **American Embassy,** Boltzmanngasse 16 (☎ 01 313 39-0; www.usembassy.at). **Canadian Embassy,** Laurenzerberg 2 (☎ 01 531 38 3000; www.kanada.at). **British Embassy,** Jauresgasse 12 (☎ 01 716 130; www.britishembassy.at). **Irish Embassy,** Rotenturmstrasse 16–18 (☎ 01 715 4246; www.embassyofireland.at). **Australian Embassy,** Mattiellistrasse 2 (☎ 01 506 740; www.austria.embassy.gov.au/vien/consular.html). For other embassies and consulates, consult the Austrian Foreign Ministry website, www.bmaa.gv.at.

CUSTOMS Anyone arriving from outside the E.U. is allowed to bring into Austria up to 200 cigarettes, two bottles of wine, and one bottle of liquor, duty free. There are no limits for anyone arriving from another E.U. country. For specifics on what you can bring home with you, Americans should consult **U.S. Customs** (☎ 202 354 1000; www.customs.gov). Canadians should contact the **Canadian Customs & Revenue Agency** (☎ 800 461 9999; www.cra-adrc.gc.ca). British citizens should contact **HM Revenue & Customs** (☎ 0845 010 9000;

www.hmce.gov.uk). Australians should contact **Australian Customs Services** (☎ 02 6275 6666; www.customs.gov.au). New Zealanders should contact **New Zealand Customs** (☎ 1800 428 786; www.customs.govt.nz).

DENTISTS See "Emergencies."

DINING Breakfast in Vienna traditionally consists of a cup of coffee accompanied by a bread roll or croissant with butter, jam, and sometimes a selection of cold cuts and cheeses. If your hotel doesn't include breakfast in its rates, it's the perfect excuse to indulge at one of the city's legendary coffee houses. Most cafes and coffee houses open from 7am to midnight, although some stay open later. Restaurants generally open 11am to 3:30pm and 6pm to midnight. Some remain open all day. Dress codes are relaxed, except in a handful of more upmarket restaurants. Many restaurants require table reservations in advance, but they are not necessary in cafes, *Heurigen*, and less formal eateries. Ask your concierge to help with any arrangements on arrival in Vienna. Young children are welcome in most venues, with the exception of the more exclusive restaurants.

DOCTORS See "Emergencies."

ELECTRICITY Like most of continental Europe, Austria uses the 220-volt system (two round prongs). American (110-volt) appliances will need both a transformer and an adapter plug. Some electronic items, including most laptops, have built-in transformers but will still need a simple adapter. U.K. 240-volt appliances need a continental adapter, widely available at home but difficult to find in Austria.

EMBASSIES See "Consulates & Embassies."

EMERGENCIES Dial ☎ 133 for **police,** ☎ 122 for **fire,** ☎ 144 for an **ambulance,** ☎ 141 for an **emergency doctor.** Hospitals (*Krankenhäuser*) with emergency facilities (open 24 hr. a day, 7 days a week) include: **Allgemeines Krankenhaus,** Währinger Gürtel (☎ 01 40400-0; www.akhwien.at); **Unfallkrankenhaus Meidling,** Kundratstrasse 37 (☎ 01 601 50-0; www.ukhmeidling.at); and **Lorenz Böhler Unfallkrankenhaus,** Donaueschingenstrasse 13 (☎ 01 33110-0; www.ukhboehler.at). A **dentists'** emergency service operates after hours and at weekends on ☎ 01 512 2078. See also "Pharmacies."

EVENT LISTINGS The English-language monthly magazine **Metropole** lists a selection of events for non-German speakers but also all the highlights of the month that don't require understanding the language. The main German-language listings magazine for what's on in the city is ***Falter*** (www.falter.at), published every Wednesday and available from kiosks and newsagents. The Tourist Office produces a monthly events listing covering theater, concerts, film festivals, spectator sports, exhibitions, and more. Look out for the free monthly magazine ***Enjoy Vienna*** available in bars and hotels, and the Friday edition of the free newspaper ***Heute*** (in German) for further listings. Online, www.hauptstadt.at is a useful site to source information on nightlife, pop concerts, and cinema venues.

FAMILY TRAVEL Vienna is a surprisingly child-friendly city, with lots of attractions that appeal to youngsters. Look for the items tagged with a **kids** icon in this book. There's even a tourist office, WienXtra-Kinderinfo, devoted solely to kids (see "Tourist Offices").

GAY & LESBIAN TRAVELERS The best gay and lesbian resource in Vienna is the ***Gay Guide,*** available in various bars and at the Tourist-Info Wien office in Albertinaplatz. The **Rosa Lila Villa,** Linke Wienzeile 102 (www.villa.at) offers information, advice, and counseling in its Lesbian Center (☎ 01 586 8150) and the Gay Men's Center (☎ 01 585 4343).

HOLIDAYS Most shops and all banks and services are closed on public holidays, listed here: New Year's Day, Epiphany (Jan 6), Easter Sunday, Easter Monday, Labor Day (May 1), Ascension Day (sixth Thurs after Easter), Whit Monday (sixth Mon after Easter), Corpus Christi, Assumption Day (Aug 15), National Holiday (Oct 26), All Saints Day (Nov 1), Feast of the Immaculate Conception (Dec 8), Christmas Day, and Stefanitag (Dec 26).

INSURANCE It is important to take out adequate personal travel insurance for your trip, covering medical expenses, theft, loss, repatriation, personal liability, and cancellation. Private medical insurance is essential for all non-E.U. visitors. However, thanks to a reciprocal agreement, citizens of the U.K. and other E.U. countries are entitled to reduced-price medical treatment on presentation of a valid European Health Insurance Card (EHIC—apply online at www.dh.gov.uk/travellers). Dental care, except emergency accident treatment, is not available free of charge and should also be covered by private medical insurance.

INTERNET Most Viennese hotels have Internet access in guest rooms or an Internet terminal in the lobby. Many cafes offer the opportunity to log on to the Internet via Wi-Fi with your own wireless-enabled laptop. Internet cafes are scattered around town. A popular one is **Surfland Internet Café,** Krugerstrasse 10 (www.surfland.at; daily 10am–11pm; €2.90 for 15 min., €5.90 for 1hr., special rates for Vienna Card holders).

LOST PROPERTY Inform all credit-card companies immediately if your credit card is stolen, and file a report at the local police station for any missing items if you intend to make an insurance claim. For help in finding lost property on a train, phone **Südbahnhof** (☎ 01 580 03 5656) or **BahnhofCity Wien West** (☎ 01 580 03 2996); or on a tram or bus, phone the **Wiener Linien General Information Office** (☎ 01 7909-100). Otherwise, try the central lost property office, **Zentrales Fundservice,** Bastiengasse 36–38 (☎ 01 4000 8091; Mon–Fri 8am–3:15pm (until 5:30pm Thurs).

MAIL & POSTAGE Austria's postal service is generally swift and reliable. Stamps (*Briefmarken*) can be bought at post offices, tobacconists, and some newspaper kiosks. Letter boxes are plentiful and easy to find—they're bright yellow. Most post offices open Monday through Friday 8am to noon and 2 to 6pm. Some also open on Saturday 8am to noon. The post offices at Südbahnhof, BahnhofCity Wien West, and Franz-Josefs-Bahnhof have longer opening hours (including Sat and Sun mornings), and the main post office at Fleischmarkt 19 (☎ 0577 677 1010; www.post.at) is open daily from 6am to 10pm.

MONEY Austria's currency is the euro, with notes issued in denominations of 5, 10, 20, 50, and 100 euros, and coins of 1 and 2 euros and also 1, 2, 10, 20, and 50 cents. Credit cards are widely used in Vienna (especially Visa and MasterCard), but it is a good idea to carry cash to use in bars and cafes, and to check the payment methods available before you order a meal or run up a bar bill. If you do get caught short, there are numerous money exchange booths around town, and most international banks' cash cards can be used to obtain cash in local currency from ATMs. For up-to-date currency conversion information, go to www.xe.com.

ORIENTATION TOURS See "Tours."

PARKING In most streets within the *Gürtel*, you need a 30-, 60-, 90-, or 120-minute *Parkschein* (parking ticket), available from tobacconists, banks, train stations, and Wiener Linien ticket offices. To validate it, cross out the appropriate time, date, and year, and leave it visible on the dashboard. Parking restrictions are in force in the Innere Stadt from 9am to 7pm (maximum 90 min). If your car gets clamped for illegal parking, the fine for releasing it is around €400. Car parks are marked with a blue "P" and charge around €3 to €8 per hour. You'll find further information on parking in the Transportation section of www.wien.gv.at.

PASSES The **Vienna Card** (available from hotels and tourist offices, €21.90/24.90) provides 48 or 72 hours of unlimited travel by subway, bus, or tram plus 190 discounts at a variety of museums, attractions, cafes, restaurants, shops, and *Heurigen*. The card is available from the Tourist-Info Wien office in Albertinaplatz, hotels, at all ticket offices of the Vienna Transport Authority, and at www.wienkarte.at. (High-school kids and students are already eligible for discounts at various Viennese sights with their international student card and so may not benefit from a Vienna Card.)

If you are planning to visit the Imperial Apartments, the Sisi Museum and silver collection at the Hofburg, Schönbrunn Palace, and the Imperial furniture collection (20 min. from Schönbrunn at Andreasgasse 7; ☎ 01 524 3357-0; www.hofmobiliendepot.at; Tues–Sun 10am–6pm), you should invest in a **Sisi Ticket** (€28.80 adults, €17 kids, valid for 1 year), to save around 20% on the normal admission prices. It also means you don't have to wait if there are queues for any of the attractions—a big bonus during peak season.

PASSPORTS Citizens of the U.S.A., Canada, the U.K., Ireland, Australia, and New Zealand need only a valid passport to enter Austria. Take a photocopy of your passport's information page, and keep it somewhere separate. This will speed up the replacement process at your embassy if it gets lost or stolen. While in Vienna, keep your passport and other valuables in your room/hotel safe.

PHARMACIES Pharmacies (*Apotheken*) are recognizable by their red serpentine "A." Most open Monday through Friday 8am to 6pm, and Saturday 8am to noon. After hours, there is a rota system. Either dial ☎ 1550 for information, or check at a local pharmacy—they all display a sign indicating the nearest one open. There is also an app called Apo-app, which shows the closest pharmacy on duty. It's available for free download for iOS and Android.

SAFETY Crime rates are low in Vienna although it is advisable to take sensible precautions against petty crime: Don't carry excess cash, and use the hotel safe for valuable goods; don't leave anything visible in a parked car; beware of pickpockets in crowded places (especially in the Naschmarkt); and stick to well-lit, populated areas by night. In particular, steer clear of parks after dusk (especially the Prater and the Stadtpark) and Karlsplatz underground station at night, which is a notorious drug-dealing hotspot. If you need a police station, ask for a

Polizeistation. For emergency police assistance, dial ☎ 133.

SENIOR TRAVELERS Discounts for seniors (ages 61 and up) are available (with proof of age) for most museums, public transport, and entertainment.

SHOPPING See "Business Hours."

SMOKING The Viennese are big smokers and unlike many countries in the E.U., at the time of publication a ban on smoking in public places is planned, but has not yet come into force. There are no-smoking (*Nichtraucher*) restaurants, and many others have no-smoking areas. There are green and red smoking symbols at the entrances to cafes, restaurants, and bars to show the options. Smoking is banned in all Austrian airports and railway stations.

SPECTATOR SPORTS The Austrians are football-crazy, with the national football league running from the fall until early spring. Two of the nation's top teams—FK Austria Wien and Rapid Wien—are based in Vienna. The main stadium is **Ernst Happel Stadium** in the Prater, which seats nearly 50,000 (Meiereistrasse 7; ☎ 01 728 0854; U-Bahn 2 (Stadion)). Also in the Prater is the **Freudenau race course** (Rennbahnstrasse 65; ☎ 01 728 9531; www.freudenau.at; races Mar–Nov), and **Krieau trotting arena** (Nordportalstrasse 274; ☎ 01 728 0046; www.kreiau.at; races Sept–June). The **Stadthalle** (Vogelweidplatz 14; ☎ 01 981 000; www.stadthalle.com; U-Bahn 6 (Burggasse/Stadthalle) hosts a variety of sporting events (and pop concerts), including ice hockey (Sept–Feb).

TAXES Visitors from non-E.U. countries are entitled to reclaim VAT (20%, called *Mehrwertsteuer*), which is included in the price of any purchase over €75. To claim, a tax-refund check must be filled out by the shop at the time of purchase (remember to take your passport). This is then stamped by border officials when you leave the E.U. The refund is most easily claimed when leaving the country—there's a counter for instant refunds at Vienna International Airport, also one at BahnhofCity Wien West, Südbahnhof, and at major border crossings.

TAXIS See "By Taxi," p 161.

TELEPHONES **Austria's** country code is ☎ 0043, **Vienna's** is ☎ 01. When calling a Viennese number from a landline within the city, the local code is not required. Avoid making international calls from your hotel as hefty surcharges are often added. For **directory enquiries** in Austria and the E.U., dial ☎ 118877; for **international directory enquiries,** dial ☎ 0900 118877. International country codes for calling home are as follows: **U.S.A. and Canada** ☎ 001; **U.K.** ☎ 0044; **Irish Republic** ☎ 00353; **Australia** ☎ 0061; and **New Zealand** ☎ 0064.

TICKETS See "How to Get Tickets," p 137.

TIPPING There are no fixed rules for tipping, but a tip of around 10% is expected in taxis, and €1 per bag is normal for porters in hotels. It is customary to give a 10% tip at restaurants or to round up the bill. Announce the total sum (including tip) to the waiter when they take your money. They will normally pocket the tip and return your change.

TOILETS There are over 300 public toilets throughout the city (marked WC), mostly open daily 9am to 7pm, although some are open 24 hours a day. Those with attendants cost around €.50. At some stage, be sure to visit the Jugendstil toilets on Graben, which still retain their original 1905 green railings, lanterns marked Damen (for women) and Herren (for men), and brass washstands.

TOURIST OFFICES Vienna's main tourist office, **Tourist-Info Wien,** Albertinaplatz/corner of Maysedergasse (☎ 01 24555; www.vienna.info; daily 9am–7pm), provides maps, pamphlets, hotel bookings, souvenirs, and a ticket booking service. There's also a small tourist information office, **Tourist-Info Wien Airport,** in the airport Arrivals hall (☎ 01 7007 32875; daily 6am–11pm). **WienXtra Jugendinfo,** Babenbergerstrasse 1 (☎ 01 4000-84100; www.jugendinfowien.at; Mon–Wed 2–9pm, Thurs–Sat 1–6pm) is an information service aimed at visitors ages 14 to 26. It also sells reduced-rate tickets for various events and pop concerts. **WienXtra-Kinderinfo,** MuseumsQuartier (☎ 01 400 084 400; www.kinderinfowien.at; Tues–Thurs 2–7pm, Fri–Sun 10am–5pm) is devoted solely to kids, with a small indoor playground and stacks of information on kids' activities.

TOURIST TRAPS Be careful not to be taken in by the sales pitches of the smooth-talking ticket touts dressed as Mozart lookalikes, who hang around the main tourist attractions waiting to pounce on unsuspecting visitors. The concert packages they offer tend to be touristy and overpriced. A couple of the more reputable establishments are listed in chapter 8, "The Best of Arts & Entertainment."

TOURS Vienna has several tour companies. **Cityrama,** Opernpassage (☎ 01 504 7500; www.cityrama.at) offers tours lasting from 1 hour (in central Vienna) to longer excursions to the Vienna Woods and nearby cities, including Salzburg, Prague, and Bratislava. A great way to explore the city is on the **Vienna Sightseeing buses,** Graf Starhemberggasse 25 (☎ 01 712 4683-0; www.viennasightseeing.at). Buy a ticket for 1 hour (€13), 2 hours (€16), or 24/48 hours (€20/€27) then hop on and off at the main sights as many times as you want between 10am and 8pm (buses run every 15 min. June–Aug, less frequently out of season). For something a little different, I recommend a nostalgic hour-long tour in a vintage open-top coach with **Oldtimer Bus Tours,** Siedengasse 32 (☎ 01 503 744 312; www.oldtimertours.at; departing Heldenplatz May to mid-Oct daily at 11am, 12:30pm, 2pm, and 4pm; adults €19, kids €10) or, for the energetic, a 3-hour **City Segway Tour** (☎ 01 729 7234; www.segway-vienna.at; departing from the Staatsoper Apr–Oct daily at 2pm (also May–June daily 10am, and July–Sept Fri–Sun 10am; €70 per person, must be at least 12 years old). **Pedal Power,** Ausstellungsstrasse 3 (☎ 01 729 7234; www.pedalpower.at) offers two guided bike tours daily between May and September—Classic Vienna and Culture & Danube. Each tour is 3 hours, and takes in many of the city's historic sights.

TRAVELERS WITH DISABILITIES Vienna caters reasonably well for travelers with disabilities (*Behinderte*), although some of the older museums and attractions have limited facilities. Most museums have ramps, and many U-Bahn stations have wheelchair lifts, but buses and older trams don't. The newer trams have doors at ground level. A plan of U-Bahn stations for sight-impaired visitors is available from **Wiener Linien.** The tourist office website (www.vienna.info) has helpful advice and detailed information on suitable hotels, restaurants, and attractions with disabled facilities, together with parking information, toilet locations, and much more in their "Specials" section.

VAT See "Taxes," above.

WEATHER See "The Best Times to Go" and "Climate," p 156.

Vienna: **A Brief History**

2000 B.C. First Indo-Germanic tribes settle in the region.

400 B.C. Celtic tribes create a settlement called Vindebona at Hoher Markt.

15 B.C. Roman legions occupy Vindebona. A further settlement (in today's Belvedere district) becomes a Roman garrison town.

280 The Romans introduce viticulture to the region.

433 Vindebona is destroyed by Huns, leading to a period of invasions by Goths, Avars, and Slav tribes.

8TH CENTURY Charlemagne deposes the Duke of Bavaria and founds the Carolingian Empire. First mention (in the Salzburg Annals) of the name "Wenia" on the borders of the Eastern March or *Ostmark* (later renamed Ostarrichi).

976 The Babenbergs become margraves of the Eastern March.

1137 Vienna receives its town charter; construction of the Stephansdom begins.

1200 The city walls are erected.

1246 The last of the Babenbergs, Duke Frederick II, is killed. Control of Austria passes to King Otokar of Bohemia.

1278 Otokar is killed in the Battle of the Marchfeld against King Rudolf I von Habsburg. This marks the start of the Habsburg dynasty (which rules until 1918).

LATE MIDDLE AGES The Habsburg court becomes a cultural hub of central Europe, attracting numerous musicians and minstrels.

1349 The Plague almost wipes out the entire population of Vienna.

1365 Vienna University is founded.

15TH CENTURY A period of political and economic instability follows the massacre and expulsion of the Jews in 1421. After the Hussite Wars, Vienna temporarily falls under Hungarian rule.

1438 Albrecht V is elected Holy Roman Emperor and Vienna becomes the seat of the Empire.

1469 Vienna is made a bishopric and the Stephansdom becomes a cathedral.

1493 Emperor Maximilian I drives the Hungarians out of Austria.

1498 Maximilian I founds the Vienna Boys' Choir.

1521 Ferdinand I becomes sovereign of Lower Austria and abolishes Vienna's special privileges. The citizens revolt and Ferdinand responds with violent suppression. Following the King of Hungary's death, Ferdinand I lays claim to the Hungarian crown and attempts to expand his authority throughout the region. In reaction, the Sultan of the Ottoman Empire declares war on the Habsburgs.

1529 The first Turkish siege takes place. After the withdrawal of the Turks, Vienna is transformed into a fortress to protect it from continued Ottoman threat.

1571 Following the Reformation, Protestant Maximilian II allows religious freedom. At this time, 8% of the city is Protestant.

1618–48 A Bohemian rebellion starts the Thirty Years' War. In 1623 the Counter-Reformation begins.

1629 A further plague claims 30,000 lives.

1638 The Turks invade again, bringing with them a lasting "gift"—bags of coffee.

1683–1736 Prince Eugène of Savoy leads the Imperial Army to victory against the Turks and the French, and reasserts the Habsburg Empire's status as a major power. Vienna becomes an international center of arts and music.

1740 Maria Theresa—the greatest of all Habsburg rulers—ascends the throne. Her 40-year reign ushers in a golden era.

18TH CENTURY Vienna develops from a court-based feudal society into the dazzling bourgeois capital of a great European power. The death penalty is abolished, and there is greater tolerance toward Jews and non-Catholic Christians. Majestic palaces, churches, summer residences, and parks spring up throughout the city.

1750–1830 Music flourishes in Vienna. Gluck, Haydn, Mozart, Beethoven, and Schubert all live and work in the city.

1792 The reign of Franz II begins. He is later appointed Holy Roman Emperor.

1805 Napoleon lays siege to Vienna; Franz II gives up the title of Holy Roman Emperor in 1806, becoming Franz I of Austria.

1809 Napoleon invades again and takes up residence in the Schönbrunn Palace. In 1810 he marries Franz I's daughter, Archduchess Marie Louise.

EARLY 19TH CENTURY The onset of industrialization leads to a rapid increase in Vienna's population.

1825 Johann Strauss forms his first waltz orchestra, and his two sons, Johann and Josef, follow in his footsteps.

1848 The citizens rise up against political repression. Ferdinand I abdicates in favor of his nephew, Franz Josef.

1848–1916 Franz Josef transforms Vienna into a magnificent modern metropolis. The Ringstrasse becomes a grand boulevard with elegant public buildings.

1867 Franz Josef becomes the dual monarch of Austria-Hungary.

1869 The State Opera House opens with a performance of Mozart's *Don Giovanni* on 25th May.

1897 The association of artists known as the "Secession" is founded, led by Gustav Klimt.

1897–1910 New mass political parties start to emerge, including German Nationalism and the Social Democrats. Anti-Semite Karl Lueger, leader of the Christian Socialist Party, becomes Vienna's mayor.

1903 The Wiener Werkstätte is founded.

1914 Archduke Franz Ferdinand is assassinated in Sarajevo, starting the chain-reaction slide toward World War I.

1918 World War I ends. The dual monarchy collapses, and Austria becomes a republic on 12th November.

1920–34 Socialism prevails in so-called "Red Vienna."

1938 Anschluss: Hitler annexes his home country, and Austria becomes his "Ostmark" in the Third German Reich.

1945 World War II ends. The Russians occupy Vienna on 11th April, followed by the other Allies.

1955 A treaty signed in the Belvedere Palace marks the end of the Allied occupation and guarantees Austria's sovereignty and neutrality.

1979 With the building of the International Center, Vienna becomes the third United Nations city, after New York and Geneva.

1995 Austria joins the E.U. and the Eurozone.

2006 Austria assumes presidency of the E.U. for a term of 6 months.

2008 Vienna hosts the 2008 European Football Championships.

2009 Vienna celebrates the 200th anniversary of Haydn's death.

2011 Vienna celebrates the 100th anniversary of Mahler's death.

2015 Vienna hosts the Eurovision Song Contest, one of the world's longest-running TV shows.

2016 Vienna celebrates the 250-year anniversary of the Prater Park.

Vienna's **Art & Architecture**

Few cities can match Vienna's architectural riches. Indeed, the entire city center has been declared a UNESCO World Cultural Heritage Site due to the remarkable diversity and quality of its buildings.

Early Architecture

Little survives of Vienna's earliest architecture except some Roman remains at **Michaelerplatz** and in the **Römermuseum** in Hoher Markt. Few buildings retain any Romanesque features either. The rounded arches, thick walls, and small windows typical of this period were mostly replaced by the medieval Gothic style in the 13th century. The finest example is the city's oldest church—the **Ruprechtskirche.**

Gothic: 1150–1550

The Gothic style imported from France enabled builders to make walls thinner and taller, with large windows to let in more natural light. Other Gothic features included pointed arches, delicate stonework tracery, flying buttresses (free-standing exterior pillars to support the building), and elaborately constructed ceilings, using the newly acquired techniques of cross-vaulting and fan-vaulting.

The intricate filigree work of the **Maria am Gestade Church** and the soaring proportions of the magnificent **Stephansdom** are both textbook examples of the Gothic style.

Renaissance: 1550–1650

The Renaissance style was first developed in Florence, Italy, as a conscious revival of certain aspects of ancient Greek and Roman design, with an emphasis on geometry and regularity, enlivened by decoration.

Symmetry, proportion, and the use of a classical "vocabulary" of columns, lintels, arches, domes, and niches are the main characteristics of this architectural style.

Surprisingly few Renaissance buildings survive in Vienna. The city was frequently under attack during this period, so precious resources of building materials were used to strengthen the fortifications. Fine examples include the **Stallburg,** the **Schweizertor,** and the striking gabled facade of the **Franziskanerkirche** (the interior is a mishmash of Gothic, Renaissance, and baroque styles).

Baroque & Rococo: 1650–1800

Vienna is best known for the splendor of its baroque palaces and churches. This was Vienna's golden age, and baroque became the favored style of the Habsburgs who, finally freed from the financial burdens of repeated wars and invasions, embarked on an unprecedented building spree. Originating in Italy, the baroque style modified the classical ground rules of Renaissance architecture, using them in a more theatrical way, which appealed to the emotions. Running in tandem with the Counter-Reformation, the baroque style also clearly underlined the wealth and power of the Catholic Church and the Habsburg rulers. Key features of baroque include classical forms enhanced by grand curving lines, exuberant ornamentation and carving (often in gilt, stucco, or marble), monumental ceiling frescoes, a dramatic use of color, light and shade, plus illusory effects like *trompe l'oeil.*

The rococo style developed in the early 18th century as an even more ornate, blousey version of baroque, involving vast quantities of gilded stucco and brightly colored frescoes. This was the favorite style of the Empress Maria Theresa, hence Austrian rococo is sometimes referred to as "late-baroque Theresian style."

Karlskirche is the crown jewel of Vienna's baroque treasures, designed by the Austrian architect Fischer von Erlach, who also built the **Schönbrunn Palace** and the **Prunksaal**—Austria's finest example of secular baroque—in the Nationalbibliothek. The **Belvedere Palace, Schwarzenberg Palace,** and **St. Peter's Church**—all impressive baroque edifices—were created by his successor, Lukas von Hildebrandt. To see the finest rococo interiors in the city, visit the **Schönbrunn Palace** and the **Academy of Sciences.**

Biedermeier: 1815–50

A new bourgeois culture known as Viennese "Biedermeier" emerged after the Napoleonic Wars and the Congress of Vienna in 1815. This left its mark not only on architecture, but also on interior design and the visual arts, paving the way for the later styles known as Jugendstil and the Secession. The main characteristics of the Biedermeier style are simplicity, elegance, and functionality of design.

Splendid examples of Viennese Biedermeier architecture include the **Stadttempel** and the **Dreimäderlhaus.**

Historicism (Neoclassicism): 1800–80

At the peak of his power following the 1848 Revolution, the young Emperor Franz Josef I set about upstaging Napoleon III's radical makeover of Paris. He invited the most famous architects in Europe to create a magnificent new boulevard right round the heart of Vienna's historic city center, or Innere Stadt. Known as the Ringstrasse, it became a showcase for bombastic imperial buildings, which lined it on either side. The fashionable style at that time was a version of neoclassicism known in Vienna as "Historicism." This was a reaction against the fussy complexities of baroque and rococo architecture, and a reversion to the purer classicism of yesteryear. Historicism was characterized by clean, elegant lines, balance and symmetry, and the use of neoclassical motifs and columns.

Typical examples of Viennese Historicism on the Ringstrasse include the **Burgtheater,** the **Kunsthistorisches Museum (KHM)** and the **Naturalhistorisches Museum (NHM)** epitomizing the Italian neo-Renaissance style. The **Parliament Building** evokes a Greek interpretation of Historicism with its columns and statues of Greek philosophers. Also along the Ringstrasse are several fine neo-Gothic edifices, including the **Votivkirche** and **Neues Rathaus.**

Jugendstil & Secession: 1880–1920

The collision of tradition and modernity in Vienna around 1900 created an unusually fertile climate for the arts. Architects felt constrained by neoclassicism, although they found the clean lines and elegant styles appealing. As the Art Nouveau movement emerged in other parts of Europe, Vienna spawned its own distinctive version, known as "Jugendstil" (Young Style). Classic hallmarks of the style include simple, functional lines; organic, flowing motifs (often flowers, flames, waves, or flowing hair); and extensive use of iron, stucco, and stained glass.

In 1897, an iconoclastic splinter-group called the Secession was formed, led by Klimt, Wagner, Olbrich, and Hoffman. This uniquely Viennese style stripped away some of the more decorative aspects of Jugendstil, focusing instead on functionalism and geometry.
The best examples of the style in Vienna include the iconic **Secession Building,** Wagner's **Pavilions,** the **Postsparkasse, Majolikahaus,** and Loos's **American Bar.**

Modern Architecture

The post-war years marked a lean architectural period in Vienna as Austria struggled to cope with the ignominy of military defeat and economic recession. However, during the early 1970s and '80s a new generation of architects emerged to create some highly imaginative structures. Pre-eminent among them was the eccentric genius, Friedensreich Hundertwasser, whose multicolored **KunstHaus Wien, Hundertwasserhaus,** and **Fernwärme** incinerator brighten the modern cityscape. Hundertwasser died at the turn of the millennium, but this creative trend has continued into the 21st century. No single style predominates, but the use of glass and steel is widespread. The innovative **Gasometer** development and Hans Hollein's hugely controversial **Haas Haus,** right at the heart of the UNESCO-protected Innere Stadt (city center), are noteworthy examples of the quirky modern style.

Useful **Words & Phrases**

ENGLISH	GERMAN	PRONUNCIATION
Good day	Guten Tag	goo-ten tag
How are you?	Wie geht's?	vee gait e see-nen
very well	Sehr gut	zair goot
thank you	Danke	dan-keh
you're welcome	Bitte sehr	bee-teh zair
goodbye	Auf Wiedersehen	owf vee-der-zain
please	Bitte	bee-teh
yes/no	Ja/Nein	yah/nyn
excuse me/sorry	Entschuldigung	ent-shool-di-gung
Where is/are . . .?	Wo ist/sind . . .?	Voh ist/zint
left/right	links/rechts	links/rekhts
straight on	geradeaus	ge-raa de-ows
I would like . . .	Ich hätte gerne . . .	Ick heh-teh ger-neh
Do you have a . . .?	Haben Sie ein . . .?	Hah-ben zee eyn
How much is it?	Wie viel kostet es?	Vee feel kos-tet es
When?	Wann?	Van
What?	Was?	Vas
yesterday	Gestern	ges-tern
today	Heute	hoi-teh
tomorrow	Morgen	mor-gen
good/bad	gut/schlecht	goot/shlekt
better	besser	beh-ser
more/less	mehr/weniger	mair/vay-nigga
Do you speak English?	Sprechen Sie Englisch?	Shpre-khen zee eng-lish
I don't understand	Ich verstehe nicht	ich fer-shtaia nikht
The bill please	die Rechnung bitte	die rekh-nung bee-teh
I'm looking for . . .	Ich suche . . .	ich zoo-khe
the station	der Bahnhof	dair baan-hof
a hotel	ein Hotel	eyn ho-tel
the market	der Markt	dair mahrkt
a restaurant	ein Restaurant	eyn res-tow-ron
a toilet	eine Toilette	ey-neh toi-le-teh
a bank	eine Bank	ey-neh bank
a pharmacy	eine Apotheke	ey-neh a-po-tay-keh
a doctor	ein Arzt	eyn artst
breakfast	Frühstück	froo-shtook
lunch	Mittagessen	mi-taak-essen
dinner	Abendessen	ar-bend-essen
coffee and cake	Kaffee und Kuchen	kah-fay unt koo-khen
The menu please	die Karte bitte	dee kaar-teh bee-teh

Numbers

ENGLISH	GERMAN	PRONUNCIATION
1	eins	ains
2	zwei	tsvy
3	drei	dry
4	vier	feer
5	fünf	funf
6	sechs	zeks
7	sieben	zee-ben
8	acht	akht
9	neun	noin
10	zehn	tsen

Days of the Week

Monday	Montag	mawn-taag
Tuesday	Dienstag	deens-taag
Wednesday	Mittwoch	mit-vokh
Thursday	Donnerstag	donners-taag
Friday	Freitag	fry-taag
Saturday	Samstag	zams-taag
Sunday	Sonntag	zon-taag

Index

See also Accommodations and Restaurant indexes, below.

Photo **Credits**

All interior images © Teresa Fisher, with the following exceptions:

p 12, Gerhard Roethlinger/Shutterstock.com

p 13, Cortyn/Shutterstock.com

p 16, Tupungato/Shutterstock.com

p 17, Manuel Hurtado/Shutterstock.com

p 35, With Courtesy BAWAG P.S.K.

p 54, Gert Krammer/WestLicht

p 55, © Eva Ellersdorfer-Meissnerova

p 65, bottom: Marco Scisetti|Dreamstime.com

p 93, America Studio/Shutterstock.com

p 109, Restaurant Steirereck GmbH

p 118, © Fabios

p 119, © Labstelle

p 121, Restaurant Steirereck GmbH

p 122, WRENKH Restaurant & Wiener Kochsalon

p 123, © Lavendertime|Dreamstime.com

p 124, www.meinlamgraben.at

p 129, bottom: Sofitel Vienna Stephansdom/Vincent Thibert

p 130, 1516 Brewing Company

p 138, © Wiener Konzerthaus/LUKAS BECK

p 141 and 149, DO & CO Aktiengesellschaft

p 148, top: © Daniella Baranek/Alstadt Vienna

p 148, bottom: © Victoria Schaffer/Hotel Das Triest

p 150, © Hollmann Beletage

p 151, HOTEL DANIEL VIENNA

p 153, Kempinski Hotels

p 154, © Strandhotel

p 155, Valentyna Holovan/Shutterstock.com.

Notes

Notes

Notes